MV NORLAND

SECRET WEAPON OF
THE FALKLANDS WAR

REG KEMP AND MICHAEL WOOD

MV NORLAND

SECRET WEAPON OF THE FALKLANDS WAR

FROM NORTH SEA FERRY TO TASK FORCE ASSAULT SHIP

The
History
Press

Front cover: Painting of the *Norland* based on a photograph taken by steward Graham (Hoss) Edwards, painted by Larry Malkin, which was commissioned by Reg Kemp and Michael Wood for this book's front cover. See page 253.

First published 2021

The History Press
97 St George's Place, Cheltenham,
Gloucestershire, GL50 3QB
www.thehistorypress.co.uk

British Library Cataloguing in Publication Data.
A catalogue record for this book is available from the British Library.

ISBN 978 0 7509 9712 6

Typesetting and origination by The History Press
Printed and bound in Great Britain by TJ Books Limited, Padstow, Cornwall.

Trees for LYfe

'I thought I knew all about the *Norland* but this book took me totally by surprise. A great yarn. I loved it.'

Larry Malkin. Chair of East Riding Artists Association

'This little-known account of the *Norland* has at last been told, without hype and sentimentality. The crew served with such great courage and humour. And I should know, I was there …'

Dave 'Charlie' Brown, 2 Para

'One of the best books ever for those looking to find adventure at sea.'

Chairman, Hull Independent Merchant Navy Association

'A cracking read that I couldn't put down. Very interesting and great to learn about the vital contribution civilians gave.'

Mary Brice, University of Hull lecturer on film studies

'Kemp and Wood make known the largely uncredited yet crucial role of the humble North Sea Ferry, MV *Norland*, in a time of war – and what a remarkable role it played. A thoroughly satisfying read.'

Projects Director, Hull Civic Society

'I only spent a short time on board with 3 Para at the war's end. All these years later and now learning the full story of the *Norland*, I have total renewed respect for the ship's crew and the Merchant Navy as a whole.'

Larry Little, Sergeant, 3 Para

'Out of all the books written about the Falklands Conflict, this one brought me back the most - but in a gentle and caring way. It explains the feelings of many people from the 'Class of 82' and gives readers an insight which many other books don't. Small details of the story swell our own knowledge and increase our understanding of what it meant to be 8,000 miles away from home in a war zone. Its appeal isn't just for the enthusiast but for the interested bystander too.'

Paul R. G. Haley, Photographer, Class of 82

CONTENTS

FOREWORD

BY CAPTAIN RN (RETD)
CHRIS ESPLIN-JONES CBE,
MV *NORLAND*, SENIOR NAVAL OFFICER

On 2 April 1982, most of the United Kingdom listened in amazement to the BBC News covering the invasion of the Falkland Islands by Argentina. Reg Kemp is a man with an enthusiastic and inquisitive nature, used to acting on his own. As a crew member, this book is his personal record of the taking up from trade of MV *Norland*, a ferry operating between Hull and Rotterdam, for the Falklands campaign. He describes her modification, logistic and assault tasks in war, her handling of prisoners of war and finally her role as a South Atlantic ferry until she arrived home in February 1983.

We saw little of each other in the ship and would certainly have viewed events as they unfolded with a differing perspective. He was carrying out his vital night work, while the Royal Navy role was to provide a link with the Task Force Command and to supply some specialist warfare skills, such as anti-submarine manoeuvres and helicopter control. He describes the tensions, rivalry and eventual melding of Army, Royal Air Force, Royal Navy and Merchant Navy people, while the ship carried out a wide range of tasks – as he and his fellow ship's company experienced it.

The story reveals the slow realisation by a crew that their unarmed civilian ship was to play a key part in the recovery of a British Overseas Territory, and that it was to go to war taking part in the initial force landings, while living with the frustration of ever-changing military plans.

MV *Norland* has been described as a lucky ship. It was her crew who made her lucky. Reg Kemp's account is very well told and a valuable addition to the many excellent publications on the Falklands War.

MAPS

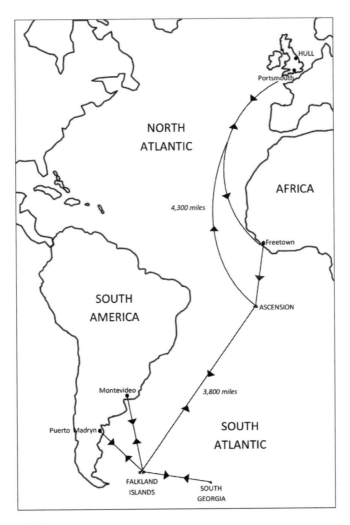

World map.

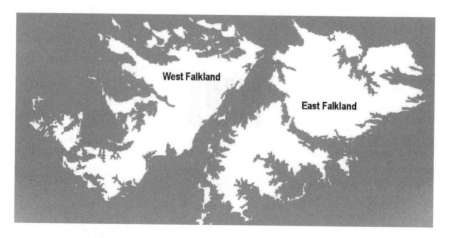

West and East Falklands.

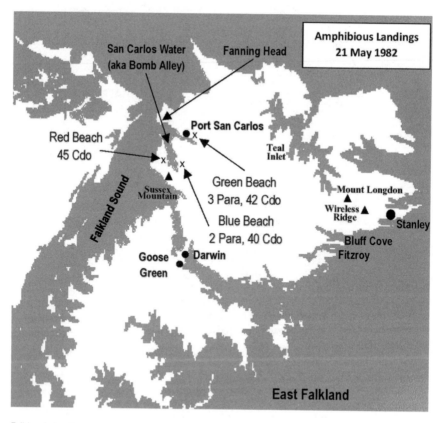

Falklands landings.

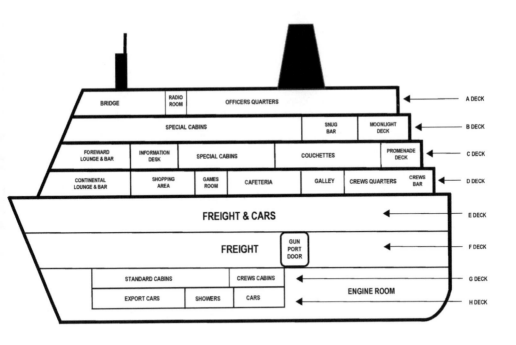

BRIDGE | RADIO ROOM | OFFICERS QUARTERS — A DECK

SPECIAL CABINS | SNUG BAR | MOONLIGHT DECK — B DECK

FOREWARD LOUNGE & BAR | INFORMATION DESK | SPECIAL CABINS | COUCHETTES | PROMENADE DECK — C DECK

CONTINENTAL LOUNGE & BAR | SHOPPING AREA | GAMES ROOM | CAFETERIA | GALLEY | CREWS QUARTERS | CREWS BAR — D DECK

FREIGHT & CARS — E DECK

FREIGHT | GUN PORT DOOR — F DECK

STANDARD CABINS | CREWS CABINS — G DECK

EXPORT CARS | SHOWERS | CARS | ENGINE ROOM — H DECK

INTRODUCTION

BY MICHAEL WOOD
WARRANT OFFICER ONE, YEOMAN OF SIGNALS (RETD),
ROYAL CORPS OF SIGNALS

I have always been interested in tales of war. This is not solely through having a military background; it began as a youngster when I was totally gripped listening to my father and uncle's adventures during their time in the Second World War. I deliberately use the word 'adventure' as most people I have met who have found themselves heading off to war initially believed that's what it would be. Usually after a skinful of drink, the tales told by my father and uncle were tragic and, depending how much they had drunk, heavy with anger. The reality of war is that it's a filthy, rule-breaking, dealing-in-death business; a business that many don't survive and, of those who do, most want to forget.

I first met former merchant seaman Reg Kemp in 2011. We both live in the same housing complex of fifty self-contained flats for retired people in Willerby, East Yorkshire. Initial nods of hello then led to conversations in which I learnt that Reg had been through the experience of going to war in the Falklands on the North Sea ferry, MV *Norland*.

My younger brother, Grahame, worked as a barman in that same conflict on the P&O cruise liner SS *Canberra* (in the Meridian Room serving NCOs and the Century Bar serving the Sergeants' Mess). As my brother and I worked in different parts of the world, I never got the chance to record his experiences before he sadly passed away. In my second career as a writer, I regretted not being able to do so.

On hearing Reg's exploits of his time aboard the *Norland*, which, like the *Canberra*, was requisitioned by the Ministry of Defence (MOD) as a troop-carrying ship, I immediately knew he had a great story to tell. Reg wasn't much interested when I urged him to do so. 'Produce a book of your experiences, if only to have something as a family legacy,' I said. As I am a former paratrooper, he trusted me to understand the relationship between the 2nd Battalion Parachute Regiment and the merchant crew he sailed with. Reg finally agreed. The more I interviewed him about his time in the Falklands, the more I realised that he had an important and enthralling story to share.

Reg had a front-row seat to the campaign. He worked as a night steward and observed a lot of after-dark military activity. As someone who only needed minimum sleep, he pushed himself to stay awake to observe as much day-time activity as he could. The nickname of 'Nighthawk' for night stewards aboard the *Norland* couldn't have been more apt, in particular for Reg, whose natural curiosity led him to witness many key events unfold.

My army experience taught me that if you wanted to know what was going on, you didn't rely on oral or written orders filtering down from above; you spent time in the Sergeants' Mess with your fellow non-commissioned officers. That is where conversations reflected reality and not probabilities. Often denied reliable information from his own superiors, Reg spent time in the equivalent of the Sergeants' Mess where he was privy to many revealing conversations prior to battle, and after battle, which is what makes his story so compelling.

Making it his business to know as much as he could not only fed Reg's curiosity, but also ensured he was prepared for the worst … whatever that might be. He and his fellow crew members got involved with aspects of preparing for and dealing with war far beyond their normal civilian duties. In conversation with soldiers of 2 and 3 Para, the Royal Navy and *Norland* crew members, but especially with Reg, what was considered to be everyday detail was fascinating to me. This detail, along with the ever-present danger in which the *Norland* had been placed, is a valuable insight into what it is to be faced with a so-called war 'adventure' and in Reg's case as a 'volunteer'. (Oh, and anyone thinking that the phrase 'swears like a trooper' was created for the military, wait until you spend an hour in the company of Merchant Navy personnel – men and women.)

I asked Reg if he knew that the MOD had decreed, 'the fallen in the Falklands would be buried there, that there was a no-repatriation policy. This therefore meant that any casualties at sea would probably result in them being buried at sea!'

He was surprised he hadn't known. Reg said:

> Well, that was just typical of never being told the full picture. Maybe it was best some of us didn't know because then we wouldn't have had to worry, not for ourselves but for our families at home coping with such information. But that's all behind us now; what matters is we made it.

It was this non-sensationalist, unsentimental manner from Reg that drew me in from the start. His concern was wanting a guarantee that what he had to say would serve as a salute to his fellow crew and his ship, as well as to smaller Merchant Navy ships that received little or no recognition.

Another reason for wanting to write this book was to tell something new about the Falklands War, and from the point of view of not only non-combatants, but personnel often thought of as being at the bottom of the pecking order: i.e., the cooks, the barmen, the storemen, the able seamen, the 'down below crowd' in the engine room, the stewards and stewardesses. Whilst this book has testimony from paratroopers at the blood and guts end of the fighting, and though the *Norland* and its crew were not asked to 'fix bayonets', nonetheless, they were still involved in the thick of the action in many other significant ways. Being caught up in a time of war, each one of the crew bore their responsibilities with remarkable good humour and resolve. Their accounts are all utterly engrossing and, now, rightly given a voice. Indeed, the importance of these accounts from those often overlooked in a time of war are affirmed by the contribution of a Foreword and an Afterword, respectively, by the attached senior Royal Navy Officer and the acting Commanding Officer of 2 Para.

In concluding this introduction, it is to Reg whom I give the final word with something that he said a couple of times which sums up the story of the *Norland* and its crew: 'You haven't only got to fire a gun to be able to fight for your country.'

1

A PEACEFUL LIFE

When not at sea, my main interest was to go rock climbing and scrambling. In 1982, on board the North Sea passenger ferry MV *Norland*, some of my fellow crew members wanted to take on the well-known Lyke Wake Walk, in North Yorkshire. I knew this could be a tough task, even for the experienced walker but certainly for the beginner. It would be a 40-mile trek over challenging terrain and not something you do on a whim. As I had always fancied doing it myself, after several requests from the lads to join them, I agreed to go along. Before I knew it, I found myself the leader of our small walking expedition.

Our ship's policeman, Ron Marshall, had wanted to come along but he didn't want to do the actual walk. Instead, he offered to drive a minibus that we'd hired, which I was delighted with, as I liked and trusted Ron – and him being a policeman! With a team of eleven, mainly cooks and stewards, I knew that some would have difficulty finishing the walk. But to give them their due, they were all raring to go.

At 3.45 a.m. on an April morning, we entered the village of Osmotherley, our starting location. On parking up our minibus outside the village, the conditions were ideal – dry with a clear sky that made it a delight to see the night's stars. Osmotherly is located in the west of the North Yorkshire moors and we were to head east, across country, to our finishing location at Ravenscar on the North Sea coast. I'd decided on such an early start in the hope of reaching the finish before dark. The lads had been briefed about packing the basics of water, snacks, a torch, plasters, and advised to cut their toenails. I carried the necessary maps and a compass.

We started the walk at 4 a.m. From the off, I ensured stragglers didn't drop behind in the dark. This was strenuous as I was forever up and down the line cajoling everyone along, keeping them together. Five miles into the walk, one of the less fit lads gave himself a rest break. Once he'd sat down, he didn't want to get up. In all seriousness he asked me, 'Reg, I'm completely knackered. Can you get me a helicopter?' He knew the answer when I laughed out loud and slowly shook my head. Thankfully he pushed on to complete another mile until the first pre-arranged stop with Ron, where he became our first walker lost to the comfort of a seat in the minibus.

Our team of ten carried on. Helped by the dry conditions, initially all was going well. Everyone enjoyed seeing the dawn breaking, which was spectacular. The terrain was sparse, with the lack of trees very noticeable. Near to midday, we approached a small dip by a stream. As we got closer to the dip, we saw that there were four other walkers taking a rest. They were heading east to west. A friendly conversation ensued when we discovered that they were army lads. The conversation had a common bond; the delight of walking and the sense of freedom it gives. We respected their situation as soldiers who were in training. They respected our situation as lads from a seafaring background without training but giving it a go. After sharing a few stories about life at sea and life in the military, we all shook hands and went our own way. Little did any of our group of walkers know that in several days, our ship would be playing host to a large contingent of the British Army who were greatly famed for their walking – or rather their marching abilities.

For now, our group of walkers were just over the halfway stage and unfortunately more of them were suffering. At the next meet-up with the minibus, steward John Kamis decided not to go on. He was sitting inside the vehicle when he shouted, 'Reg, can you take a look at this?' He'd taken his boots off and his white socks were stained red, not due to dye from his boots but from blood. I said, 'John, just put your boots back on and pretend it's not there. Didn't I say to cut your toenails?'

'It's a bit late for that now,' he said with a strained smile.

It wasn't without good reason that others decided not to go on. Though the weather was kind, as we slogged on yet more dropped out and by 4 p.m. there were only four of us left. I called a quick halt to chat with the other three lads, Johnny Lambert, John McWatt and Dick

Johnson. 'Look, fellas,' I said, 'we're going to finish this thing. We've got to get to the end before nightfall. You're going to have to keep up a good pace, a faster pace. You have to stay with me, okay?' No one argued and so with quiet determination we continued.

With 5 miles to go before the end, we stopped for an unscheduled rest. Dick Johnson was normally a real 'live wire', but I could see he was suffering for he had gone very quiet. Johnny Lambert, a big powerful fellow, had asked me before the walk what he should do to get through it. 'Just stick alongside me all the way,' I advised him. This is what he'd done and if I'd said to him, 'John, when we get to the end of this walk, we are going to turn around and go straight back the way we've just come,' he would have shrugged his shoulders and done just that. Not so with John McWatt. He'd had enough and he didn't want to go on.

'Look, it's only 2 more miles to go from here,' I lied. 'And anyway, you have got to finish it because how else are you going to get to the end? The minibus can't get here to pick you up. Oh, and before you ask, a helicopter isn't going to turn up and neither is mountain rescue with a St Bernard dog carrying a small barrel of rum round its neck.' I didn't know if my words were registering as there was a long pause before he spoke.

He looked at me blankly and said, 'You're a bastard, Kempy. I hate you. And no matter what you say, I am not moving.'

In response, I spouted one of those motivational movie speeches in which I talked about the embarrassment of failure, of how everyone on the ship would know he had given up with only a couple of miles to go, of how they would take the piss out of him big time and for a long time to come.

'Do you know what, Kempy, I fucking hate you even more. In fact, right now, I don't think I could hate anybody in this world as much you,' he said. Then dragging up his aching bones, swearing and muttering away to himself, he began shuffling along until falling into a walking rhythm again.

I was amazed that I'd managed to persuade him to continue. On long walks like these you inevitably hit a pain barrier and that had happened to us all. To their credit, everyone dug in deep, including me. We finished just after 6 p.m. under ugly grey clouds, with a drop in the temperature setting in.

We may not look it, but we were definitely happy at finishing the Lyke Wake Walk. Left to right are stewards John McWatt, Johnny Lambert, Dick Johnson and me.

I was proud of all the lads for taking on the walk in the first place, but I was especially proud of those who'd finished it. We'd covered 40 miles in just over 14 hours. What a pleasure it was on arriving at our final destination of Ravenscar to be greeted by familiar territory, the North Sea. As far as I was concerned it had been a successful venture. I couldn't have been more pleased, though, to see my wife, Jean. She had driven to Ravenscar to drive me home to Hull. Other family members had also turned up to drive some of the lads back. Before we headed off, either in Ron's minibus or in private cars, we spent a good hour in the pub replenishing fluids lost en route. I am not someone who usually needs a lot of shut-eye but that evening, on arriving home, I felt at peace with the world as I fell into a deep welcome slumber.

(The 40-mile walk that we covered gets its name from the Lyke Wake Dirge. This is a traditional Yorkshire song describing the soul's passage through purgatory, which is what many walkers feel when taking on the challenge. Not only does one have a great sense of self-esteem in completing it, one also earns an entry to the Lyke Wake Club. The song has it that male finishers of the walk are called Dirgers, women finishers are called Witches. And why this is, no one really knows!)

2

THINGS ARE ABOUT
TO CHANGE

The morning after our walking trip my wife, Jean, woke me with a cup of tea and a look of concern. 'Morning, love, hope you slept well. Listen, something's up,' she said. 'I've just had a phone call from North Sea Ferries. I don't know what's going on but you have to go to the ship. They are calling all hands to a special meeting on board the *Norland* at 10.30 this morning.'

The date was 17 April and as I was on leave, I thought it a bit of an inconvenience. I realised, though, that such an unusual request meant it had to be something important. I grabbed some breakfast and hurriedly made my way to King George Dock.

There were two civilian crews who manned the *Norland*: one crew on the ship, the other on leave. It was therefore quite surprising to see people from both crews assembled in the ship's restaurant at the same time. Also, there were two captains for the ship: Don Ellerby and Derek Wharton. After a lot of gossip and guesswork as to why we were there, Captain Don Ellerby appeared with several of his officers. He called out for attention. Straight to the point, he announced that the MOD had requisitioned the ship to do service for the military. The reason that we had all been called in was that the military wanted North Sea Ferries personnel to crew it, though it wasn't compulsory to do so. 'You either go or you don't!' said Captain Ellerby. He explained that if we decided not to go, the ship would be manned by Royal Navy personnel. The military didn't really want this to happen and so they were hoping we would provide sufficient volunteers from the two crews available.

For me, it was easier to volunteer than not to. It just seemed the right thing to do and, anyway, others said they would go. We were assured it would only be a preliminary kind of exercise in that we'd be taking troops as far as Ascension Island. Someone then had the sense to ask the reason for all of this.

'It's because the Argentinians have invaded the Falklands,' a military person piped up.

There was a long silence and someone near to me said, 'What the fucking hell are the Argentinians doing in Scotland invading us up there?' This was greatly amusing to those who knew the location of the Falklands. It was quickly explained that they were located in the South Atlantic. This was followed by a brief of the political and military situation, which those of our crew members with an interest in world current affairs were broadly aware of. Several hundred miles off the Falklands lay the islands of South Georgia, which belonged to the UK. Under the disguise of being scrap metal merchants, the Argentinian military had landed and raised their flag. This was later followed by an invasion of the Falkland Islands from the sea by full-on Argentinian troops. The Falkland Islands belong to the UK and they were home to around 2,000 people who considered themselves totally British. The UN had condemned the unprovoked aggression of Argentina and called for a withdrawal, which was ignored. The UK then declared a 200-mile exclusion zone around the Falklands. An Argentinian Junta headed up by the country's President, General Galtieri, imposed its own South Atlantic operations zone in reply. General Galtieri had claimed that *Las Islas Malvinas* (The Falkland Islands) belonged to Argentina. It was political posturing by him to revive his waning popularity and to be seen as a strong leader by his people. Margaret Thatcher was about to put him right about ownership of the Falklands and, through a quickly assembled 'Task Force', she had already sent some of our military down to the area, including aircraft carriers HMS *Hermes* and HMS *Invincible*. A couple of days prior to our requisition, the ocean liner SS *Canberra* had been dispatched with the Paras and Marines on board. And when the heavy gang of the Paras and Marines gets involved, it's more than serious.

We weren't given time to go home and think before making any decision. It was 'make your mind up' there and then. Some of the crew said they had bad backs, holidays booked or other reasons not to go. Fortunately, my close pal Dave Aistrop, whom I had worked with on nights for some time, volunteered. Of the three lads with whom I had finished the walk, Dick Johnson and Johnny Lambert volunteered to go, but John McWatt was gutted that he couldn't because of matters to do with his union position. He was deemed to be of better use on the *Norland*'s replacement vessel, whatever that was going to be. His younger brother, Pete McWatt, was allowed to volunteer instead, but this wasn't without great resistance from his father, who thought that it was a dangerous decision to make and that he shouldn't go.

An assurance for those who would be going was that we could all keep our same jobs and run the ship, within reason, in the same way we did on our normal run across the North Sea. Though under overall military control, the ship's pecking order would remain in place, from the Captain down to the lower ranks. After a lot of soul searching, those of us who would be making up the volunteer crew had our names registered and we were allowed to leave the ship.

Technically we were 'STUFT', which is an acronym meaning Ships Taken Up From Trade. This is an arrangement for supplementing the Royal Navy fleet in time of war, under which a merchant ship takes aboard a naval officer to command it, and sometimes a few other naval personnel to help run the ship.

Earlier that morning I'd arrived with a friend of mine, Russ Turnbull, who had given me a lift to the dock. Before going home, it seemed a good idea for everyone to go to the local pub to discuss the situation and he came along. It was a pub off the dock called The New Inn and that day it was absolutely packed with crew members and dock workers. By now news had filtered through on the local radio that the *Norland* had been requisitioned by the MOD. The beer began to flow. I suggested to Russ that he shouldn't be drinking as he was driving. Russ wasn't the type of bloke you could ever tell what to do. After a couple of hours in the pub, we got back into his car to drive home. It would have been wiser not to do so. But, anyway, he convinced me he was okay and we headed off home. Immediately, I noticed he was driving erratically and I advised that he took it easy. Like I said, Russ wasn't the type to be told anything. Before we knew it, a police car had pulled us over. As the copper approached, Russ wound down the window and I told him just to try to play it cool.

The copper said, 'Hello, fellas. I am going to ask you something. Have you been drinking?'

Russ brazenly answered, 'Yes we have!'

Taken aback, the copper said, 'Oh, have you?'

Russ replied, 'Yeah, and you'd have gone for a drink if you'd just done what we've done.'

'What's that?' asked the copper.

'We've just volunteered to go to the Falklands,' explained Russ.

Now as it happened, Russ wasn't going. The Purser, John Crowther, had firmly decided on this. The copper then asked me, 'Is that right?'

'Yes, I'm going as well,' I answered.

The copper thought for a couple of seconds and said, 'Look, I am not going to make any charges against you. Pull your car over there to the side, lock it up, get a taxi home and pick your car up another time.'

I thought this was extremely kind of the copper. We then got a taxi home where I broke the news about volunteering to my wife and two young sons. Jean wasn't happy but she was understanding of my decision. She was used to me being away on ships, not only on the short runs of the *Norland* but also in my earlier days on deep-sea voyages. This trip, though, was likely to be unlike any other I had been on.

(Many months later, it amused me to learn that Russ was stopped by the copper, who was in plain clothes. He was walking along the same street when he recognised Russ. 'I thought you was supposed to be away on the *Norland*,' he snapped at him.' Russ was groping for an excuse when he was told in no uncertain terms by the copper: 'Don't you ever let me catch you for anything else, whatsoever. Do you understand?' Russ said he gave the copper an earnest look of apology and five minutes later he just laughed it off without further thought. This was typical of the carefree way that not just Russ but many people enjoyed living their lives.)

The next day I went aboard the ship and it was a hive of activity with minor alterations taking place. Lots of military people were running about looking busy. This continued for a couple of days until the ship was ready to sail with the addition of personnel from the army and navy, who had carried out reconnoitring duties of the ship's facilities in readiness for what the future had in store.

Norland Radio Officer, Brian Lavender, was due to go on leave on his arrival at Hull on the ship on 17 April. He was the first to know we had been requisitioned by the MOD when he received the message on the night of the 16th, which he handed to a very surprised ship's captain, Don Ellerby. In the morning, to Brian's relief, Bob Jenkins took over, but due to company policy, which came to light later, Bob was unable to go as his wife was pregnant. The company rang Brian and asked if he was prepared to go at forty-eight hours' notice. He said, 'yes' and he had a heck of a rush to get his affairs together before leaving Hull.

To a boisterous farewell with lots of folks on the dockside, on 21 April we were ready to sail to Portsmouth. Roy (Wendy) Gibson, one of our long-standing crew members and a keen pianist, had acquired a piano from the Flying Angel Mission to Seamen located near to King George Dock. This was put on to the afterdeck. Roy tickled the ivories and was accompanied by lots of singing as we pulled out through the lock gates of King George Dock, with an underlying uncertainty as to what lay ahead.

The aim of heading to Portsmouth was to carry out major alterations, for transporting military manpower and equipment down south, which was the main reason it had been requisitioned. The soldiers that we'd be carrying were to be the Second Battalion, The Parachute Regiment (2 Para), and other units.

In Portsmouth, during the major refit and remaining final adjustments, I was doing my normal job on nights with Dave. Things were, however, anything but normal, and the ship was swarming with personnel who had taken part-control. I had done my first nightshift and the following morning, not wanting to go straight to sleep, I decided to visit Portsmouth. I vaguely knew the place but had never visited HMS *Victory* and fancied doing so. It was a lovely day and, as it was only a mile or so away, I arrived by foot at its berth at around 10 a.m. Strangely, I was the first visitor there. The only people on the ship other than me were two Royal Marines, who were acting as guides. I learnt that the Royal Marines and the Navy take it in turn to man HMS *Victory* and look after tourists, just as they were doing then. But on this occasion, I was the only tourist so far. In conversation with the two Marines, just before one of them vanished he said to the other, 'Take him into Nelson's cabin.' On arriving there, the Marine who'd vanished then reappeared. He seemed to have been drinking. Nelson's sleeping cabin surprised me for it was a pokey little space as opposed to his main quarters where he did his planning and briefings. I was further surprised when the Marine who had been drinking produced a bottle of rum and three glasses. I'm not a rum drinker myself and it was a bit early in the day, but I wasn't going to turn down this offer. We each had a decent tot and a toast was made to the memory of 'good old Nelson'. What an enjoyable experience this had turned out to be and, even as a non-rum drinker, I found it very palatable. By now, other tourists were coming on board and the Marines needed to return to their proper job of meeting and greeting them. I thanked them for their hospitality and moved on to enjoy wandering about the ship on my own, with a warm feeling in my stomach.

The ship leaving Hull for Portsmouth. (Courtesy *Hull Daily Mail*)

Portsmouth is traditionally one of the major homes of the Royal Navy. In April of that year the town was busy, busy, busy, with work being carried out on numerous ships, none more so than the *Norland*. Our fuel tanks had to be enlarged to accommodate more fuel, water tanks enlarged to take more fresh water, further space found for numerous containers, mostly with food to feed 1,000 men for sixty days, but one of the main jobs was the construction of two helicopter decks. These decks had to be in place as soon as possible and so construction workers worked around the clock. I'm not technically minded but I did notice some kind of special satellite and navigation equipment being installed. With so much happening on board, people like myself who were working nights found it near impossible to sleep the next day. Dave had accommodation on G-deck in the lower part of the ship, well below the waterline and considered not a very good place to live, but at least it was away from most of the noise. My cabin was higher up on D-deck, closer to the activity. I decided to spend a day away from the ship and stay in a local hotel to get some peace and quiet.

The morning after my second night shift, I packed a small bag and went down to the quayside hoping to catch transport to the town. As I walked down the gangway, a taxi arrived to drop someone off. I asked the driver, 'Are you free?' The driver, a woman with a friendly smile, said, 'Yes, where do you want to go?'

'I am looking to get some sleep and need a nice quiet hotel.'

'No problem, I know just the place. Come and sit up front,' she offered. 'There is a hotel nearby where I live that I can recommend.'

'Yeah, well okay, whatever you think,' I said.

Conversation ensued and I revealed my reason for being in Portsmouth. She was knowledgeable about what was taking place and told me her brother was in the Marines and due to go to the Falklands. I was already aware that the whole town was very conscious of its naval roots and had a deep pride in its naval traditions. We arrived at the hotel and I asked if there were any pubs open early as I fancied a beer or two before getting some sleep. Living nearby, she suggested a pub she sometimes used for her breakfast. I booked into the hotel, leaving my small bag behind, and then made my way to the pub just around the corner. I was surprised when the taxi driver lady walked in and asked to join me. As I was the last fare of her night shift, she stayed to have a couple of drinks. There is something about the people in port towns that, like Hull, they are welcoming and friendly. This lady was definitely friendly and made it clear she was single. We enjoyed each other's company and had a few good laughs but at the end of our drinks we went our separate ways.

Later that day after a decent sleep, when it was time to go back, the hive of activity preparing the ship was still in full flow. I noticed that senior naval officers had been coming and going. Three days later we took on troops in large numbers. By the time they were all on board, they totalled near to 1,000 men. On a normal North Sea run, the ship would be busy loading and discharging people, cars and cargo, but this was something else.

While we were in Portsmouth, radio, television and newspapers reported that nothing was getting better politically. One development was that South Georgia had been recaptured by our Marines and, with no British casualties, near to 200 Argy troops had been taken prisoner. A meeting was held in the mess room, which I missed, when the Captain had come down to speak to the crew at 'smoko'. (This is a sea term for a short break, usually at 10.30 a.m.; the army equivalent is a Naafi break.) He put it directly to the crew: 'Anyone who wants to go home, now's the time to do so. If anyone has cold feet, come to my cabin and I'll make arrangements to get you back. This is your last chance before the ship sails from here. After that it'll be too late.' Three stewardesses who had volunteered back in Hull were not scared off by the old man's words. Two male crew members took up his offer: a steward and an able seaman off the deck department. A replacement was immediately found for the able seaman's job but not for the steward's role.

Unlike a few days earlier in Hull, the farewell at the dockside in Portsmouth on 26 April was one of near hysteria. This send-off didn't really mean much to our crew; we'd had our send-off back in Hull. But it did matter to our military passengers, who had countless family and friends blowing kisses, waving flags and tearfully saying goodbye. The ship let go and we proceeded across Portsmouth harbour, heading for open water. Amongst all the people milling around, I remember a small jetty with one man standing on it alone. It was strange to see him standing in his own company. I thought I recognised him. Struggling to recall who he was, I suddenly realised he was one of the main bosses of North Sea Ferries. What thoughts did he have? Did he know something we didn't? It was too late to concern myself with that right now, for the ship was heading south and I had plenty of other things to think about – mainly that without all the banging and crashing of the alterations going on, I could get some proper sleep.

3
SAILING SOUTH

Once we were at sea and with the manic preparation behind us, the crew settled down into their usual work routine. I was pleased to see that three stewardesses made up part of our crew. I admired their pluck in not having hesitated to volunteer. The skipper probably viewed it differently in that he would rather they hadn't. He had previously tried to persuade them to go home but they had refused, and he couldn't do much about it because they had gladly volunteered right from the off. With the potential of going to war, he probably viewed it as being a man's environment. Yet there was a carefree feeling, almost a carnival atmosphere, as we headed south. With Wendy entertaining us on the piano, it was all jolly good stuff.

During the early part of the voyage, a chain of command emerged between the military and our civilian regime. The crew had wanted to carry on as they had when in civilian mode, but now we were in military mode and heading to possible conflict it begged the question: 'Who would be giving out the orders?' The top military man on board was Royal Navy Commander Christopher J. Esplin-Jones, with his second-in-command, Lieutenant Commander Ian Hughes. They had overall control of the vessel in that they outranked our skipper, Don Ellerby, who would be working under their command. The crew as a whole hoped that Don would be no pushover. Don was a nice guy but on this particular trip we had to hope he'd be a tough one too. Don was responsible for the overall running of the *Norland* as Master of the Ship, but the supreme command for military purposes was firmly in the hands of the Navy.

The chain of command for the crew, as in all British Merchant Navy ships, is that we took orders from our skipper through his officers.

On this trip, we didn't have to take any orders whatsoever from high-ranking Royal Navy or Army officers. In fact, we didn't have to take orders from any military person, whatever their rank. Had they attempted to tell us what to do, we wouldn't have listened to them anyway, and it would have only caused confusion if someone else had been giving us orders as well. It was very important to us that we stuck with our own chain of command, which was agreed back in Hull at that first meeting when we all volunteered. The ship's company had three departments:

- **Navigating Department.** Also known as the 'deck department', the skipper commands the entire ship's company and is directly responsible for the navigation of the vessel. Under him are a Chief Officer, 2nd Officers and a radio operator. Non-officers but still part of this department are a Bosun, the ship's carpenter and the role of able seaman (AB) of which we had ten.

- **Engineering Department.** This consisted of the Chief, 2nd and 3rd engineers, two electrical engineers and four motormen, who were nicknamed 'donkey men'.

- **Catering Department.** Under control of the Purser, this department consisted of the most men and women in the crew, made up of cooks, stewards, stewardesses, barmen, storekeepers and gift shop personnel (it was deemed useful to keep the gift shop open as a NAAFI-style outlet for the sale of everyday items). The ship's storekeepers, Chris Sutcliffe and his assistant, Kevin Hornsby, had a mammoth task in ordering and maintaining stocks of food, mountains of it, as well as a crucial order of 100 tons of beer. This worked out at approximately 22,400 gallons, making five pints per day for 1,000 passengers over a thirty-day period: we were worried it might not be enough! Overseen by George Rimmer, our very experienced chief cook, the galley staff would be flat out serving three big meals a day to hungry soldiers. And what pressure it would be keeping soldiers happy with one of the things they love the most, good grub.

Captain Don Ellerby, MV *Norland*, Master of the Ship. (Courtesy *Hull Daily Mail*)

The stewards in the catering department were not all seasoned seafarers; many had only worked on the short runs of North Sea Ferries (what we call 'home trade'). Leaving behind the short crossing of the North Sea for the ocean travel of the Atlantic waters (what we call 'deep sea') would be a big change for quite a few on board. That said, many of the *Norland*'s crew were very experienced 'old hands', and I think the MOD was very lucky to have this calibre of Merchant Navy personnel sailing for them on this trip, particularly in the deck and engineering departments.

Going across the Bay of Biscay we were blessed with decent weather. The soldiers during this time worked up healthy appetites through weapon practice, first aid and physical training. Each morning after breakfast they were on the open decks doing static exercises or running.

On finishing my night shift at eight o'clock in the morning, and after a light breakfast, I took to jogging with several of the ship's barmen, Alan Eastwood and Tony and Geoff Palfreman. We liked to keep a level of fitness but, in truth, we were further inspired to do so on seeing the soldiers keeping fit. Initially, we jogged around the car deck when the weather wasn't so good. As the weather turned better, and as the barmen got too busy with other tasks, I found myself joining in with the soldiers on the open deck. Nobody stopped me, but why would they? For some reason many thought I was a soldier anyway. I began to strike up conversations with several of the soldiers who had seen me joining in. Some were surprised to discover I was a crew member and someone just trying to keep in shape. But nobody kept themselves in shape more than a paratrooper. It amused me to hear their expression 'beasting the body'. Often, they would exercise to the extreme with weighted rucksacks. My nearest equivalent was carrying cases of beer to the bar and taking away the empties.

A soldier I managed to get on with really well was called Chris. It was pleasant to have conversations with military people and the soldiers probably thought it equally refreshing to have the same with sea-farers. Many of the crew had gone from nodding terms to speaking terms and relationships were starting to form. However, during a conversation with some soldiers, one said, 'I see you've been hobnobbing with one of the officers.'

'What do you mean hobnobbing?' I asked.

'Well, you know, you're getting friendly with one of the higher rankers.'

Wishing he would get to the point: 'Who are you referring to?' I asked.

It turned out he was referring to Chris Dent, who had the rank of Army Captain. He seemed a very popular officer whom all the lads liked and respected.

The first few days at sea I spent time wandering around on the car decks and was amazed at the amount of equipment that had been packed into the ship. There were dozens of refrigerated containers with food in frozen form, and masses of other foodstuffs. There were enormous black rubber water containers and thousands of tons of army equipment of one type or another; all the car decks were full, with little room to spare.

During these first few days at sea we caught sight of a Royal Navy ship accompanying us. It was HMS *Intrepid*, sailing a couple of miles astern. On this same day, after jogging with Chris Dent, I went to get my head down and fell into a deep sleep until I was woken up by a horrendous noise. I went into the alleyway and asked one of the lads who was passing by, 'What the hell's going on?'

'Go and have a look on the arse end,' he said, without revealing why.

I quickly got dressed and went aft to realise it was gunfire. A dozen or so Paras were lined up on the handrail, firing weapons into the sea, although there didn't seem to be any visible target. Talking with some of the lads, we wondered if this is what we'd have to put up with every day (bearing in mind 2 Para are an infantry unit and small arms are their stock-in-trade). It wasn't long before the army invited the crew to participate, even though we'd had no weapon training. Before I knew it, along with the ship's barman, John Foster, we were firing their army-issued weapons. After being shown the basics of an SLR (Self Loading Rifle – their standard issued weapon), like the Paras, we were firing away at imaginary targets. It seemed strange that we were openly encouraged to use their weapons.

Later that day I approached an army officer about it and was told, 'Nobody really knows what lies ahead but it's possible it's going to become a shooting war. If that happens and we leave the ship, would you want the ability to defend it?'

'Against who?'

'Against the Argentinians, who do you think?' he replied with a look of bemusement at my naïve question.

It seemed to me a noble gesture that we could defend the ship, but surely it wouldn't be feasible – would it? Whatever the prospects ahead, we could still have a lot of fun by using the army's weapons. On handling a Browning 9mm pistol, I figured I knew how James Bond felt, and handling an SMG (submachine gun), how Al Capone felt. This became a daily routine until other things took over. The crew were being slowly initiated into army ways and what an initiation it was.

What struck me was the amount of ammunition that was used with no restriction. All the brass cartridges would apparently have been recycled off the range when practising back on land. It should have been the same at sea, but instead they were swept up and shovelled over the side without a second thought.

Not every member of the crew wanted to join in. One said, 'Why the hell should I? I'm not a soldier!' One of the gay lads in the crew was equally reluctant, remarking, 'Good heavens no. What do you think I am, dear?'

My workmate on the ship, Dave Aistrop, and I had worked together on nights for some time. We had a good relationship. What we did was a two-man job but if one of us was tied up with other business, we knew the other would carry on regardless. I couldn't have asked for a better workmate and personal friend. Dave and I differed in that, after breakfast and a natter, I would go to search out something to do before turning in, whereas Dave headed to his cabin on G-deck to turn in straight away. For me there was too much happening, and I wanted to witness some of it.

Normally on nights, we would use the information desk on C-deck as our base, which was also the base for the ship's policeman. That was normal for the three personnel who did nights. On this trip the police-man was deemed unnecessary because the military had their own form of policing, as well as their military discipline.

The information desk was open all night for passengers' inquiries when sailing in civilian mode on North Sea crossings. Either Dave or I would man this desk until relieved by the Purser and his staff the next morning. But now that this desk had been commandeered by the army for their use, we had to move to a corner in the restaurant on D-deck as our new base. The nature of our job as night stewards gave us licence to roam pretty much anywhere on the ship, when required. There are some areas we wouldn't normally go, such as the bridge or on the fo'c'sle, being forward of the bridge. Neither would we go in the engine room unless we had a good reason. We carried various pass keys that allowed us to get into cabins, store cupboards or wherever we needed to be. One of the reasons I was on nights was the freedom it gave me to carry out the job. The immediate boss to Dave and me was the Purser, John Crowther, the head of the catering department. He had two Assistant

Pursers, John Graham and Keith Thompson. Normally they wouldn't interfere with our work unless we needed them in an emergency. One example is a passenger falling down one of the stairways, which happened a lot on booze-cruise crossings.

Around the clock, we had watchkeepers on deck and watchkeepers down below in the engine room. They worked four-hour watches covering 12-4, 4-8 and 8-12. These were done as four hours on, eight hours off.

For any problem that arose regarding safety of the ship, such as a fire, whatever working hours each of us had were irrelevant; you were called out to deal with it. We called it Emergency Stations, signalled by the ringing of bells throughout the ship. Little did we know at this stage that a new sound was to be introduced to us – the dramatic sound of a klaxon, which the military had brought on board the ship for when they would be signalling their own emergency stations known as a red alert.

Aside from watchkeepers, the rest of the crew were day workers. Everything described regarding the running of the *Norland* was pretty much general for all British merchant ships.

Something new to our ship, however, was that the sheer volume of food needed on board to provide soldiers with three meals a day now required a night staff in the galley. Food was prepared and cooked during the quiet hours to ease the workload of the galley staff during the day.

The ship's officers were lucky because administering discipline in the crew was rarely necessary; everyone simply got on with their work, unlike in the army which mostly achieved it by giving out orders with lots of shouting as part of the process. In conversation with the Purser, I asked, 'What do you want us to do, particularly on nights?' His answer was, 'Reg, I want you and Dave just to carry on and do whatever you think is right.' He added, 'If there's any change in that, I will let you know.' This suited Dave and me fine.

Not unique to the *Norland*, there is a distinct line between the Merchant Navy officers and the ratings. Generally speaking, they moved in their circles and we moved in ours. Both groups were happy with this situation. Though the officers were in charge of the running of the ship, in my opinion as well as that of many other ratings, it was us who really ran the ship, or so we liked to think.

On board, civilian passengers had access to the Continental Bar, the Forward Lounge and Bar, and the Snug Bar. These three bars were utilised by the military. It has to be remembered the *Norland* wasn't a luxury liner like the *Canberra* or the *QE2*. That said, the standard was still high. The Snug Bar, the smallest of the three, served as the Officers' Mess. The Forward Lounge and Bar became the Sergeants' Mess. The Continental Bar served the junior NCOs and private soldiers (this bar was the largest, boasting a sizeable area with a disco dancefloor during normal runs). The military had decided it would not be a 'dry ship'. An allocation of alcohol was imposed with a method organised by the military that (in theory) controlled the amount each soldier drank.

Two more bars existed which were the ship's Officers Bar and a Crew Bar. Many military officers used the former and soldiers the latter, mainly because these two bars had the cheapest prices. Leisure time was allowed on the ship sailing south; during free time what else was there to do on board except have a drink in the evenings? All drink for the soldiers was facilitated by the use of a voucher system. The barmen were popular and never stopped working when they were on bar duty.

When it became clear we were sailing to Sierra Leone, one of the stewardesses – a good friend of mine called Carol Ewart, the eldest of the three female volunteers and a person everyone liked – wanted a private word with me. She said the skipper had called her in for a chat. He wanted the three stewardesses to leave in Freetown and fly back to Britain because from the political situation it looked more likely that there would be conflict. They had already been pressured in Portsmouth not to sail, but the girls were adamant they wouldn't leave. My view was that Margaret Thatcher wasn't going to back down to a military junta in South America. I told Carol, 'It's not going to be good. It will get worse, I'm sure, and if I was you, I'd go home while you can because it might become impossible to do so at a later date.' So that was my advice to Carol, which I felt other crew members told her as well.

Several days into our journey, I think we had a happy ship. Everyone had firmly settled into a routine, though some of the soldiers struggled to find their way around the ship with all its decks, stairways and corridors. Leisure time saw lots of drinking – probably too much drinking.

Several of the ship's stewards were gay. The term 'queer' was commonly used at that time by the old school, whereas 'gay' was the much-preferred description. We all knew each other and got on well. One of the gay stewards, Wendy, organised for the piano to be put in the Continental Bar, where the 2 Para soldiers drank. Wendy set up a singalong session after he had finished his normal work. Without care to what anyone thought, he did this in camp, colourful clothing and eyeliner. With his tuneful piano skills and boisterous voice, he became quite the celebrity at these fun times. Once the soldiers had accepted his flamboyant way, Wendy became well thought of. In fact, his engaging personality was helping to break down barriers between the machismo of the military and the other gay crew members on board.

Though there was definitely a carnival atmosphere on the ship, I felt there was also an undercurrent of uncertainty about what was happening in the wider world. We were cut off from the main sources of news with only scant information filtering down.

I kept up my jogging and I also enjoyed shooting practice. Somebody came up with the bright idea of putting a target in the water that could be towed. A beer keg was chosen. It was placed on the end of a 40–50m rope and it bounced around in the wake of the ship. The keg had so many holes in it, and the line itself got shot up so badly, that it inevitably parted company from us. But we still had plenty more beer kegs to use – empty ones, of course. One time after shooting practice, I was up on the open boat deck and there was activity going on everywhere with the troops doing one thing or another. What caught my eye were three Paras sitting down blindfolded. Puzzled, I asked one of the sergeants in charge, 'Why are they like that?' 'Stay and watch,' came the reply. It turned out they were taking their personal weapons (SLRs) apart. I marvelled at how, with their blindfolds still on, they reassembled them by sense of touch. This action would help if they were in total darkness and needed to do the same. This quite impressed me. The emphasis was on small arms until they brought out anti-tank weapons for practice – bazooka-type things (anti-tank weapons) that two men had to operate. Now that was interesting to watch!

One thing that fascinated me was that if it came to war, along with their basic first aid dressing (which the medics called a 'puncture repair kit'), they would be issued with morphine. For some reason, hearing this word seemed to heighten the impending seriousness of the situation, not just to me but to the Paras as well. It was emphasised that each man would carry morphine for personal use only. If a soldier found his mate wounded, then they had to use that casualty's morphine but not their own. This and other serious instructions did not bode well for anyone who thought that war wouldn't happen. The importance of having excellent first-aid skills was realised when training films were shown of battlefield wounds. Some officers wondered if it was wise to show these films because it could scare the troops. The medics on board must have thought that was a crazy way to think. It's okay going into a war and inflicting casualties, but you have to accept that you'll also have your own to deal with. The medics looked to be doing a good job of driving home that first aid mattered. As serious as this subject was, what brought some amusement was the suggestion that, if a vein couldn't be found for an intravenous drip, an alternative technique could be used of placing it up a casualty's backside. I have no idea how much this was being practised as part of their training!

What we wondered, as a crew, was would the Paratroopers go into possible conflict like the Marines do, by sea, or would they fly in and parachute down? At this stage, no one knew. But the next day we would be arriving in Freetown, which was something I looked forward to and that gave us something else to think about.

4

FREETOWN TO ASCENSION ISLAND

The weather had changed from pleasant sunshine in the area surrounding the Canary Islands to being uncomfortably hot once we entered the tropics on sailing further south. Throughout the ship we had an efficient air-conditioning system. This facility, like all air-conditioning systems, was only any good if its users understood the best way to manage it. If you drive along a road in a car on a hot day with the windows wide open and then switch on your air-conditioning, it isn't going to be efficient. On the ship, many doors were left open due to the constant movement of 1,000 men. This meant the air-conditioning during the day was under pressure to perform properly, whereas during the quieter period in the evenings, it started to do its job. Those who were not used to tropical heat really felt it. Inside the ship, at times, it was almost as bad as out on the open deck.

The day before we docked in Freetown, I had a private farewell with Carol, knowing that she'd decided to leave. Maybe she was the only one making the right decision. Then in her early sixties, many years earlier as a teenager she'd embarked on a career in the entertainment business as a successful singer during the latter part of the Second World War. Having already experienced that war may have been a further encouragement for her to leave. Parting meant that an opportunity was missed for her to accompany Wendy on the piano. They could have been the new Elton John and Kiki Dee!

I made my way to the upper deck, as I often did, and it was there that I picked up a strange aroma. Thick and scented, it was hard to describe exactly what was in the air. Not everybody noticed this smell. I had come across something similar several times before at sea. The first time for me, I was aged 17 and sailing east through the Arabian Sea when a thick, not unpleasant, smell filled the early morning air. At the time I asked one of the old hands on board what it was. 'That's India!' he said.

If you have heard people say that you can smell India long before you arrive there, now you know what is meant by that expression, which is not meant in a disrespectful way. But after all, we were now in the tropics where these kinds of aromas are enhanced by the climate.

What I could smell this time around on a prevailing wind was Sierra Leone. The next day we docked in Freetown, the capital city. I wasn't sure exactly what we were doing there, probably to take on fresh water and rations. Kingston upon Hull chose to be twinned with Freetown through its associations in helping with the abolition of the slave trade in the early 1800s by the sterling work of Hull-born politician and emancipist, William Wilberforce.

The continuing alterations on the ship had finally been completed and the two civilian workers involved with them left along with Carol. One of the gay stewards, Frankie Green, was very close to her and I'm sure that the farewells between the two of them involved a few tears. Most of us were sorry to see her go but we thought it was for the best. I was glad I had said my goodbyes the day before because I didn't get to see her again. There was real sadness in having this popular woman leave. The other two stewardesses, Shirley Howlett and Jean Woodcock, stayed on.

Shirley was the partner of steward Bill Moody and there was no way they were going to end up being apart. Jean was simply along for the ride, being the bubbly, energetic lover of life that she was. Middle-aged, Jean was for sure an eccentric force of nature. You always knew when she was present. Everyone liked her as much as she liked everyone else. People aside, she particular enjoyed a tipple (or two), and after a tipple (or maybe three) she enjoyed flirting for a bit of fun. One time she made to give me a kiss and I made my escape by leaping over a bar. I am not a tall bloke and this was quite a feat for me, but it reflected my determination to avoid, let's say, her charismatic grip. It made me think that if there was to be any fighting against the Argies, in Jean we had a surprise advantage card. If the Argies ever dared to board our ship, on meeting her they'd immediately be leaping over the side and retreating back to their trenches quick time. All of the 'Toms' took to Jean straight away. (Toms is the name given to the young Para lads.)

Without much to say about Freetown, we soon found ourselves back at sea the following day and it was business as usual. When out jogging I bumped into Captain Chris Dent, with whom I had a good natter. Chris and I didn't have that much in common, him being a commissioned officer in an illustrious mob like the Parachute Regiment, me being a steward on a Merchant Navy ship. But that said, we felt at ease in each other's company and we enjoyed each other's conversation. I learned he was married with two kids, the same as myself.

What became noticeable was a greater sense of urgency on board. News had been leaked to us that talked of no improvement on the political front. The Toms were training more intensely now. Dave and I carried on as usual and during the late hours we always had plenty of visits from soldiers asking favours of coffees or teas. We weren't open for this service as such, but we were glad to look after them; it was a good way for us to get to know some of them better and especially to get information. On civilian runs we would have charged for serving hot drinks, but we'd decided through the Purser that on this run we would never charge the soldiers for any coffee or tea. One paratrooper, Stuart Cardy, was on first name terms with us and he always enjoyed a natter whilst having a brew. He was a fit-looking, broad-necked type and a very serious soldier. He didn't drink much alcohol and was always training hard. He was typical of the professionalism that a lot of the soldiers showed.

A few days after leaving Freetown, Dave and I had sat down for a cuppa, and when talking with some of the Toms, one of them complained, 'These useless bastard boots are killing me.'

I'd noticed the army-issued boots had a design that didn't look at all comfortable. I hadn't given this observation any more thought until this moment. 'They're shit-useless things,' the Para moaned. He took one of them off to show me and they looked to be of poor quality. He pointed out where they chafed. I was amazed to see that the tongue inside the boots was loose, in that it flopped to the left or right. Good boots should have a built-in tongue. I had brought three special items with me in addition to all my usual gear: a compass, a pair of 7x50 binoculars and my sturdy pair of walking boots. In a sort of Crocodile Dundee way, I told the Para, 'Call those a pair of boots, I'll show you a pair …' As my cabin was only 20yds or so from where we sat, I went to get them. The pair I showed him, made by Scarpa, I had worn for a couple years and they were quality walking/climbing boots. A good pair of boots will have a tongue designed so that it is stitched at the sides up to the top of the boots, better to repel water, like mine were.

'Christ, I like the look of them!' he said with envy. 'What size are they?'

'Size eight,' I said.

'That's my size. Can I try them on?' he ventured, to which I thought, I need to be careful here.

He put them on and loved them. 'Can I buy them off you?' was his response.

'No, sorry. I broke them in and they're staying mine.'

'I'll offer you twenty quid?'

I shook my head. 'No, they're not for sale.'

'Twenty-five then?' he chanced. That was a fair amount to offer for a second-hand pair, but I wasn't going to budge.

I told him, 'Look, I'm showing you them not to wind you up or anything, and it's certainly not to sell them. I just wanted you to see what else you can get that's available if you shop around.' I then thought it best to take them back to my cabin so that I wasn't tempted to sell them for an outrageous sum or, even worse, that I wouldn't have to fight to hang on to them.

I was amazed that these soldiers were possibly going to war and they didn't think much about some of their army kit – and not to be happy about boots, of all things, seemed crazy to me. Paratroopers are famous for marching long distances. For this very reason, some of the more experienced (or probably better paid) Paras had purchased their own civilian boots in place of their army-issued boots.

Several days after the boots conversation and before reaching Ascension, we crossed the Equator, known as 'crossing the line'. Normally those doing this for the first time would have some kind of ceremony. I wasn't around to see it, but from what I'd heard, 2 Para celebrated it with great gusto. Such a ceremony meant we had left the North Atlantic and we were now in the South Atlantic. The next day, in the distance, land could be seen that appeared mountainous. As we got closer, using my trusty binoculars it looked, to my eye, like volcanic terrain. Indeed, there was only vegetation on the upper quarter of this mountainous island, having been watered by cloud formations. I had looked forward to going ashore there and really wanted to do some exploring. Annoyingly, there was no shore leave whilst at Ascension.

We dropped anchor and soon got absorbed in busy activity. There were quite a few other ships at anchor. What was very apparent was the number of aircraft constantly coming and going, which were mainly UK and US types. This indicated to me that we were possibly receiving help from the Americans. Some may have been happy with support from them, but as far as the Paras were concerned, one individual was not at all enamoured by them and said, 'Fuck John Wayne and his heroics! Whatever happens we don't ever want the Yanks involved with us.' I think this had most to do with 'friendly fire' from trigger-happy Americans in previous wars.

Over the side of the ship, the sea was crystal clear with countless fish visibly swimming about. It absolutely teemed with them. A delight for everyone was spotting hammerhead sharks. It felt like a really nice place to be, but frustratingly, we were confined to the ship. The next day someone said to me, 'Kempy, go on deck and have a look at what's going on.' I went on deck and couldn't believe my eyes on seeing naval landing craft alongside us. Soldiers of 2 Para had life jackets on and were all clambering down the side of the ship and getting into these landing crafts. I thought, wow, they're converting these guys into Marines, there's no way they're going to be parachuting in anywhere. Of all the rumours circulating the ship, the biggest rumour had been that once we arrived at Ascension Island, we would be saying goodbye to the troops as they went on their merry way. We were then supposed to return to Britain. But my gut feeling had told me that the *Norland* was going to take the Paras all the way down to the Falklands – which meant us with them. What I didn't know is that similar thoughts were had by some of our officers on A-deck. These thoughts were enough that a twenty-two-page document was produced by the Royal Navy listing the 'distribution of responsibilities' between the military and Merchant Navy. In time, I would obtain a copy of this document. When I did, I was disappointed that I hadn't got to see it earlier due to its interesting contents. Its distribution was limited only to senior military and Merchant Navy personnel who had a 'need to know'. Produced by Commander Esplin-Jones and his naval team, the document covered all conceivable situations on board, from messing to medical to lifeboat stations. I would also later discover that these orders were produced on the insistence of our Chief Officer, Bob Lough, and the Chief Engineer, Lloyd Newell, who both wanted full clarity on board of the relationship between the Royal Navy and the Merchant Navy. Apparently, there were often tensions between Commander Esplin-Jones and the ship's officers over key decisions to be taken. Lloyd Newell was particularly keen to have such a document produced, revealing that it formally made clear that: 'We were now under naval command and we would be court martialled if we didn't do what we were told!'

(On 15 May, a state of active service was declared in the South Atlantic. This meant the crew of *Norland* became subject to the Naval Discipline Act, but it was made clear that this only applied for operational efficiency of the fleet. The Merchant Shipping Act continued to apply for day-to-day discipline.)

Since 1941, all naval deployments/operations in peacetime and war have been given a 'Naval Party' number. The number allocated to the *Norland* was 1850. As well as Royal Navy personnel, Naval Party 1850 included members of the Royal Corps of Signals (Corporal Barnet and Signalman Winning), who carried out communications tasks; and Warrant Officer Two, McKenzie, from the Royal Corps of Transport, who allocated accommodation and organised movement of personnel on board. Worthy of mention is the name of Alan Richardson, who did not appear on the Naval Party 1850 or the ship's crew list. Alan was a Royal Fleet Auxiliary, radio officer, who happened to be a local lad from Hessle near Hull. One of the cabins (4th Engineer) directly next to the ship's radio room was commandeered and fitted out as a second radio room with all manner of secret equipment installed. Our ship's Radio Officer, Brian Lavender, mainly sent and received messages over normal

M.V. NORLAND.
(LPH 169)
WAR
ORDERS

MAY 6 1982

commercial shipping communications links, whilst military communications were through the second radio room overseen by Alan, employing two Royal Navy and two Army signals operators. The guest operators and our Radio Officer all liaised closely.

Back Row

LA Luckett	CPO Woods	PO Thomas	LMEM Spall	CPO Pilcher	Lt Cdr Hughes	Lt Cdr Shorter	Cdr Esplin Jones	Lt Cdr Wingate	RO Green	CPO Marriott	CPL Barnet	SIG Winning	WO McKe

Front Row

LWTR Philips	NA Mills	NA Welsh	LRO Cooper	AB Griffiths	LA Oakley	LMA Hearnden

Naval Party 1850: formed on 17 April 1982. (photo courtesy Lt Cdr Cliff Shorter RN)

5

ASCENSION ISLAND TO THE FALKLANDS

All the crew, by now, felt that 2 Para would be going all the way by sea, not by air. Would we be going all the way with them, or only to a rendezvous outside the Falklands? At what point would the troops be transferred from a possible meeting point to other ships such as HMS *Fearless* and HMS *Intrepid* for a beach landing? Which ships would be our escorts if needed?

Yet more confirmation this might be true came in the form of a paint job to the exterior of the ship. Most of the ships surrounding us were coloured battleship grey. This might mean if anyone was to attack the Task Force, they would likely go for the grey ships first. Then again, they might instead go straight for a ship that looked an easier target, especially one with a bright flashy livery like ours. Someone else must have had the same thought and realised that having the large, bold white letters of NORTH SEA FERRIES emblazoned along the length of starboard and port side of the ship was not a good idea. It wasn't long before lifeboats were lowered down the side of the ship to paint out these words with black paint. This job was given to several soldiers and they seemed to revel in the task as it was a break from their normal routine whilst at anchor in Ascension. Another necessary job was the painting out of the ship's bright red funnel, which was like the centre target of a bullseye. This job was begun but never completed because a wind of around 20 knots kept blowing the paint all over the place. So, we could be heading into possible conflict with the Argies in a ship that was not presented at its best. Considering the military and its love of bullshit attention-to-detail, I could only think that there were more important priorities than painting parts of the ship, which again was an indication that we'd be going all the way.

Something of interest that electrician Brian Burton talked of was when the Chief Engineer had put out a request to see what experience any of the troops might have that could come in handy. A Para corporal professed to have been a welder in civvy street. This kind of work on the ship was always cropping up. The corporal was tested and up to par and thereafter gainfully employed. Brian reckoned the corporal was actually quite brilliant at some of the welding tasks he'd been given, which he did in-between his soldierly duties. Oddly, he was always accompanied by a Para sergeant, a minder/assistant-type figure, and apparently they were both big pals.

I laughed when Brian told of how, as a thank you to the corporal and the sergeant, they were invited into the ship's Officers' Mess for food and drink. This mess was also used by the Navy and Army officers. The Navy went nuts about this. The *Norland* officers didn't care and Brian found Commander Esplin-Jones very unhappy about it, but Brian thought that Esplin-Jones was never happy about anything. In fact, as a wind-up, some of the *Norland*'s officers used to greet Esplin-Jones and his fellow officers with words such as 'Good morning, sunshine', which greatly amused Brian.

We were back at sea all too soon and the next day the weather got even hotter, as did the training of the troops, who were going all out to achieve maximum fitness, along with constant weapon handling and shooting practice. Looking out in all directions from the ship, we could see an even bigger build-up of Merchant Navy and Royal Navy ships surrounding us. One afternoon, I was woken up from my sleep by a red alert alarm. I quickly dressed and went to my emergency station. The Purser, John Crowther, was there. 'What's happening?' I asked.

'We've had a submarine sighting,' said John.

This was a strange situation as it could have been one of our own submarines that had been sighted. Someone had spotted what they thought was a periscope. Regardless, the whole ship had reacted and whether this was a way to keep everyone on their toes or an actual threat, no one really knew. Either way, it served to put a jolt up the crew – the military as well.

On this trip, the catering department was fortunate to have John Crowther as our boss. John and I had met each other ten years earlier when I first started on North Sea Ferries. I was new to the company and John was a senior steward with them. The company recognised his talents and urged him to go for promotion. His conscientious manner led to his current role as the ship's Purser. Responsible for the *Norland*'s catering and the control of around fifty men and women, he had to be a lot of things to a lot of people. He coaxed the best out of his department with his friendly style, but he was no pushover. Both the same age, I liked and respected him. John was in the Liberal Club on Anlaby Road in Hull when he received a phone call from North Sea Ferries. On finally tracking him down to ask if he would volunteer to go, without hesitation he said yes. When asked who he wanted as his two Assistant Pursers, John volunteered John Graham, whom he had been mentoring, without the latter's knowledge. The other Assistant Purser who'd readily volunteered was Keith Thomson. Anyone else in the company available at Purser level would be required to find a replacement vessel and a crew for it in the *Norland*'s absence.

After the red alert stand down, John and I stepped on to the outer deck. He took out a pack of cigarettes and offered me one. Out of habit, I lit it up but immediately realised I had chucked smoking about a year earlier. Maybe it was that our current trip was on my mind and it had me forgetting I had quit, but there was no way I was going to start again, no matter what was to come. As John happily puffed away on his cigarette, it was good to speak with him and get his take on what lay ahead. He said, 'Before the final decision was made to commission the *Norland*, the MOD had initially reported it as not being suitable for the purpose. Mainly, there wasn't enough water and fuel storage for a long trip. The ship was really all they had at such short notice and the MOD reconnaissance party was told to go back, make another appraisal and damn well make it work!'

Thinking over John's comment, I knew the ship's design was for short overnight crossings, not deep sea, hence the conversions that had taken place. Some of the other stewards were only used to 'home trade' on 'rock dodgers' like the *Norland*. But I had confidence in our ship that it would be up to the job, whatever it might be.

This confidence was reinforced by a comment from the Chief Engineer, who'd told John, 'Feed the engine properly and it'll go like a baby. I'll be happy with it because we've got better fuel. P&O normally purchase the cheap stuff but now we are on par with Royal Navy ships and we are getting the best there is.'

John had sailed with the *Norland* skipper, Don Ellerby, for many years. John was fond of telling a joke about how Don's three brothers were also skippers but on big Merchant Navy cargo ships. Because Don was the skipper on a 'rock dodger' car ferry, they called him a 'car park attendant'. Don took this teasing in his stride. Easy going as he was, like John, he was no pushover – and this trip was to be no pushover. Forget about shuffling cars and people between Hull and Rotterdam, this was as big as it could get for any skipper, on any kind of ship. Don Ellerby's brothers were probably envious of the responsibility that he had right now.

'How are you getting on with the army, John?' I asked.

John said:

I'll tell you what, the skipper stuck up for our crew. Most of the Para officers are billeted on B-deck and one of them passed a remark to him that my room would have been more suitable for a senior Para officer. The skipper immediately rejected this, telling him that 'my crew will live where they have always lived, in their own cabins'.

I wasn't surprised when John added:

Initially, the 2 Para RSM didn't take kindly to the actions of Roy Gibson in his Wendy mode. On first seeing him dressed in light make-up and pirouetting around, he wanted to throw the piano over the side and Wendy after it. But he's slowly come around to seeing that it provides harmless entertainment for the troops.

'They're a tough lot,' I said, 'not the type who are used to having someone like Wendy in their company. But knowing Wendy, he can give as good as he gets.'

'Whatever they're used to or not, they strike me as the best troops to be sending to the Falklands. I'm confident in them,' said John.

'And the navy, how are you getting on with them?' I asked.

John replied:

I've been dealing with a Royal Navy bosun. I'm not keen on him. You would think being in the Merchant Navy, I'd have something in common with the Royal Navy, but to be honest I'm not keen on any of them. The real people for me are the Paras. They tell you how it is. The first one I met was the 2 Para Quartermaster, Tom Goodwin. He is a fabulous bloke. So is the straight-talking RSM, Malcolm Simpson. The RSM has a right-hand man, a Colour Sergeant called Del Amos, and he is a great bloke too, especially to have a beer with and hear his war stories. I've been working with these three a lot. It's mainly been sorting out the menu for each meal. You can't overestimate how important mealtimes are to a soldier's life.

I agreed with John on this. We were effectively on twenty-four-hour catering, and mealtimes for the troops were a social occasion as well as necessary replenishment. As is often said, an army marches on its stomach or, as is in this case, sails on its stomach.

John continued, 'I've been happy so far that no one from the Paras has asked me to have a word with any of our crew for their behaviour. Well, except for the remark from the RSM about Wendy, but he's realised that Wendy's sincere in his entertaining of the troops.'

John then came out with something quite surprising: 'You know what, Reg, this might be one of the easiest trips I will ever have to do.'

'What do you mean?'

'Before we left Britain, the union rep back in Hull demanded that the ship was manned by the full complement required. An argument against this was that from previous experience with the military as passengers, a lot of the work could be done by them. The union rep wouldn't have it and insisted that everyone who could be in work should be in work. In the back of my mind, having so many in our crew, the risk was greater if it all went wrong. There would be hell to pay if there were lots of casualties. It was a needless danger, because right from the off, I thought we would end up at war. The union rep wasn't having it.'

As the crew, we understood there would be a monetary bonus of sorts for sailing so far south. But whatever the reasons for our crew being on board, we just wanted to know what our ultimate role would be. John said:

Like you, Reg, I've sailed to Argentina before and they are very proud people. They've been hoodwinked that the Falkland Islands belong to them and that it's worth fighting for. The Paras should beat them though. Yet if for some reason they don't, we're lucky that the Argentinians are civilised people. If we're captured, we should be treated alright.

'Let's hope that we don't have to bloody well find out!' I said.

John left to resume his work and I went to get some sleep. John and I had a relationship where the truth could be told. We'd had disagreements before, but we didn't hold grudges and we'd never seriously fallen out. John was probably right about this being an easy trip for him because, early into our trip, he had wanted to get stuck in with us when we had to prepare a special buffet. He was more a hindrance than a help. I said to him, 'Look, John, will you please do us a favour and just piss off to let us get on with things?'

'You can't talk to me like that. I'm the Purser, I'm your boss,' he said.

With a smile I said, 'Well, okay, will you kindly sod off instead and just leave us to it?'

Shaking his head, but with a smile, he left us to carry on.

At this time, I also bumped into electrician Brian Burton and got a chance for a lengthy catch-up on our situation. A stocky, well-built fellow with an engaging smile, Brian and I had a good relationship in that he was fun company to have a beer with and, like me, he was an outdoors type who enjoyed hill walking. Brian's concern was that the 8,000-mile trip down south might prove too much for the *Norland*, which was only used to the short 202-mile trip across the North Sea from Hull to Rotterdam, and back again. Brian really rated the Chief Engineer, Lloyd Newell, and if anyone could ensure the ship performed at its best, it would be Lloyd. Before sailing, Brian had been tasked with ordering necessary parts for the engine as back-ups, speaking with MOD officials who dealt in logistics. Amongst the many items he'd asked for were ball race bearings for an alternator, of which the ship had four. He hadn't held out too much hope that they would be delivered before sailing from Hull to Portsmouth. He was wrong. The very next day after his order went in, a Chinook helicopter appeared hovering above the berth where the *Norland* was tied up in King George Dock. A huge forklift truck then came onto the scene and began using its two menacing, fork-like blades to pick up and move cars without the owners' consent. It wasn't long before an uncluttered area had been created for the Chinook to land and unload its spare parts and other vital engine items. The MOD simply compensated the car owners for any knackered exhausts, springs or bumpers.

Before leaving Hull, even with a list of key adjustments to be carried out in Portsmouth, an inspection of the ship's suitability to face sailing through intense warm humid tropics before enduring the extreme cold of the South Atlantic was needed. An expert arrived from the Maritime and Coastguard Agency (MCA), the organisation responsible for maritime safety in the UK, which is an agency of the Department for Transport of the British Government. The maritime expert had carried out a detailed appraisal of the ship and signed off a certificate okaying the ship's suitability. With quizzical looks from Brian and some of the ship's engineers who had reservations about the *Norland*, the MCA representative unconcernedly said, 'Oh, don't worry, it'll be alright.'

Overall, this was a hell of a risk for the MOD to be taking, but with a possible war on, they had taken it! Brian never had any lack of confidence in our crew, only the pressure that the ship itself would be under. Though some of the engineers initially thought the ship might not be capable of what was to be asked of it, that was yet to be seen. For now, like the Chief Engineer, Brian was relieved at having been issued with the best oil and, most importantly, the best fuel. 'The Queen's five-star diesel' is how he described it, and it would go some way to making the journey ahead more achievable. However, with the offhand words from the MCA representative of 'Oh, don't worry, it'll be alright' hanging in the air, in a way this was all that Brian and those in the know could do – hope that it would be alright.

Not long after the submarine sighting incident, a state of 'darkened ship' was introduced to all ships sailing south in the Task Force. As in the Second World War, there was a blackout imposed during dark hours. Most of the ship's doors leading to the outside deck had a two-door system to counteract bad weather. Nearly all ships have this system of a small foyer area between the inner and outer door. All the doors with glass on the *Norland* were blanked off with black bin liners, as were all windows. When we asked questions about this, we didn't get any answers, which wasn't surprising.

Graham Edwards, a steward, had an old radio. He couldn't get a proper signal and one evening he asked me to join him on the open deck in the dark to see if we could pick up the BBC World Service. We were tinkering away trying to tune it in when out of nowhere a voice of authority barked at us, 'Turn that fucking radio off!' Trying to be clever, we moved further down the deck to what we thought was an out-of-the-way space and again started tuning the radio. With great menace, the same voice from somewhere in the dark said, 'If you don't turn that fucking radio off, I'll shoot you both!' My reply was, 'I don't know who you are but take it easy, we're on your side.' Heeding his warning, we retreated back to our cabins. We found out later there were guards positioned all around the ship to stop the kind of thing that we were doing. We didn't try it again.

One day, in the distance, an enormous aircraft high in the sky flew past us. It was identified as a Russian aircraft. What were the Russians doing here in the South Atlantic? It was said to have been a spy plane. I found this to be very odd and another situation unaccounted for.

Thankfully, ships belonging to the Task Force included the aircraft carrier HMS *Hermes*, which was briefly spotted. Everything was escalating and I counted up to thirty ships, from tankers to tugs, when looking from all sides of the *Norland* to the horizon.

There was a constant use of choppers flying from ship to ship. It's funny how easily we got used to the droning noise of them doing their work. Sea Kings were the main helicopters in use, with the occasional Chinook also employed.

With such a build-up, it seemed inevitable to most of us there was going to be conflict. When we joined the Task Force, one of the main topics we'd discussed was knowing the Argies had a big navy. It was believed within the Task Force that the Argentine Navy's capital ships could appear anytime. One such ship called the *Belgrano* was mentioned to be in our vicinity. We were told it was an old Second World War cruiser but it still had the capability to sink us from a distance of 15–20 miles. If it sank us, with 1,000 men lost, the thinking was that it could be over, or at least for now it would be. If it sank the *Canberra* with even more troops on board than us, what a re-think it would be for Task Force war planners.

On a relatively quiet evening, Dave and I were going about our work when we heard a loud cheer from the main mess room where the lads hung out. Dave and I went to see what the fuss was about. It had been reported that the *Belgrano* had been sunk, presumably on the orders of Margaret Thatcher. For everyone, this was a major event. We later found out that it had been sunk by one of our subs. Could it maybe have been the same sub someone had spotted when we had our first red alert? Who knows? What we did know is that, at the time, throughout the ship there was an immense sense of relief. Hearing this news, we didn't know the loss of life to the Argies, hence our cheering. It was thought that if they had lost this capital ship, it would surely deter other ships from attacking us. We could only be thankful it had happened, even though it surely meant that this was it – we were now at war.

We lived on rumours and the latest one doing the rounds after the *Belgrano* sinking was that a political solution could still happen. But, after listening to countless other rumours, none of us really believed this to be the case. In truth, talking with the Paras, the sergeants and especially the Toms, none of them wanted it to be called off. All of them wanted to see action. Training was one thing, going on exercises was another, but to go into battle for real, well, that would be the ultimate test. Several of the lads had the attitude, 'Don't let us down, Maggie, don't give in … leave it up to us and we'll fucking sort it out.'

One thing that struck me was the energy and confidence of such young men who were ready to put their lives on the line. A few of the soldiers were in their late teens but mostly their age group was early twenties and thirties. The sergeants were mostly in their early thirties, with many of their senior officers near to their forties. It also struck me that , at the age of 43, I was in the older bracket of the ship's crew. Only a few of the crew were older than me from our complement of ninety-three personnel. These were the four 'donkey men' in the engine room, AB Paddy Dolan, Harold Dixon the restaurant manager, John Crowther the Purser, Billy Hookem the Bosun, as well as Les Isham, Tony McNamee and Terry Stephenson who were stewards. No doubt the skipper was in his forties but with the weight of responsibility on his shoulders he must have felt 100 years old. The Commanding Officer of 2 Para, Lieutenant Colonel 'H' Jones, was for sure near to his forties as was his second-in-command, Major Chris Keeble. They both had something about them, a definite air of authority, and not just from the rank they carried. Considering Lt Col Jones' high-ranking position in the Para battalion, whenever we had cause to address him in our work as stewards, Dave and I always found him to be quietly spoken and polite. One observation about him was that I never saw him without his beret on.

If you are captured you are required, under the provisions of Article 17 of the Prisoner of War Convention, 1949, to give your captors the information set out overleaf so that your capture may be reported to your next-of-kin. When you are interrogated, but not before, tear off the duplicate portion and give it to the interrogator. GIVE NO OTHER INFORMATION. Once this card has been issued to you you must carry it upon you at all times. In your own interest you must ensure that the particulars of your rank are kept up to date.
(Fill in your particulars in (BLOCK LETTERS)

Quiet politeness aside, any orders imposed on us, either written or orally, we were reasonably happy to comply with. However, an apparent incident told to the crew by Able Seaman Brian (Shep) Sheppard was that a day or so after leaving Portsmouth a Royal Navy rating stopped him. The rating said, 'I'll be taking over this work that you are doing, you know. My role on the *Norland* is to act as a buffer between the Royal Navy and the Merchant Navy.' Shep looked at him with scorn and asked, 'Tell me, just how long have you been at sea, lad?'

'Three years!' the rating proudly replied.

'Well, I've been at sea for twenty-five years … so fuck off and stop bothering me,' said Shep.

I think Shep was speaking for us all with his forthright manner to the rating. One thing that was making us unhappy was that no one had received mail. But at least we had Wendy entertaining us on the piano to keep up morale and maintain an atmosphere of friendliness between all those on board. Indeed, his singalong sessions were becoming an extremely popular daily event.

We observed a change of eating habits among the troops. Their portions became bigger and they seemed to be beefing themselves up even more. I asked about this and was told 'we're building ourselves up for the big event' – whatever the big event might be. One time, at an evening meal, all the 2 Para lads had eaten well. Two of them were walking out of the restaurant when they stopped at the cheese board. Instead of having cheese and biscuits in the normal way by cutting off a modest slice for it to be accompanied by a cream cracker or maybe a digestive biscuit, they each picked up a large segment of cheese that was on display and walked out, scoffing it as you would an apple. I thought, 'Fill your boots, boys.'

Music was introduced through the ship's tannoy system, which had the likes of 'Rule Britannia' and 'Land of Hope and Glory' blasting out to wake up the troops in the morning. These patriotic tunes, many of them marching band melodies, may have been entertaining for some but they were bad news for others, such as the off-duty watchkeepers who needed their sleep.

We resented the lack of real information. We felt there was a reluctance to inform the crew of truly relevant news and that we were the last to know about anything. And why would that be? The crew thought it was because the military thinkers themselves didn't know what the overall plan was. As such, we seemed to latch on to rumours more than anyone else. It was around 17 May that a message was passed to all of the crew that Don Ellerby, the skipper, wanted to come down to the mess room and speak to us. This rarely happened. Coming to the mess room to address the crew as a whole was really something. A grand entrance was made with the skipper supported by a couple of our ship's officers and some military personnel. His entrance was almost farcical for he entered the mess room wearing a steel helmet. It was a *Dad's Army*, Captain Mainwaring, moment. He imparted what knowledge he had of the current situation, mainly that a site had been chosen for the landings in the Falklands, somewhere called San Carlos Water.

So, this was it. We had finally been told that, whether we liked it or not, we were part of the military and that there would be no return to the UK until the job was done, whenever that might be. What happened next was extremely comical. One might have thought a member of the crew would have said something about this not being the deal we had signed up for, but no, the only question that someone asked was, 'Excuse me, sir, are we all going to get steel helmets?' The skipper, not appearing to acknowledge the sarcastic tone of this question, replied in all seriousness, 'No, sorry. . There aren't enough to go around for everyone.' The skipper then turned to leave with his entourage following on behind him, when one of the crew muttered, 'Thank fuck for that.'

The skipper's warlike attire aside, we knew he had meant well. More importantly, we had at last been given some concrete information.

Not long after this, instructions given to us stated that everyone should find out their blood type. A medic took a pin prick from everyone's hand to establish this. We were then questioned about whether we had made wills. If not, now was the time to think about it. Emphasising our increasingly dangerous situation, we were all advised to write home to our families. This kind of thinking from those who knew more than we did suggested it would be good to write with whatever thoughts we might have.

For a worst-case scenario of getting captured, we had ID cards produced and issued. We were told that we were now subject to the Official Secrets Act. To us, having to sign any Official Secrets Act was laughable.

This was because, should we get captured by the Argies and interrogated, what on earth did we know to tell them? Nothing except what the 'soup of the day surprise' was for each evening's meal!

An incident that provided some amusement was when the donkey men in the engine room discovered a fuel leak. They informed the engineers, who informed the chief officer, who informed the skipper, who informed the military, who informed Commander Esplin-Jones. It was explained to him that the ship would need to 'heave to' (i.e. the ship would have to stop) for a couple of hours to fix the problem. Apparently Esplin-Jones responded with the startled words, 'Is this some kind of a joke? Please tell me it is!' When realising it wasn't, he offered troops to help with the problem. 'How many do you want, five, ten, twenty?' A hundred men could have been offered up to fix the leak but only two engineers were needed and the space they had to work in was only big enough for two people anyway. But this was typical of the military mentality of throwing bodies at the problem. The ship hove to and thankfully the problem was fixed within a couple of hours.

Taking time out for a tug of war between the crew and the Paras. (Courtesy Brian Burton)

More mundane matters to think about included drinking water, which was always a problem. We had an on-board desalination unit but the water from it looked terrible. A limit on water use was imposed on everyone and we were discouraged from showering. We accepted this, for we had left the hot sweaty weather behind as we headed into the much colder climate of the South Atlantic. A welcome bonus was that, although the South Atlantic is notorious for bad weather, we were lucky that we only experienced heavy swells. Mind you, one of the Toms was looking out on a smaller vessel about half a mile away. It was bouncing around in the heavy seas and caused him to remark with amusement, 'Thank Christ I'm on this big ship and not that crappy little rowing boat thing.'

A strong suggestion from the bridge was that we stay fully clothed at all times, even when sleeping. This had some of what would normally be white coat-wearing stewards, wearing civilian coats instead when going about their jobs. The ship's heating system appeared to have been switched off and I wondered if this was to make sure we would wear more clothes without being reminded.

What we learned for real was that when the time came to make our way into the Falkland Sound (the waterway between the two islands of East and West Falkland) it would be on a non-moonlit night. There was a window of three nights that could be chosen to land the troops. It was to be our ship, escorted by naval ships, that would be leading the disembarking of the troops from the Task Force. We had gone from being a troop-carrying ship to an assault ship. And you know what, I believed that the military had known this all the time; they had strung us along until there was no turning back for any of the crew.

The night before the landing I was doing my rounds up on B-deck when I heard a strange sound. The ship had four Toms to a cabin on bunk beds and a lot of the Paras slept with the doors open. It was very quiet except for an unusual swishing sound. As I moved further along the alleyway there were a couple of Paras sitting in the corridor and they were rubbing something metallic. I asked, 'Are you alright, lads? What are you doing?' One of them produced a bayonet and said, 'I'm just sharpening this.'

I asked a dumb question: 'What are you going to do with that?'

His response was, 'I intend to kill Argies with it.'

The other Para just smiled at me. I carried on my way and thought, 'Well, I guess this is what they are here for.'

A bayonet is, of course, one of the tools of a soldier's trade but I was surprised that it might go down to hand-to-hand combat. All the troops had been psyched up and were mentally prepared for whatever was to come. They were still openly praising Maggie for being strong and not backing down. They were ready for a fight, which for many could be a fight to the death.

Thinking of the brave face put on by the lad holding the bayonet and how primitive war could get, I tried to imagine my own two lads as soldiers. I don't know what might have made them want to join up. I hope it would be for a more exciting life than civilian street had to offer. I would dread to think that they wanted to go to war to kill people, but that is it how it felt with some of those in the Paras, especially the young fit Toms, which I guess had to be a good thing in order to get the job done. The overall sadness in all of this was that some wouldn't be coming back and they all looked so young to be prepared to give up their lives. I guessed that secretly most were never expecting it to happen for real, but now that war seemed inevitable, they had to psyche themselves up for it. Our crew also had to psyche ourselves up for whatever was to come, but not in the same, intense, gut-wrenching way as the Paras.

As well as hearing the names of the Falkland Sound and San Carlos Water, a landmark often spoken about was Fanning Head, a high headland overlooking San Carlos Water. Fanning Head commanded strategic military control over this area. All the military thinking was that this headland needed to be controlled by us. It was reckoned that the Argies had taken this location, but it wouldn't be for long once our Special Forces were called into action, namely the SAS and SBS. At least this is what we hoped would happen, for entering through the Falkland Sound and heading into San Carlos Water was going to be a damn scary situation otherwise.

6
TAKE COVER!

My cabin was at the end of an alleyway with six other cabins. After we'd heard that HMS *Sheffield* had been hit, suffering heavy casualties (no doubt in retaliation for the *Belgrano*), I started to ensure that my cabin door was never completely shut. I achieved this by wedging something under it so that it was left ajar with a 3in gap and didn't swing about. My reason for doing this was that before we sailed from Hull, I visited my parents. My father had some very strong views on Margaret Thatcher and her politics. He believed there was no way she was going to suck up to the Argentinians – a tin pot regime in South America. He was an old seafarer who had survived the Second World War while serving in the Merchant Navy. He'd made countless trips across the Atlantic in the risky convoy system and he was also on a ship at the Normandy landings. Like many other crew members on our ship whose past relatives had served in the convoy system, I knew the sacrifices they'd made. We were very aware of the high mortality rate suffered by British Merchant seamen during the Second World War. Over 32,000 were lost and this figure was higher than the losses in the British Army, pro rata. My father advised me, 'If they don't back down, Maggie will be going all the way. Should it be the case, I want you to bear in mind that when any shooting starts and the shit is flying about, never close your cabin door.' He explained that once a ship gets hit with high explosive, the shockwave can vibrate throughout the vessel. This can cause the door frames on board to bend and warp; the impact can result in doors jamming and becoming difficult, if not impossible, to open. Whoever is inside could be trapped and unable to get out, resulting in lives being lost. That's why I'd decided to leave my door ajar. Some of the lads had noticed this and asked me why. Some weighed up my explanation and copied me; some didn't. I also sorted something on a private level that maybe others did too. I put together a small emergency bag of food, a bottle of water, a compass, my walking boots and some odds and ends; the idea being that if the ship got hit and we had to take to the water, I wanted to give myself the best chance of survival. Then if we made it to land, my boots would hopefully help in that situation. I felt that these thoughts going through my mind were going through those of other crew members too.

Early in the morning of 20 May, I had a mooch about. We knew the landing was imminent, that it would be sometime in the next day or so. Trying not to overthink the situation, I'd done my shift and got what sleep I could. I'd had a good few hours and woke up around 1 p.m., when I went into the mess room. One of the stewards, Tony Palfreman, saw me and said with excitement, 'Reg, I've got something to tell you.'

'Yeah, what's that?'

'We're going in. Tonight's the night!'

Earlier in the day, Tony and all other available crew had been briefed that, when going into San Carlos Water, those not working should put on a life jacket and go and lay down on their bunks for safety reasons. If we hit a mine, the shock could shake the ship so violently that if anyone was standing up, it would increase their chances of getting hurt. Tony said, 'The enormity of what we were involved in as a crew had finally hit home with me, more than any other time. I knew then that this was war for real.'

'So, they've finally made a decision,' I thought. We were not a troop carrier any more. Without doubt, we were an assault ship.

Wondering what lay ahead, I was on the upper deck when our ship was going dead slow and I saw on the port side that HMS *Broadsword* had come up, sailing dead slow, very close to us – unusually close. Dead slow for a ship is like walking speed. Our ship's bridge was higher than the frigate's bridge. I saw a naval officer on the frigate with something in his hand. He tossed a container from his ship to ours. It bounced on our upper deck and this pre-arranged action had someone dash out to pick up whatever the package was. We knew we were on 'radio silence', so communication between ships required that it be achieved in a different way. I'd guessed that orders had to be delivered by hand and this is what I had likely witnessed. Luckily, the person throwing it had a decent arm on him. Who knows what would have happened if he hadn't and instead it had fallen in between our two ships! (What I didn't know is that on this critical day, HMS *Broadsword* had come alongside because we had only received half a secret signal when some equipment failed, and simultaneously radio silence had been declared. She sent over (by packet) a copy of the signal which stated, 'H hour 210630Z MAY for the landings', i.e., the next day.)

Sometime in the late afternoon, I did the unusual thing of going back to my cabin to get a couple of extra hours, knowing that it was going to be a busy night. I read for a while and, surprisingly, I managed to get some decent sleep. On turning up for my shift at 9.30 p.m., I went into the restaurant and, though the main meals were all over by then, it was jam-packed with troops and their equipment. Piled up high were enormous rucksacks and assorted gear. All the troops had blackened faces from camouflage cream that disguised their pale skin. Two or three were walking about with their rucksacks on, bursting full of kit. They had drawn their weapons and were loaded up with ammunition too. The rucksacks looked enormous. In my limited 'outdoor pursuit' kind of way, I was used to carrying a rucksack, but what these guys had on was something else. The weight I might carry could be around 20lb. What these lads were carrying must have weighed 100lb or more. Amongst the hundreds of Para lads, a strangely dressed individual caught my eye. He was festooned in imitation foliage, grass-like camouflage. I went up to him and said, 'That's a strange get-up. Are you all right, mate?' He didn't answer but smiled and winked. I guessed that he was a sniper.

What was noticeable to me is that all the Paras had finally been issued with their field dressings and morphine, which were attached either to their bodies or to their helmets. This was the final bit of military 'kit' that to my view defined them as being ready for battle. One of the sergeants I knew was relaxing by his rucksack, ready to disembark. I asked him, 'Are you ready for what's ahead then?'

'Yeah, as ready as we can be,' he replied without hesitation.

'And your lads, are you happy with them?'

'Yeah, I'm okay with my squad, but I have reservations about one of 'em. He's a young lad of 19 from Yorkshire. He hasn't been in the Airborne for long and I'm apprehensive for him. The rest I'm happy with, or as happy as I can be under the circumstances.' The sergeant was in the mood for a natter, so we chatted about several topics before I moved on.

It was unclear to us exactly what time they were going to disembark, though the word was that we were getting close to where we needed to be. Dave and I went out on open deck and, sure enough, no moon was to be seen, which was part of the plan. On watch on the bridge was Mike Failey with Mick Templeton at the wheel. I later found out that, in addition to using radar, their orders were to look straight ahead, eyeballing a small light. There were no other lights to be seen apart from the one they had to follow, which was on the stern of the frigate HMS *Plymouth*. We were later told that for some reason the frigate had to drop behind and the *Norland* had to carry on without the escort in front. If this is true and not just a bit of bravado from our ship's crew, it meant that, for a brief period, technically the *Norland* led the invasion to take back the Falklands. At the time any thoughts of who might be leading the charge was the least of our worries. Our concern was Fanning Head. Had it been neutralised? We had to pass directly by it, almost under it. Surely, we wouldn't be making our way through the Falkland Sound on the way to San Carlos Water if this strategically dominant position hadn't been secured?

Prior to the troops leaving the restaurant area for the car deck to disembark, they were in that army state of 'hurry up and wait'. A lot of the crew were up and about. Whilst it was a scary situation, at the same time it was thrilling. Someone suggested that while everyone was waiting for something to happen – it was just after midnight by then – why not give them a sarnie! The troops didn't know when their next meal would be and it would also give them something to occupy their minds. Boxes of eggs and loaves of bread were produced, and egg sarnies were made by the hundreds. A couple of slices of bread with a couple of fried eggs placed in the middle were gratefully wolfed down. There was an old advert on television about 'going to work on an egg'; this was a case of 'going to war on an egg'. Credit has to be given to the cooks and stewards who turned out to give the 2 Para lads this last impromptu meal before leaving the ship.

Dave and I went out on the open deck where we strained our eyes to see what was going on in the dark. When our night vision had kicked in, we could see the vague outline of land rising up on either side of the ship. A big shape appeared on our port side and I guessed it was the infamous Fanning Head. It was a nervy time. Nothing happened. The ship continued on and then there was some kind of explosion in the near distance. 'What the hell's that?' I asked Dave. 'How the fuck would I know?' he replied, along with a thin laugh. Was it friendly or enemy fire? My heartbeat had quickened. Maybe it was a diversionary tactic? The situation was eerily tense. We were told mines could be laid all along San Carlos Water. Furthermore, was someone looking at the *Norland* right now through night-binoculars, waiting to give a command to open fire, with either small arms or artillery? As civvies we had these thoughts because the military certainly had them and they'd rubbed off on us. After about an hour of, thankfully, nothing else of consequence happening, we went back inside. In the restaurant, the troops had dwindled to about half the number we had seen earlier because they were slowly making their way down to the car deck for disembarking. On the *Norland*, as on many ships, there were special doors called Gunport Doors, large heavy doors sitting a few feet above the waterline. On hydraulic hinges they can be pulled to one side. It was through these doors that the troops would leave us.

By now the anchor had been dropped. I went down on to the car deck and the only way to get to it was from a stairway where sliding doors gave you access. I opened the sliding doors and a voice shouted, 'Turn that fucking light out!' I quickly nipped through the doors and it slid closed behind me. On the car deck was a spooky kind of dark red lighting. All the normal lights on the car deck had been covered with red filter material to create this effect. I believe it's the same lighting they operate in a Hercules aircraft on a night jump for the Paras to help them get their night vision quicker. All the Paras were standing with rucksacks on their backs, armed to the teeth, waiting their turn to board the landing craft ready to get ashore. As I looked through the Gunport Doors, I estimated that land was 400–500yds away. The key thing was that there had been no enemy fire. This was an absolute bonus.

The procedure of the landing craft ferrying the troops from ship to shore continued for several hours. On nearing the end of the last troops leaving the ship (wishing good luck to as many of them as I could), I made my way back up to the restaurant area. Looking around, the transformation was amazing because all equipment had gone, leaving only a strange quietness. There was not one single military person to be seen. All the cooks and stewards had thinned out and there was only Dave and I left in the quietness of the restaurant. We sat there having a coffee, contemplating all that had gone on. It was well past midnight when, as I sat with my back to the door that led into the restaurant, Dave said, 'Hey, Reg, look who's coming in.' I turned around to see at the far end of the restaurant Commander Esplin-Jones, who was making his way through. I wondered what he was doing here. I told Dave, 'I'll be back in a minute.' I went to approach him and cut across the route he was taking. 'Excuse me, sir,' I said.

'Yes, can I help you?' he replied in the way of someone who is burdened with great responsibility and hasn't really got time for small talk.

'Can you tell me what today has got in store for us?' I asked.

He looked around and then looking back at me he said, 'You know, that is a very good question. There's one thing that we would like and that's lots of low cloud. I cannot really tell you what's in store for us but something for sure is that people are going to die.'

I don't know why but inanely I said, 'Oh, thank you very much, sir.'

With that, he just walked off and I thought, 'Bloody hell, that's the top man telling me that!'

I walked back to where Dave was sitting and he asked, 'What did he say?'

'According to the man there, he reckons that at first light, people are going to die.'

Dave said, 'Oh, piss off. He wouldn't say that.'

'Well, I'm telling you that's what he told me.'

We still had our night shift to finish and so we tidied up all the rubbish left behind. We then set to preparing the morning breakfast for the remaining small military contingent left on board. We went to some of the bar areas and tidied up rubbish left behind here and there. The atmosphere felt weird. It was an empty ship without all the noise and energy it had been host to while leading up to the beach landings.

Life went on as normal for the ship's crew in that the watchkeepers did their watch as usual. The cooks and stewards prepared breakfast with the welcome thought that the workload was reduced. Our precious cargo, so to speak, had been safely delivered. We had ferried them, fed and watered them and disembarked them. It was around 4 a.m. and it seemed they had all safely made it ashore. The ship had done its job. In military terms, we had accomplished our mission.

I wanted to be out on deck at first light. Dave was with me and, looking up at the sky, we couldn't believe it. There wasn't a cloud to be seen, which dashed the hopes of Commander Esplin-Jones and made it yet more dangerous for the military. What surprised us as the day broke was seeing nearly twenty other ships in San Carlos Water, mainly naval war ships. At the entrance to the bay, way out in the distance, I was even more surprised to see the *Canberra* cruise liner. Painted white, she was unmissable. If the Argies came to attack, they couldn't help but spot her as well. As a target we were bad enough, but the *Canberra* was even worse. I wondered what thoughts its crew were having.

With only a handful of troops left on our ship, there was a kind of relaxation for us. The galley staff and stewards were not under so much pressure now. Dave and I were getting some breakfast, when suddenly rest time was over as an alarm sounded. We had been briefed about yellow alert and red alert situations; this was the latter. Ignoring instructions to go to my designated emergency station, I rushed to get my binoculars from my cabin and made it out on to the open deck. There were even more ships in San Carlos Water by now. I was trying to figure out what the commotion was and then I spotted an aircraft way up high. It seemed to be propeller driven, flying relatively slowly. Other members of the crew were looking up and we took it to be an Argy aircraft. With that, there was a plume of smoke from one of our naval ships. A white object shot up into the sky, spiralling as it went. I followed its route and there was an explosion in the air. Debris trickled down from where the aircraft had been. It was totally destroyed. Commander Esplin-Jones was right that men were going to die. This happened to be an Argentinian one.

Shortly after this incident I bumped into a Royal Navy fellow in the Forward Lounge and Bar. 'Excuse me, what did you make of that aircraft?' I asked.

'It's almost certain it was a reconnaissance aircraft and it's equally certain it will have radioed back that British ships are in San Carlos Water,' he said. 'So, soon we can expect pretty much anything. Don't bother going to bed if you're the night steward.'

Dave had already gone to bed, but I wanted to hang around to see what else was going to happen. Half an hour later there was another red alert. The *Norland* tannoy system had a distinctive 'ding dong ding' sound. The crew had heard it a thousand times and so on hearing it you knew there was going to be an announcement. Forget about telling passengers 'the duty-free shop is now open', this announcement, like many to come, was different. An unfamiliar voice spoke: 'Everyone to their emergency stations. It's a red alert and we've confirmation of four Skyhawks approaching from the west.'

The idea was that you had to go to your emergency station on an alert and mine was deep down on G-deck below the water line. It crossed my mind that it was about the worst place you could be. But like good boys, several of us decided to go there to await further instructions. Whilst down there we felt, and heard, bumps and thuds somewhere in the distance. The voice on the tannoy then announced: 'There's more enemy aircraft coming in from the northwest, TAKE COVER, TAKE COVER ...'

Down in the passenger accommodation on G-deck, we were thinking, 'What the hell are we supposed to do?' We were clearly under air attack and what were we doing down there? One of the lads, Dick Johnson, said, 'Ah well, there's a first time for everything.'

I told him, 'Actually, this isn't the first time for me.'

'Why is that?' someone asked.

'I can remember the Blitz during the war, when I was a child,' I said, which wasn't a joke. At that point, memories came back to me of running to air raid shelters during the Second World War in Hull, which was one of the most bombed cities outside of London. Sadly, loss of life in Hull was huge and the city was never justly recognised for its suffering and stoicism during the war. I was only a child at the time, but these thoughts came flooding back to me, as I'm sure they would have done to anyone else on board who'd experienced the Blitz.

'Bollocks to this!' I thought and I told the others, 'I'm going up top, I'm not staying here.' Several followed me. We were wise enough to use the stairs and not the lift. As we went out on to the open deck there was a noise that I wasn't familiar with that signalled a lot of activity was taking place. The noise was in fact several General Purpose Machine Guns (GPMG) on our ship and other ships blasting away.

Our ship's carpenter, Derek Zeese, appeared and I asked if he was okay. He said he didn't know and we just smiled at each other. We should have been taking cover but we wanted to see what was going on. Not really knowing what to do, we remained transfixed. An Argy aircraft then zoomed overhead, maybe 500yds away, 200ft or so above the water. Every gun was firing at it. It disappeared towards the end of the bay and was followed by a second Argy aircraft.

From a nearby frigate there came a plume of smoke from its foredeck. I thought, 'Bloody hell, it's been hit!' It hadn't. Instead, a missile appeared from out of the smoke and it looked to be searching for its target. The second Argy aircraft that had followed the first was now being pursued by the missile. It caught up to the aircraft and disappeared into its exhaust. A quick double explosion followed, causing a 'dum dum' sound. The aircraft totally disintegrated. All the debris was still moving forward until it lost momentum and, like the first aircraft that got hit earlier in the day, the debris eventually trickled down. That was another dead Argentinian, or however many crew members had been in the aircraft. It was a shooting gallery right in front of us. A further jet then came over with another missile pursuing it. The Argy jet seemed to initiate an extra burst of acceleration and it pulled away from the missile. Both it and the missile disappeared over the hills. With all this happening, I thought about getting my head under cover inside the ship. I owed it to my wife and kids not to be sticking my neck out, but it was all too compelling to miss. Looking around me, I could see along the length of the ship that other crew members were taking in this spectacle as more Argy aircraft continued to fly over us.

Instead of showing the usual ship's plan of where restaurants, bars and the duty-free shop could be found, the plan opposite displays the position of our military defences. MILAN is a hand-held anti-tank guided missile and BLOWPIPE is a man-portable surface-to-air missile.

Geoff Palfreman, the head barman, was a very fit guy. The temptation to drink was always there in his job, but he had shown great willpower when he'd decided at the start of the expedition to 'go on the wagon'. On this trip he wanted his wits about him at all times. A former keen amateur boxer and someone who kept himself in shape, his strength came in handy during our first red alert. One of the crew, who'd finished his work, had enjoyed a couple of beers too many. He'd gone back to his bunk to sleep it off.

Concerned for the crew member, Geoff went to check on him. The crewmember was flaked out and Geoff was unable to wake him. Putting him over his shoulder, he carried him all the way down to G-deck, our alert station. By the time the all-clear came, the crew member had come round and was able to make his own way back to his cabin. Geoff pointed out that, if the ship had been hit, it would have been a massive job for anyone deep down in the lower decks to carry someone injured, up ten flights of stairs to the upper decks. This was especially appropriate to the lads working in the engine room, which under the current circumstances was considered one of the most dangerous places to be.

Not long after this first red alert, 3rd Engineer, Derrick Begg, spoke of a vibration that shook the engine room, which was accompanied by a rattling alongside the ship. It was from a bomb that had exploded close by and which Derrick 'felt through to the soles of his feet'. This happened around the same time that some of the crew thought the side of the ship had been strafed by gunfire. Geoff Palfreman and several others were in the crew's mess when they heard an horrendous racket. To them it sounded like bullets hitting the ship. The noise was so loud and scary that everyone immediately hit the deck and sheltered under what tables were available. It wasn't known if it was cannon-fire from enemy aircraft or quite possibly friendly fire. Derrick Begg later got the likely answer from Commander Esplin-Jones, who reckoned it was probably super-heated bubbles bursting against the ship's hull, caused by evaporation from the explosion.

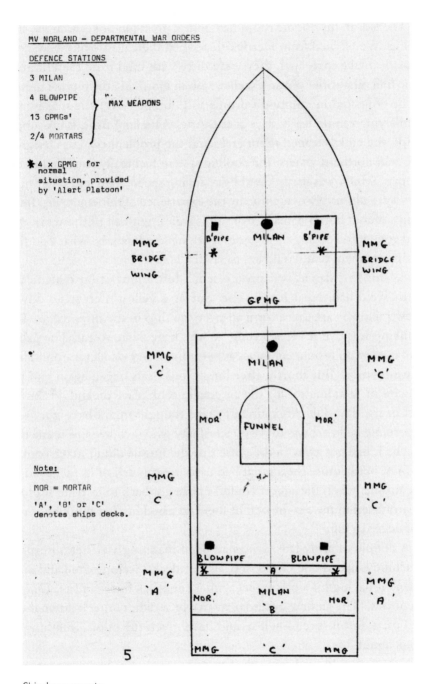

Ships' armaments.

The lads in the engine room had done a great job of keeping the ship going. We learned from Derrick that when the ballast tanks were converted to take spare fuel, they were dirty with mud from the Humber. The fuel oil purifier did an excellent job in removing the mud. This had to be collected in empty oil drums and dumped over the side by the donkeymen in the early days at sea. After refuelling from RFA supply ships, the tanks cleaned themselves and the problem ceased. Designed for cold northern waters, the cooling system had really struggled in the tropics, which was partly eased by reducing speed. This and other matters were ultimately overcome by the experience of our engineers. If the ship suffered bomb damage from the Argies, with all of the work that had gone into keeping the engines working so efficiently, what a gutting disappointment that would be, to say the least!

As this first day at war progressed, I lost count of how many red alerts we'd had. Near lunch time, during a yellow alert stand down, crew members appeared from all over the ship in the mess room. The thinking was that it's lunch time, so let's have a bite to eat. The galley staff carried on producing meals as per normal and we all sat around like it was natural. But shortly after lunch, red alerts began again and the process of 'standing to' for the air attacks took place on and off for the rest of the day. The Argy aircraft that I thought might have got away apparently hadn't. I was told by a naval guy who saw the same scene that maybe it had got away in the sense that the missile didn't make contact with it, but because the aircraft had used up so much of its fuel evading the missile, it was thought it couldn't have got back to its base. It probably ditched in the sea for lack of fuel and based on that thinking it was considered a kill.

A couple of army lads, who had been manning a General Purpose Machine Gun on one of the ship's upper decks, were excited and confident at having hit a passing jet with a couple of bursts of fire. One of them said, 'The jet flew on and okay maybe it didn't bring it down there and then, but it sure as hell would have given the pilot something to think about.'

Information filtered through that more naval ships had been hit. We already knew that HMS *Sheffield* had been sunk a couple of weeks earlier. Later in the day we learned that HMS *Ardent* had been under attack. Someone remembered that up on the afterdeck of the *Norland* there were two important containers, one on the port side and one on the starboard side, both holding military explosives – possibly phosphate, which was apparently as deadly as napalm. On the lower car decks there were still hundreds of tons of army equipment including ammunition. Any major hit by aircraft, or another source, could have penetrated through the flimsy metal of our ship and the army containers. This would have been catastrophic for us. It must have been the same situation for all the ships in San Carlos Water carrying ammo.

On the yellow alerts, helicopters appeared from out of nowhere. On red alerts, they disappeared into the hills because they were easy targets for Argy aircraft. Their main task was ferrying equipment from ship to shore. Landing craft were also ferrying troops and equipment from ship to shore. It was bizarre to see the industrious military going about their business in between these raids. When we had to take cover, the voice telling us to do so belonged to Lieutenant Commander Ian Hughes, the second in command to Esplin-Jones. Towards late afternoon it all quietened down. The Argies had knocked off for the day. Everything was peaceful. The tannoy then sounded and the voice of Lt Cmdr Hughes informed us that it was, 'Argentina nil, Great Britain four!' I surmised that he meant four aircraft shot down. It was all very well him saying this but a lot of the crew were thinking, it's not a case of *if we* get hit, it is a case of *when we* get hit.

That first day I hadn't gone to bed at all. I had some concern for Dave, who was down in his cabin on G-deck. I was tempted to go and wake him up. If we did get hit, I felt that Dave, being deep down in the guts of the ship, would never get out. Worryied about him, I went to his cabin and, not wanting to alarm him, carefully opened his door. He was doing what he enjoyed doing most, sleeping. In the end, I didn't have the heart to wake him, so I closed the door as carefully as I had opened it. Come our evening turn to, Dave was there as usual at 9.30 p.m. 'So, what's been happening?' he casually asked. By that time, which was dark, it had been confirmed that HMS *Ardent* had been sunk with a large loss of life. We were all shocked at this but nobody more so than Dave.

In general conversation, we experienced an increase of military terminology, such as Seacat and Seadart, which were missile systems present on most of the naval ships. It was reckoned these missile systems were okay but the best was another system called Sea Wolf. The military informed us that we shouldn't be worrying as yet another missile system called Rapier was being positioned on the high ground surrounding the ships in San Carlos Water. No matter how good the Rapier system was thought to be, it was temperamental. It was a delicate bit of kit and all the movement of it from ship to shore by helicopter hadn't helped its performance. New to this kind of war situation were the Sea Harrier jump jets. They had yet to prove themselves. Sidewinder was another name we learned, which was an air-to-air missile used by the Harriers. We hardly saw any of these aircraft and wondered why. What we didn't know was that they were proving themselves efficient in shooting down Argies in air-to-air combat. If all else failed, we had the good old General Purpose Machine Gun.

That night in the crew's mess, stories unfolded about who had seen what and where. One story doing the rounds was that Wendy had gone down to the car deck to wave off the troops as they left through the Gunport Doors. Getting carried away with the excitement, one of the Toms suggested that Wendy should join them – and this he did! He apparently jumped into one of the landing craft and, when reaching the shore with the troops, he was spotted by a Para sergeant who went nuts. 'What the fucking hell is he doing here? Get him back to the ship on the next available landing craft, NOW!' screamed the sergeant. Whether or not this incident was actually true, it should be.

One story that would go down in Merchant Navy folklore is that AB Brian (Shep) Sheppard was forward in the ship's bow with the 2nd Officer, Alan Woof when it entered San Carlos Water. He'd been ordered to drop the anchor. The ship having been at sea for so long, when he made to release the holding clip for the anchor to fall, it wouldn't. The chains had rusted up. With the whole of the Task Force dependent on the *Norland* establishing safe anchorage to get the troops off, this was a panicky moment. Shep then got permission from the skipper to set the chains loose with physical force. This was quite a decision considering it was the still of the night and any untoward noise could give away our position. Suddenly this didn't matter because, when in the state of not wanting to make a noise, the sound of the hammer whacking the chains was superseded by the actual sound of the chains dropping, which seemed to take an eternity. As the last piece of chain rattled through its housing, to everyone's relief, it went quiet again. Then inexplicably, as the troops were ready to disembark, the skipper addressed them on the ship's tannoy. The sound of 'ding dong ding' was followed by the skipper amiably announcing, 'I'd like to take this opportunity to wish our troops well on their mission. We do hope you all come back safely. Good luck.' Gasps of disbelief along with gasps of laughter were experienced and this kind of thing could only make someone think, what a strange but funny business going to war can be. Furthermore, how odd to be discussing the events of the day in the same way we would have discussed a normal day of incidents on the ship during a civilian run. We had to remember that people were losing their lives or getting seriously injured. In a way, we admired the bravery

In the distance, at sunset, we could the see *Canberra* and, like us, it had also come through the bombing in one piece. (Courtesy Brian Burton)

of the Argy pilots who came in for attack after attack, facing our missile defences knowing they might not make it home. The mixed emotions we had as a crew had been affected by having been drawn into thinking like the military over the last several weeks.

Up until now I hadn't had any sleep throughout this first day. Overwhelmed with tiredness, in the early hours after midnight, when nothing out of the ordinary was expected to happen, I asked Dave to cover for me whilst I crashed for a couple of hours.

1

TAKE COVER WHERE?

Early next morning, feeling refreshed, I was back with Dave getting breakfast ready and we speculated about what this second day would have in store for us.

I spotted the Purser and asked if he knew anything about what was to come. John said:

I wish I could tell you but I don't know. Like you I've lived off scraps of information. What I can say is that the only time I'd been invited to an official briefing was the night before we went in. Cmdr Esplin-Jones stressed that the priority was to get the paratroopers ashore. A discussion was had about what to do if *Norland* was badly damaged. In such a case, Esplin-Jones emphasised the importance of getting the stores and ammunition ashore using mexeflotes (a type of landing raft) and, if we could, preserve the accommodation/dry space asset of the ship. He said: 'Beaching her bow first was possible on the gradual sloping beach where 2 Para intended to land.' The skipper, Don Ellerby, shot straight back telling him, 'If you do that, you'll break the ship's back!' Lloyd Newel, the Chief Engineer, interrupted to ask a damn obvious question: 'If that happens, where do all of us, the crew go?' In a matter-of-fact way, Esplin-Jones said, 'You head for the trees.' At this remark, we all looked at each other. The Chief Engineer then rightly said, 'Trees ... what trees? By all accounts there aren't any!' The briefing then moved on to other issues without the further implications of grounding the ship being discussed. I don't know how the hell we'd have dealt with it had it come to that situation. Thank God it didn't.

I said to John:

Maybe it was good none of us knew about this. Imagine if we *had* run the ship aground. Okay, the Paras would have been the ones off first, followed by us lot. But what might we be carrying for weapons? The Chief Cook had a big carving knife, but what would the rest of our catering department use – soup ladles and spatulas?

We laughed at this ridiculous thought. I also thought that bringing my walking boots on this trip could be a godsend if we abandoned the ship and had to march alongside the Paras to safety, somewhere ashore.

John said:

Here's something else amusing for you. The army paymaster has been based in my office and I asked if there was anything the Paras might need before going ashore. Of all things, he wanted sweets. He was referring to our gift shop on board. I told him to go down there, tell the stewards it was okay and as long as he didn't take anything electrical, he could help himself to whatever he liked, and he did alright. He just about cleaned out the place, not just of sweets but confectionery as well. The paymaster was really chuffed and emphasised that these treats were invaluable out here in the middle of nowhere. It amused me to think of those hairy-arsed Paras happily sucking on a fruit pastille when heading out to face the unknown.

'From what I saw, the lads were raring to go,' I said. John replied:

You're right. I was talking with a quiet, unassuming navy bloke. He reckoned he'd done both the Para and the Marine course. When I asked how he rated them, he thought the Marine course was much harder, but he would never have said that to a Para. I wasn't sure I agreed with him on who was the toughest. When we were waiting for the decision of whether to go in or not, the navy bloke also said he hoped to hell they wouldn't call this thing off. If they did, the Toms would go insane. I agreed with him on this because I could see they were so highly strung and ready for it.

Aside from John's thoughts, a comment that struck me was when the crew were talking about the day's events and someone pointed out that we went in first with HMS *Intrepid* and HMS *Fearless* following some-where behind us. One of the lads then cracked a line about it 'not being that intrepid or fearless of the military'.

Shortly after daylight on the second morning I went out on to the open deck with my binoculars. I scanned the top of the surrounding hills, trying to spot the Rapier system. I couldn't see anything but that was probably a good thing because it meant their camouflage was working. When looking at the terrain, how similar it was to that of the Pennines and North Yorkshire moors, where I had spent time on outdoor pursuits. The biggest surprise was the lack of trees. This was not a good thing because when the troops needed to take cover, where the hell would they go? They were left to do what they had all been trained for, I supposed: to dig trenches/shell scrapes.

What I could see around me were navy ships and, of the navy personnel on view, they had a form of protective clothing. They looked to be well wrapped; some even wore gloves. At least they had something to help them against flash burns. We had nothing. Whether our crew would have worn similar is another thing. We were reminded to ensure that we continued wearing extra clothing as the next best alternative, which we felt was a joke.

I didn't know what time it was, but sure enough early on that second day we got a red alert. Going down on G-deck was a non-starter for me; the same for a lot of lads who wouldn't do it either. When the aircraft attacks came in, we had to figure out whether to cover our faces or take the risk of watching events unfold. Quite a few of the lads were braving it by going out on deck and standing or crouching near a part of the ship's structure that might give some protection. It was amusing to see the overall reaction of the crew. One of the lads went into a toilet, shut the door and sat and hoped everything would be okay. Steward Joe Wheelan, on hearing the order to go to our emergency stations, was making his way down an alleyway quite briskly with a lifebelt hung over his shoulder. With a silly grin, he was comi-cally singing, 'We're all going on a summer holiday'. What was going through his mind as he made his way to his emergency station, I can't imagine. Some of the others who didn't really know what to do ended up with half a dozen of us in the mess room just sitting, awaiting our fate. Nervous chatter always ensued. One of the ABs, Tommy Clark, a steely guy, came in and looked around with an expression on his face as if to say, 'What is all the fuss about?' For Tom, it was 'carry on regardless'. Feeling unsettled, I went out on deck to see ABs Paddy Dolan and Brian Shepherd strolling around as though they were looking to do a bit of painting somewhere, while aircraft were tear-arsing overhead. They didn't seem to be concerned with what was happening or the potential danger of the situation.

I had made my way back down into the mess and was making myself a hot drink when there was a loud, dull explosion and the ship lurched. In truth, it was terrifying to be out on the open deck watching the aircraft come in. To come down to the mess and have a cup of tea didn't really lessen the situation. For many it wasn't just a cup of tea, it was a bottle of beer or something stronger. During another air raid later in the day, John Foster and Pete Samson appeared. 'Christ almighty, did you see what just took place over the ship?' one of them said.

'No, what was it?' we asked with excitement.

'An aircraft just blew up over the top of us.'

'Oh shit, I missed it!' said one of the lads sitting close by.

This last comment was spoken in the same way that someone would have been upset if they had been watching a football match, turned the wrong way and missed seeing a goal scored. Such thinking was remarkable considering a life had been lost, which didn't seem important; it only mattered that another enemy aircraft had been shot down, making it one less to shoot at us. This prompted, yet again, the thought that sooner or later it was going to be our turn to get hit.

Of this incident, engineer Derrick Begg said:

There was such a bang and the whole ship seemed to bounce up and down a few inches. I was in the ship's hydraulic room when I rang the engine room to ask what had happened. The Chief Engineer told me, 'I think we've been hit; you stay there and I'll ring you back.' I thought to myself, so, here I am, in a steel box, 8,000 miles from home, pacing up and down and wondering if this could be the end of the Begg dynasty. It was the longest three-minute wait of my life. Then the phone rang and the Chief said, 'It's okay, it was an aircraft blowing up above us, we're just clearing up the mess now.'

Furthermore, John Foster and Pete Sansom, who'd witnessed the aircraft blowing up, had been lucky. They had walked out onto C-deck at the same time that the ill-fated Skyhawk was flying towards the ship. They could see the pilot's face before seeing the aircraft's undercarriage as it headed their way – with a missile chasing it. John turned to run back into the doorway that they had just come out of. He didn't make it. This is because Pete had decided to do the same and he was that quick in his movements, he crashed into the back of John. They both fell to the deck with Pete sprawled on top. At that very moment, above them, the missile had caught up with the Skyhawk. An explosion followed and shrapnel scattered everywhere. They were both okay, except that John suffered bad bruising from Pete's unintentional flying rugby tackle from behind. One of our merchant crew could now claim to be our first casualty! And so could someone from our ship's Royal Navy contingent. Shrapnel had hit one of their lads on the upper deck and he was taken off to the hospital ship, SS *Uganda*, for treatment. (The injured navy lad had the unusual title of 'goofer', which is defined in naval terms as 'a spectator watching aircraft operations in a "carrier", standing in the *goofing gallery*'.)

Chief Officer Bob Lough said:

I was on the starboard Bridge Wing and saw the aircraft approaching from astern over the top of the funnel. Just as it was nearing our stern, a missile connected with it and it blew up. The blast knocked me over and as I looked up there was a large lump which I think was the aircraft engine sailing over the top of the wheelhouse. It splashed in the water about 400 metres in front of us. The airframe was completely destroyed by the missile and fell in the water astern of us, some small bits of shrapnel landing around the aft flight deck. Immediately after this, Cmdr Esplin-Jones was concerned that the plane may have released a bomb before being destroyed, so I was dispatched to check that we did not have an unexploded bomb on board, thankfully we did not!

The draw for me to go and take a look on the upper deck of the ship was overwhelming. I was so curious as to what I might find there. Between raids, on state yellow, as I walked along the top deck, tiny particles were strewn about the place. It must have been the debris from the aircraft that blew up directly overhead. I picked up several bits of plastic that had numbers and letters printed on them. Although I was tempted to hold on to some of these as war trophies, I didn't and I left the scene thinking that a man had been blown to pieces in the process of all this. His vaporised body was probably amongst the debris.

One worrying thought I had was small arms fire. There was so much shooting, from our ship and other ships, in particular from personal weapons and especially machine guns, but where were all the stray bullets ending up? They had to fall somewhere back to ground or into the surrounding water in which we were anchored. I couldn't believe that somebody didn't get hit by any of it; a 'friendly fire' or 'blue on blue' situation as the military would describe it.

The usual routine was that we stayed in our area of work and the officers stayed in theirs. However, under the circumstances of being at war, I would have thought we might have had visits from our ship's officers, but they were rare, if at all; not that we needed to see them anyway. Okay, there might have been contact if the job required it, but that was as far as it went. Socially there was also little contact; they did their thing and we did ours.

On the second day, after more terrifying air attacks, HMS *Antelope* was hit. Around sun up, whilst she was escorting our ship into San Carlos Water, an air attack came in. Two bombs hit her. She anchored up in a relatively unoccupied area of the bay and we discovered that the bombs hadn't exploded because the Argy aircraft dropped them too low, not allowing enough time for the fuses to work. HMS *Antelope* was in big trouble and the bombs needed deactivating. Only time would tell what the answer to that was going to be. For now, the evening meal wasn't up to its usual standard. This wasn't through lack of skill preparing the food; it was the lack of enough decent food to serve up. We were running low on quality rations. Water was always an issue and orders were still in force to preserve what supplies we had. I suspected the same was true of fuel.

Electrician Brian Burton came by the crew's bar. I saw a look of strain on his face, the same look a lot of the crew had, including me. 'Have you been watching the attacks?' I asked.

'How can you not? It's scary stuff and anyone thinking different, they're kidding themselves.'

'It'll just be a matter of time before we get hit,' I said.

'Don't worry, I think they're trying to get at *Fearless* and *Intrepid*, and they're not too worried about us as a threat,' said Brian. His opinion of the situation surprised me.

'Well, I don't agree … and I don't know if you're saying that to try and make me feel at ease.' Brian was always a measured person with an analytical view of life.

'Mind you, forget missiles, we'll still be goners if we get hit by cannon fire or a land-based artillery shell,' Brian continued. 'By my reckoning, Royal Navy ships have carbon steel plating whereas Merchant Navy ships have mild steel plating. Up to a metre above the water, I believe our hull is only around 12mm; the remaining superstructure is around 10mm. It doesn't need a missile or bomb to sink us; get enough concentrated machine gun fire in the right area of the ship and that'll probably do the job.'

'Yeah, well that's as maybe, and should our time come, I don't want to be injured with loss of limbs or, even worse, badly burned. All I would want is for it to be over quickly. And I reckon a lot of our crew would think the same,' I said.

'Should anything happen, we wouldn't know it's happened,' said Brian. 'All the resupply of ammunition we've taken on board the last couple of days, there wouldn't be anything left of the ship.' This was typical of his reasoning.

'I'd always thought we'd end up fighting but I didn't imagine we'd have a front row seat like we have,' I said.

'Actually, I never thought we'd go to war,' Brian said. 'I'd heard through the ship's radio how hard the American Secretary of State, Alexander Haig, was negotiating for peace. But after the sinking of the *Belgrano*, that's when everything changed. In the final week's build-up to the Paras disembarking, can you believe that as the ship's officers we were asked for our ideas of how best to get the troops ashore quickly and safely? That kind of worried me … I worried whether those taking us into war knew what they were doing. And the number of ships we've lost so far, it's questionable whether those in charge have put the right war plan together.'

'I have to tell you, Brian, if at the start of this conversation your intention was to make me feel at ease, it fucking well hasn't!' We both laughed – what else could we do?

The transformation from what was going on during the daytime to the calm of what went on in the evenings was surreal; this was in the sense that no doubt the ship's officers were meeting in their bar like we were meeting in ours to discuss the day's events over a drink. Of the many conversations buzzing around, a new term had been coined for the area that we were anchored in. San Carlos Water was now being called 'Bomb Alley'. I chuckled at this description and I thought it was as good a term as any for our location and the situation of the last forty-eight hours.

Accompanied by the sound of a Second World War klaxon, below is an actual example of one of many air-raid warnings piped from the bridge and the stand down procedures thereafter:

> Defence state one, defence state one. Personnel not closed-up, move downstairs to G Deck. Arms to defence stations. Air Raid Warning Red!
>
> Stand down from defence stations, carry on with work, we can still expect several of these red alerts throughout the day. Be prepared to go to your stations at the rush, the probability, though, is that very few, if any, will get under our air cover.

The last sentence above proved not to be wholly true.

8

OUR NEXT MISSION

It was the third evening when Dave and I entered the restaurant and we did a double take. Part of the restaurant was taken up by people unfamiliar to us. We were initially puzzled by this. A navy officer was speaking to this new group of around 200 men. We got ourselves a coffee and sat nearby to listen in. It turned out that they were the crew of HMS *Antelope*. We learned that he was the second-in-command of the *Antelope* and his words were of encouragement: 'Okay, we've had to abandon ship, but it's not a disgrace because these things happen in war. You're now on a civilian ship in the Merchant Navy, not a Royal Navy ship. We're seafaring people and they are seafarers too, but remember they have a different way of doing things.' He was emphasising they were on board in the capacity of passengers, not navy service personnel.

I noticed that a lot of these men were not in uniform but scantily dressed. Apparently, the order had been given to abandon ship quickly on realising the severity of the situation. What they stood up in is all that many possessed. After about an hour of briefing their crew, they were detailed off to accommodation about the ship. Our new role was providing shelter for Royal Navy survivors.

As the evening progressed, I had cause to be outside on D-deck when I felt a pressured movement in the air followed by an almighty explosion. The sky suddenly lit up. I raced from the port side to the starboard side, where the *Antelope* had been during daylight. Now in the dark, all I could see was smoke and flames. It lit up the whole of San Carlos Water and was such a sad sight to see because I realised that the *Antelope* had blown up. A lot of the crew from the *Antelope* would have been on the *Norland*'s outer decks watching their ship die. Either one or both of the Argy bombs had gone off and it seemed the ship's armament too. It's likely that it took the lives of those trying to defuse the bombs at the time. That was another ship lost and a depressing thought. Trying not to dwell on it, Dave and I carried on with our work throughout the night, taking care of our new passengers. Later that night, Dave was busy doing something somewhere and I was in the restaurant when a smartly dressed figure in civilian-type clothing walked in. Somehow, I knew he must be in the military. He had a brown leather jacket on, which I hadn't seen anyone else wearing. It was similar to the one I had been wearing for most of this trip. Thinking he was making his way somewhere, I was intrigued when he approached me to ask if I was Dave or Reg.

'I'm Reg,' I answered.

'I was recommended to contact either you or Dave to help me,' he said. He introduced himself as Trevor.

'Well, Trevor, if I can, I will,' I said.

Trevor then said:

It was suggested I approach you because I'm looking for some foodstuffs to hopefully take away with me. I'm a pilot, flying Sea King helicopters. During daylight hours we're dodging Argy aircraft and we haven't eaten properly for a while now. We're snatching bits of food here and there. When we're under camouflage, it's a good time for us to eat properly but we haven't got anything substantial as rations.

'What are you looking for?'

'Maybe you could give us some bacon and eggs. Something we can easily prepare.'

'I can do that for you. Tell you what, come with me.'

He must have been tipped off that we had the keys to the storeroom, which is where I took him. 'You mentioned bacon and eggs. Do you also want some bread and butter as well?' I offered. His face lit up. 'Oh yeah, anything that we can cook quickly.'

I got a big black plastic bag and carefully placed twenty-four eggs in an egg tray with a cover over the top to protect them. I then tied them together so they wouldn't fall about. I included a 7lb pack of bacon along with bread, butter and some biscuits. I had to bear in mind that our ship was running low on provisions but I wanted to look after this guy. He couldn't have been more delighted. He asked me, 'How much do I owe you?'

'I'm not selling any of this; they're for you to have with pleasure.'

'But surely I owe you something for them?'

'No, no, let's just say it's compliments of the ship's crew.'

'If there's some way I can pay you back, I will.'

'You just go and enjoy the stuff,' I was happy to tell him. Then half-jokingly, I said, 'I tell you what, maybe I can get a ride in your helicopter sometime.'

'Oh, maybe you can,' he said.

We shook hands and I said, 'Don't let the Argies get ya.' He departed and we left it at that. Not much else of consequence happened during the night. After all, there was enough that had happened previously with the *Antelope* blowing up. It provided a fascinating but sobering sight for anyone on the *Norland* who'd seen it blow up and for a long time it lay there helplessly burning. Who would have thought that metal could actually burn? At first light, a lot of us were drawn to see what might be left of the *Antelope*. She was broken in half with the bow and the stern protruding above the water. What a terrible sight to see.

After breakfast that morning there was a lull in the action, and looking through my binoculars, I saw a navy ship that had a lot of activity taking place on its deck. A launch came alongside it with a number of people aboard. A figure stood up in the launch, who was guided by someone behind him. This figure appeared to have his hands behind his back and what looked like a bag over his head. Another member of the launch got onto the ship's gangway first and pulled the figure up after him. I tried to guess what was going on and later that day I found out. We had got the first Argy prisoner. He was a pilot who had been picked up in the sea after ejecting when his aircraft got shot up. To me this was quite a significant part of this developing war, that we were now taking Argy prisoners.

Later, after breakfast, Dave and I were approached by the Purser, who asked us to volunteer to help clear the ship of equipment. All the remaining army equipment, particularly ammunition and explosives such as boxes of grenades, were required ashore. Men were needed to cart it from where it was stored on the forward end of the car deck to the open ramp at the ship's stern. The helicopters could then get access to drop their harnesses and carry it off to where it was needed. The army had long departed by now, so all available hands were required to do this job. The crew, and any other 'volunteers' who could be raked up from around the ship, turned out. The Purser was the first to get stuck in, followed by the donkey men, stewards, cooks, ABs, barmen; in fact, anybody who wasn't on watch. Most of that morning we were humping heavy crates and boxes to the stern ramp. It was hard work but we didn't mind as we were glad to see the back of the stuff – especially the ammunition. Getting rid of all the remaining army equipment was surely an indication that something was planned for the ship.

By now everything seemed a blank slate to me. I'd lost track of time as one event merged into another. I didn't know what day of the week it was. I realised this was probably through the lack of proper sleep. After the work on the car deck, we went for a cuppa in the mess. Someone came in and told us, 'Guess what? I have got some real good news. On 25 May it is National Day in Argentina and those upstairs reckon it's likely they will be throwing everything at us, military-wise.' I didn't care. I needed some sleep, which I got that day until turning out in the evening. I found out that raids had gone on as usual and for a change I had slept through it all. It was 24 May and the *Norland* had been through a lucky escape. It had avoided being hit by two 500lb bombs that landed close alongside. Other ships in our near vicinity were not getting the same luck.

Now that we had the *Antelope* survivors on board, the rumour was that we would be taking them home to Britain. Their job was done; they were surplus to requirements. As they were already on our ship, it made sense to take them back home; they had nowhere else to go. For our crew, what a thought that was.

Some believed it would happen; others didn't. Personally, I was sceptical. We heard we were going to leave San Carlos Water. The *Canberra* would be leaving too. We were to head out into the Atlantic, roughly east by south-east, on an anti-submarine zig zag course. If we were going home it should have been north by north-east. This tactic of zig zagging didn't sound good to us. As we understood it, the Argies had four serviceable submarines. Engineer John Dent told us there had been a meeting he'd attended with the military who were worried about these Argy submarines. Even though they were Second World War leftovers, possibly ex German U-boats, John asked the military about their capability: 'How deadly are they?' In a deadpan manner he was told, 'Oh, they're deadly all right. They can still sink us.'

Though always uncertain about what lay ahead next, one development indicated something significant was afoot. We were each issued with a package. Ooh, this is exciting, we thought, until discovering the package contained a sea survival suit, better known as a 'once only suit'. This was a naval issue item which the crew would wear on top of normal clothing should we have to abandon ship. Why was it known as a 'once only suit'? – because you would never want to use it twice! Made of a pliable rubber mixture that enclosed you from head to toe by use of a zip pulled up from your crotch to your head, it was reckoned that in freezing seas it would give you a better chance of survival. Like a wet suit, but not as efficient, it might keep you alive for up to an hour or more, depending on the sea's temperature. Why had we been given this? Was the threat to our ship greater than it had been before? It's strange that for every positive such as being given something to help save your life, it had us thinking negatively that something dreadful was going to happen. That said, many of the crew members were appreciative of their survival suit, knowing that their seagoing forefathers had nothing similar in their time at war except for a life jacket. By my reckoning, even if we had made it into a lifeboat with our survival suits on, drifting around aimlessly on rough seas in the South Atlantic, we might have lasted up to forty-eight hours before hypothermia set in and finished us off. Either way, life jackets were also needed, which everyone had access to.

The *Norland* and *Canberra* rendezvoused on the evening of 24 May. We sailed about 5 miles apart but to what destination? There was a big, wide ocean out there – where were we headed? The *Canberra* sent a message to the *Norland* that, because of her greater speed, she wouldn't be hanging around and she'd be leaving us. Sure enough, she sailed off into the distance and we wouldn't see her again for several days. We were now alone in this vast southern ocean. It's an area literally at the end of the world. I always carry maps with me and I studied them to see what our destination might be. It was clear there were only two places we could be heading: South Georgia or the South Sandwich Islands. The next nearest southern landmark was Antarctica, and several thousand miles beyond that was New Zealand. It had to be South Georgia. My guess of where we were headed was reinforced by the issue of our sea survival suits. I found this part of the voyage a little unnerving in this very lonely part of the world. The temperature was dropping dramatically and we encountered heavy seas. If you had to take to the water as mentioned, you wouldn't last long. Should the chance of getting into lifeboats present itself, your chances of survival were increased, but from what I'd read of ships hit by torpedoes, they can sink quickly.

On the way to South Georgia, Radio Officer, Brian Lavender was on listening watch during radio silence when a faint Morse-code signal came through on the international distress frequency 500kHz. It was an SOS from MV *British Wye*, giving its position and that it was under attack! Its location was about 200 miles north-east of our ship. MV *British Wye* was being used as an auxiliary support tanker. Bombs had been dropped on it from an Argentinian Hercules aircraft. Brian took down the details but because of radio silence he couldn't acknowledge back to the ship a receipt of their distress call. He passed on the details to the military in the radio room next door, who dealt with the matter by informing HMS *Hermes*. Improvising dropping bombs from a transporter aircraft was a worrying new tactic from the Argentinians at the time; it was certainly worrying for Brian and others who knew of the incident. The majority of the crew didn't learn of it until later. This was probably a good thing on our long, lonely journey to South Georgia. It was enough worrying what was below us, never mind worrying about a continued threat coming in from above.

During this isolating time, we were still a darkened ship at night. Sleeping in full clothing and discouraged from showering, a lot of the lads had begun to grow beards. We were making do with what food we had. Most annoyingly, it was fresh-tasting water that was always the problem. When you turned the tap on, unwelcomingly, the water coming out was often brown.

An aerial shot for a postcard taken of the *Norland* at its launch in 1974 with bunting hung from forward to aft. (Courtesy P&O)

Troops embarking on to the *Norland* – the policeman didn't look too happy at this photograph being taken.

Carrying out adjustments in Portsmouth on the upper deck at the ship's stern, ready for one of the two helicopter landing pads.

In addition to two heli-pads, a further giveaway to the enemy that the *Norland* had special equipment aboard, and was therefore a legitimate military target, was a 1980s state-of-the-art satellite dish, mounted midships. Also seen is the funnel before its many paintjobs.

Above left: The first crew member using an SLR was John Foster who, as one of the ship's barmen, was determined no Argy invader trying to board the ship was going to get anywhere near his tip jar!

Above right: Firing an SLR was quite an experience for some crew members, but tricky for left handers like Reg. It was unnerving to think the crew might have to use them to defend themselves.

The experts were better shots, thankfully …

Bringing out the big guns – an 84mm Carl Gustav anti-tank weapon.

One of the many general-purpose machine guns positioned around the ship. With his back to the camera is Private Dave 'Charlie' Brown of C Company, 2 Para, ready for duty as Air Defence Gunner. To the ship's stern is frigate HMS *Broadsword*.

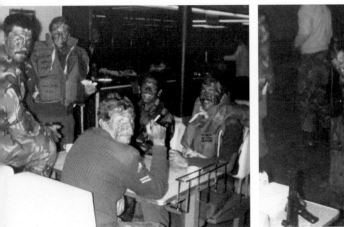

Above left: 2 Para lads find time for a final cigarette and a brew before landing.

Above right: The call came to board the landing crafts, when heavy bergens were lifted on to strong and able shoulders.

Heading down to the Gunport Doors and giving a farewell smile to the camera.

Above: HMS *Antelope* from the stern of the *Norland.* How terrible to see its back broken as it waits forlornly to sink. In the foreground is RFA *Fort Austin.*

Left: Steward, Dick Johnson welcomes a Gurkha soldier aboard.

Below left: Able Seaman, Brian Sheppard – first man into the Falklands (allegedly).

Below right: Electrical Engineer, Brian Burton – last man out of the pub (definitely).

Various forms of resupply and transport to and from the *Norland*.

Above: RFA *Tidepool*.

Right: Taxi.

Below: Chinook.
(Photos courtesy Brian Lavender and Brian Burton)

Various forms of resupply and transport to and from the *Norland*.

Left: Sea King.

Below: Lifeboat. (Photos courtesy Brian Lavender and Brian Burton)

In waters near South Georgia, passing by our starboard side is SS *Canberra*, for which we had great respect for its contribution to the war.

An honorary flypast which signalled that, at last, it was over for the *Norland* and its crew serving in the South Atlantic.

Jimmy Goodhall with a Falklands friend, Matthew, whom he had not seen for 32 years. (Courtesy Paul R.G. Haley).

Falkland Island children have a new theme park to play in from the spoils left behind after the war.

Ship's cook, Pete McWatt, and Private Dave 'Charlie' Brown, 2 Para, who both celebrated their twenty-first birthdays during the war and who have since become great friends, as well as key supporters of the South Atlantic Medal Association (SAMA 82).

Each year Dave 'Charlie' Brown visits the Falkland Islands to pay respects to his fallen comrade and best friend, Private Mark Holman-Smith. (Courtesy Paul R.G. Haley)

An Argentine Armed Forces grave in the Falklands.

British Armed Forces graves in the Falklands.

The Twenty-Fifth Anniversary Pilgrimage Convoy. (Courtesy Pete McWatt)

In 1983, the *Norland* on its return – although looking worse for wear, it was as strong and seaworthy as ever. (Courtesy Brian Burton)

"FAREWELL NORLAND"

MV Norland
Final Voyage Menu

27th February 2002

Dinner will be served from 1800 - 2200 Zulu Time

Bomb Alley Chicken Tikka (*Hot & Spicy*)
South Georgia Starter (*Cold*)
Fresh San Carlos Soup

Ascension Island Chicken
Port Stanley Rolled Plaice
South Atlantic Roast Beef
Falkland Island Lamb Knuckle
Tabbing Roast Turkey

Selection of Compo Style Indonesian Fayre

Special for tonight:-
Gurkha Curry with an accompaniment of Special Norland Rice

Hot Sweets:-
Goose Green Pie and Victory Sponge

Selection of King Penguin Cold Sweets

A Selection of Aldershot Cheeses & Ships Biscuits

Tea & Coffee
(Please bring your own Action Mug or Billy Can)

The menu card from the last trip of MV *Norland* before its sale to SNAV *Sicilia* in 2002. Note the play on words for each food course of the menu.

2 Para memorial at Darwin which overlooks the Goose Green settlement. (Courtesy Paul R.G. Haley)

The memorial's plaque lists the fallen from 2 Para (and support arms) at Goose Green and Wireless Ridge, which poignantly reflects the sacrifice made so that the Falkland Islands could continue to fly the Union flag and perpetuate the island's motto: 'Desire and Right'. (Courtesy Crown Copyright 2019, Sgt Paul Oldfield)

Above: The Norland pub, newly renamed and re-opened after a refurbishment in 1983 by Captain Don Ellerby, who pulled the first pint and where the former ship's barman, John Foster, was the proud landlord.

Left: In Hull Minster, amongst a large display of war memorabilia, a cabinet contains the *Norland*'s bell. Here we see on top of the cabinet a wooden carving, which represents the *Norland*'s battle honour: Falklands War 1982.

Left: Falklands War Medal (the rosette signifies active service within the 200-mile exclusion zone).

Below: Together with the Army, Air Force and Royal Navy, SS *Canberra* and MV *Norland* were honoured to be chosen to appear on a set of commemorative stamps.

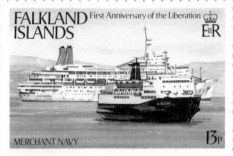

Above left: A specially produced Merchant Navy Red Ensign and Veteran's Badge.

Above right: Since 2015, Hull Minster has hosted a memorial service. A parade then follows through the city where at the Maritime Museum another short service is held. Here we see British Armed Forces and civilian Merchant Navy veterans proudly wearing their medals.

When the water restriction notices were first issued, some of the crew were made aware that it would always be available to the galley but only at certain times to the military and the crew. Tony Palfreman, a steward, not yet fully aware of the ruling, decided to take a shower. Standing under the shower head, with a steady stream coming out, he happily lathered his body with soap and was just shampooing his hair when the water stopped. He knocked and kicked the pipes, but nothing happened. Greatly annoyed with the situation, he went to the nearby crew's mess wearing only his flipflops and a towel. 'What the bloody hell's going on with the water?' he asked the lads. As he stood there dripping wet with soapsuds still adorning his hair, the lads chuckled at his predicament. Knowing there was a telephone in the mess, he rang the engine room to ask for the water to be put back on. The crew guessed the answer when Tony said in a loud voice, 'No, I'm not joking!' After a couple more seconds of listening to whoever was on the other end of the line, Tony hung up and looking at the telephone that was sat on the cradle, he said, 'And bollocks to you as well.' I was surprised no one quipped that he could always try having a beer-shower, using a bottle or two from the bar (although that would have been a waste of alcohol). Tony left the mess as he'd arrived, in a bit of a huff, but also with a bit of a smile on his face.

During the trip to South Georgia, I made the acquaintance of a navy rating in charge of the desalination plant located on C-deck. It turned sea water into fresh water, supposedly. The rating, a young lad, told me that part of the process was to add a tiny amount of a special acid into the water to kill any bacteria before it was distributed throughout the ship. This had the unwanted effect of descaling the pipes that the water was flowing through, which explained the brown water from the taps. While having this explained to me by the navy lad, I spotted what looked to be some non-brown water, beautiful clear water, ready to drink water. It was trickling out of a special tap that was part of the desalination unit.

'What do I have to do to get a drink of that water there?' I chanced.

'No way, it's more than my job's worth. I'll get court martialled if I let you have some. To give any of this good stuff away, sorry I just can't do it.' He seemed a good lad, but he was under orders and he stuck to his orders. I didn't pursue it any further.

I got in a conversation with one of the crew from the *Antelope* who was very upset about his crew's situation, and understandably so. It wasn't a very nice thing for me to see him in such a state. The *Antelope* to him wasn't just a ship; it was his home. As a fellow seafarer, I had complete empathy for how he felt, though I don't think I'd have got as emotional as him.

'Look, you've got a great consolation here,' I said.

'What's that?'

'For a start, you're still alive and one way or another you're going home. The crew of this ship would love to take you home. And who knows, we may yet do that … but *we* never know what's happening to us.' He took in what I'd said but didn't reply. I didn't know what else to say and I left it at that.

Not only were many of the *Antelope* crew feeling displaced, they had also lost their personal possessions and, in particular, spare clothing. It was suggested we help them out with this. A lot of the crew donated items of their own clothing: T-shirts, jeans, socks, anything that we could reasonably spare. On board we had a general shop from where some of the stock was generously donated to them. These were good-quality, trendy, grey sweatshirts and, one way or another, a lot of the *Antelope* crew had acquired them!

A couple of days after heading towards what felt like the end of the world, on 27 May, we found ourselves in Grytviken, the largest settlement in South Georgia. We didn't know the real reason we were there. Up on A-deck they would have known though. As it turned out, along with the *Canberra*, we were to rendezvous with the *QE2*. It was reassuring to see these ships, but I was surprised to see tugs also present. I have a particular soft spot for tugs and their crews, having worked on docking tugs on the river Humber during the winter of 1962–63. That was recorded as one of the coldest winters ever in the UK, but it was nothing compared to what it felt like here. Tugs have a very small crew – even ocean-going tugs, which these were. Who'd have thought that they would be here, so far away from home, doing their bit for Queen and country?

We assumed that the job of the *QE2* was to transport people and equipment quickly from the UK to the South Atlantic. I guessed that she could carry up to 3,000 men. Her role was as vital as any other ship but as

I understood it, she would only be sailing from the UK to South Georgia and back, not anywhere near the actual Falkland Islands exclusion zone. This made sense because, if we thought that the *Norland* and the *Canberra* were a good target, to have hit a ship of the *QE2*'s status would have been disastrous for us and a magnificent victory for the Argies.

The next day we learned that the *Canberra* and the *Norland* were to receive troops from the *QE2* to take to the Falklands. Earlier in the morning of that next day, the sheltered bay that we were in fascinated me. It was very cold with ice floes in the water and small icebergs drifting around us. The whole place had a unique atmosphere. Despite the cold, it was teeming with life. Seals were everywhere, but disappointingly I never saw a single penguin. All kinds of sea birds could be seen flying about the place, especially the famous albatross which is only found in the Southern Hemisphere. They seemed to have little fear of man. On the deck of the ship, they would walk about, 2 or 3ft away from you. It was a treat to see such wildlife. With my trusted binoculars, I scanned the surrounding terrain of black rock, capped by snow and ice on low-range mountains. This part of the world was first made famous by Ernest Shackleton and his fellow explorers, somewhere back in 1914. I thought it a wonderful place to be and for a while it gave me my first feeling of being safe.

I put down my binoculars whilst standing outside on A-deck. None of the other crew were about as I watched a tug come alongside. Not giving it too much thought, I saw some people on its deck and I gave them a wave. A short while later the tug pulled away and by now quite a lot of people were standing on its afterdeck. I realised they were the *Antelope* survivors. The tug was transporting them from our ship to the *QE2*. As the tug pulled away, some people looked up and again I gave them a friendly wave. With that, as they waved back, a loud voice announced, 'THREE CHEERS FOR THE *NORLAND* … HIP HIP HOORAY! … HIP HIP HOORAY! … HIP HIP HOORAY!' I felt moved by this. With it being so cold, most of our crew were inside the ship and I was alone on A-deck to enjoy this moment. There might have been an odd member of our crew on the open decks below also to wave the tug farewell and enjoy hearing the shout of thanks. Whatever, that was the last any of us on the *Norland* saw of the *Antelope* survivors.

9

BACK TO BOMB ALLEY

With the *Antelope* survivors gone, once again the ship was quiet like it was after 2 Para had disembarked. Because of this, it seemed Dave and I wouldn't have a lot to do that night, so we found time to roam about and we ended up on the car deck. It still had all the large food containers lined up, most of which were empty by now, as well as numerous smaller boxes and different items laid around. Here in South Georgia, the darkened ship rules were relaxed. It was reassuring to know the *Canberra* and the *QE2* were close by for company. Dave and I had noticed that the Gunport Doors had been opened. There was a series of lights that we call a 'cluster' (a round dish with several high-wattage bulbs) giving a lot of intense light to the sea below. This got our attention and we went for a closer look. Through the Gunport Doors, in the water where the light was concentrated, it was amazing to see how it attracted all kinds of fish. This had us fascinated, watching them dance and jostle so close to the surface. There was a mist beyond our cluster light which prevented us from seeing much further out into the bay where we were anchored. Suddenly a shape appeared through the mist. It was a tug that looked like it was coming alongside. Getting closer, we could see the afterdeck of the tug was crowded with troops. As it slowly came alongside, we saw that the troops were in a war-like state with their steel helmets, weapons and rucksacks. Once the tug was in place, the troops started to prepare themselves to come aboard as Dave and I looked on. Our ship took a line from the tug and made it fast. The first man who made to come on board seemed to be struggling, due to the amount of equipment he was carrying. Seeing his difficulty, I shouted, 'Here, give me your hand.' I bent down to help him but he was reluctant. Getting a better balance,

I leaned down as far as I dared and made a grab for his rucksack. I then heaved him up and he scrambled aboard. Dave had come over to help pull him onto the ship as well. When he stood upright to acknowledge us, he gave a polite little bow and said, 'Thank you, thank you!' I told him, 'There's no need for that.' We noticed he had handsome oriental features. He was a Gurkha. By now others were clambering aboard whom we also helped. They then helped each other. So, this was our introduction to the famous Gurkhas (7th Duke of Edinburgh's Own Gurkha Rifles Regiment), who'd been transported from the *QE2*.

A figure that was often seen around the ship was a Liaison Officer. He had the rank of Sergeant Major and was known as Movements McKenzie. He had a lot of say in administration matters on the ship and his influence was on the military but not our crew. On this occasion, his task was to allocate accommodation to the Gurkhas. There was lots of confusion as many of the Gurkhas had been sent the wrong way to find their cabins. Dave and I knew where each and every cabin was situated. We offered to help McKenzie, but because of his military standing and misplaced personal aloofness, he didn't want to take advice from anyone in civilian clothing. At least that's how it seemed to us. We thought, 'Ah well, bollocks to you!' Unlike with the Gurkhas who didn't mind a helping hand, we let McKenzie struggle through on his own.

More and more soldiers arrived throughout that night and the early morning, including 16th Field Ambulance as well as various other cap badges that I couldn't identify. I assumed that we would be taking these many hundreds of men to the Falklands, but to where exactly? When first turning to in the evening, our ship had been quiet, but by the next morning she wasn't any more. All the ship's crew were flat out preparing breakfast and then getting back into the routine of looking after soldiers, once again heading into a war situation. The pressure was back on, especially for George Rimmer the chief cook and his lads in the galley. The storekeepers, Chris Sutcliffe and Kevin Hornsby, also had to do their magic of finding extra food for all these new troops. Making ends meet from our ever-dwindling stores was a constant challenge. The stewards and the galley staff had to up their game once more for this new influx of troops.

One of the true workhorses of the Task Force: a tug. (Courtesy Brian Burton)

The Purser stopped by and we caught up for a chat on our current situation. The Gurkhas had a mystique and John, like me, was intrigued by them. He told me:

> I'm pleased to say I am getting on with Esplin-Jones and on the first night of hosting the Gurkhas we had a walk around the accommodation. Every cabin we went in had a Ghurkha with his gun aimed at the door. They certainly take their duties seriously. We'd heard that the first thing they did on the *QE2* was to take themselves down to the very bottom of it. They then familiarised themselves with every inch of the ship. It's what they've done on our ship too.

'I really like them,' I said.
'Yes, I do too. But not everyone else does.'
'What do you mean by that?' I asked.

He said:

When we brought the Gurkhas on board, there was a small RAF party with them. I didn't know where Movements McKenzie had gone. Anyway, I was sat in my office when this big bloke, an RAF sergeant, burst in and in his words, he wanted to know why these 'wogs' were in an outboard cabin and why he was in an inboard one? Whilst he was talking to me, two Gurkhas were present, one was a young man and the other middle-aged. You couldn't see what rank they had under their large outer combat-jackets. So, as this RAF sergeant is giving me grief, all of a sudden, the older Gurkha pulled his jacket off and you could see he had the pips of an officer. 'I hold the Queen's Commission and you are completely out of order,' he told the sergeant. 'You will apologise to the Purser now … and apart from that you are on a charge for insulting me,' he added.

'What a wanker of a Brit!' I said angrily. John said:

I felt the same, I've never seen a big bloke like that RAF guy drop so quick. Something else that has greatly annoyed me is our problem with laundry. You know we only have half a dozen domestic washing machines, which can't really cope with the number of men we're looking after? We've always been in need of fresh bed linen and towels, never mind the problem of cleaning personal clothes. The *Canberra* was a big help with this back in San Carlos Water. From what I'd heard, it was only a man and his wife on board the *Canberra* that did all the laundry for us, and they did this whilst under fire. Whereas here, the *QE2* spurned our request. When we took on the Gurkhas, I asked the *QE2* for anything they could give us to help with our journey, especially food – would you believe it, we got nothing.

The next day we were back at sea, heading in a westerly direction. With South Georgia behind us and surrounded by the vastness of the South Atlantic, once again I got a feeling of vulnerability. Where exactly were we headed to in the Falklands? We guessed it might be the dreaded Bomb Alley! This was not good news; the ships anchored there were still constantly under attack from the Argies. The *Canberra* would be doing the same as us, taking soldiers on board to ferry them to the Falklands, whereas the *QE2* had headed off to Ascension with the *Antelope* survivors.

Long days spent at sea give one time to reflect on many things. A lot of the crew felt, so far, we had been lucky in the war. We were heading back to where action was taking place and maybe it was only a matter of time before the inevitable happened. Fortunately, we all had jobs to keep us busy and take our minds off the situation. One time when moving about the alleyways in the lower decks, I heard the sound of crying. One of our crew members was having a good sob. Not wanting to intrude or make the individual feel embarrassed about their emotional state, I didn't stop to offer any comfort. It did make me realise the pressure that some were feeling more than others. Overall, it had long since dawned on the crew what we had let ourselves in for. But if we thought our lot was somehow tough going, it was worse for those in the thick of the fighting in the war on land.

Reports had filtered through about 2 Para, who had been locked in a tough battle. There had been talk of quite a few casualties and this really hit home with us because we felt that the Paras were not only our ship's adopted soldiers, but also our friends. Goose Green was a name mentioned where 2 Para had taken some losses. We didn't know exactly what Goose Green was: a village, a town, a hill or a mountain.

Our immediate problem before getting back to the Falklands was heavy seas. A lot of the troops didn't like this. They had been spoiled sailing on the enormous *QE2*, which could cope better with big waves. Seasickness can be quite debilitating for those who suffer from it. Land-locked Gurkhas had to acclimatise themselves quickly to it. More difficult still, they had to get used to the ship's menu and those who couldn't had come up with a plan. Dave and I were called to the galley one evening. Certain foodstuffs had been specially allocated to the Gurkhas from what little resources we had available. They'd been given permission to prepare food familiar to their diet, mainly curry-type dishes. These very pleasant people were in the galley preparing their food when Dave and I got into a conversation with them. I asked, 'This special knife that you possess, the Kukris, it holds a great myth — what's the story behind it?' Smiling at me and lowering his voice in a secretive manner, the Gurkha said, 'Well, it has several uses but its main one is that it is good for chopping up vegetables.' I burst out laughing at this, as did the Gurkha.

Round about this time, terrible news had come through that the Commanding Officer of 2 Para had been killed. It was awful news for anyone to lose their life but I didn't expect it would be Lt Col Jones, the one in charge. This led to a conversation that I had with one of the Gurkha sergeants whom I had spoken to several times. He came up to me and said, 'Is it true that 2 Para have lost their Commanding Officer?'

'Yes, that's what we've been told,' I answered.

There were two or three other Gurkhas standing with him and he spoke to them briefly in his own tongue. With a very serious face, he then turned to ask me, 'Is there any mention of taking prisoners?'

'I think there's news of Argy prisoners being taken in addition to a lot of them being killed as well.'

Again, he had a word with his fellow soldiers. Then with utter frankness he said, 'If we had lost our Commanding Officer, we would have killed them all.' He turned and just walked away.

I thought, 'Bloody hell, these nice, polite people are maybe not so nice and polite after all. I'm glad they're on our side!'

On passing each other, the Purser asked me, 'Hey, Reg, did you hear about what's happened with 2 Para?'

'Something yeah. What do you know?' I asked.

The Purser said:

When I'd heard them say that Sunray had gone down, I was a little shocked but not totally surprised. I didn't have any real connection with Lt Col Jones … every time I saw him, he was going 100-knots an hour down a corridor to see someone. It's so sad to say it but he gave me the impression that if some of the Paras were going to get killed, he might be one of them. He struck me as a bold kind of person who would go charging in everywhere, into machine-gun posts and the like. How terrible that this actually happened.

'Who do you suppose is in charge now, John?'

He said:

It'll be the second-in-command, Chris Keeble. He seems a bit calmer to me, a bit more measured. Let's hope they're doing alright. I was having a beer one night with Colour Sergeant Del Amos and I asked him, 'Who are the best paratroopers in the world?' I thought he was going to say, 'We are' but instead he said, 'The Israelis are first, the French second and we're third.' I asked him about the Americans. He laughed and said, 'We might be third but at least we're not, and we never will be, like the Americans!' I agreed with him on that.

'You've always thought the same as me, that our lads will get the job done,' I said.

'Oh, we will. It'll come at a price though,' John said.

One evening, still as a darkened ship, a very strange incident took place. I didn't know our exact location when Dave and I were in the Forward Lounge and Bar and we heard what sounded like an aircraft. A chink of light from outside appeared through the curtains from the foredeck. A terrifically bright light was shining down from an object, about 50ft above. The light was constant and stable, even though the ship was still moving forward. This threw Dave and me because we couldn't figure out where this kind of light was coming from, here in the middle of nowhere in the South Atlantic. We looked at each other and I'm sure we had the same thought … is it a UFO? It couldn't have been a helicopter, because it would have hovered over the heli-decks, which were mid-ships and astern. And anyway, we were way too far out for a helicopter to reach us. So, what the hell was it? Then abruptly, the light went out and the noise disappeared. What on earth was going on, we wondered, especially as lights were absolutely forbidden on the foredeck at night? I rang the bridge to see if they could explain. The best answer they could give was that probably a Sea Harrier had paid us a visit. But it was still a long way even for a Sea Harrier, and what would that kind aircraft want of us anyway? Maybe the bridge was being evasive and they didn't want us to know the reason. If it had been a Sea Harrier, it might have been that the pilot didn't know who we were and he'd come in for a closer look to check us out. Thank goodness we didn't end up as a friendly fire incident. The whole thing was a mystery.

What I hadn't given much thought to was the two stewardesses on board, until I bumped into one of them. Even though we were on the same ship, due to Dave and me being on nights, I hadn't seen either one of them for weeks. I then got to thinking about something my father had told me of his war years, of how it was frowned upon to sign up men on ships who were members of the same family. This was for the obvious reason that if the ship was lost, then it would be a double tragedy for the family. For one family it could have been a triple tragedy. On board, we had two brothers, Geoff and Tony Palfreman. There was another Palfreman brother called Glen, who worked as a steward and who had volunteered. He was very upset when North Sea Ferries firmly drew the line, only allowing his two elder brothers to sail but not him. We also had a father and son on board, Les and Steve Isham. These thoughts crossed my mind as we got closer to the Falklands. On arrival there, like the operation with 2 Para, thank goodness all the troops had safely disembarked, which included a special bomb-disposal section. Next day, once again we were subject to red alerts and we hoped good fortune would stay with us. The month of May had given way to June and, anchored in San Carlos Water, the air attacks continued; yet, somehow, we became nonchalant about them. A red alert became an alert not to take cover but for some to go out on deck and see what was happening. It was hard not to. Some cheery news that filtered through was that, although we'd suffered significant losses to our navy, the Argies had suffered huge losses to their air force. We'd had a couple of RAF observers on board for some time and they mentioned that our forces had taken out near to eighty Argy aircraft. This sounded impressive. I didn't know if it was true or just propaganda to keep our spirits up.

Whenever we were desperate for fuel and water, the *Norland* sailed out of San Carlos Water to join the main part of the Task Force at sea. Tankers were in the area carrying fuel and fresh water. 'Replenishment at Sea', a system called RASing (pronounced 'razzing' by the Royal Navy), transferred these supplies. The razzing would take place mostly at night, when a ship would pull up alongside, leaving only a narrow gap and at a speed of dead slow. One can imagine how vulnerable any two ships would feel in a war environment carrying out such a procedure. By now, any mention of our ship going home was laughed at, for the latest news filtering through was that we would be taking Argy prisoners on board. With all that was going on, the main question the crew wanted answering was,

'Are we winning this war, or what?'To us, it was unclear how things were going. Were we gaining or losing ground in the land battle? In taking prisoners one might think we were in fact winning. All I knew is that we had been a troop-carrying ship, an assault ship and a survivor-carrying ship, and now we were to be a prisoner-of-war ship. Reports of other navy ships being hit did not instil great confidence that we were winning.

When finishing my night shift, as usual I went down on to the car deck for a look around before getting some sleep. Starved of information, I did this to find out what might actually be going on. One morning I arrived on the car deck to see the Gunport Doors open and bedraggled troops climbing into the ship. These were not our troops, they were the Argy prisoners whom we would be looking after. They were to be guarded by armed Royal Marines. The Marines looked fearsome and very imposing to me. The repeated word the Marines used with the Argy prisoners as soon as they came aboard was 'rapido' (Spanish for 'quickly' or 'move'). The prisoners were made to sit cross-legged with their hands behind the back of their heads. Of course, the Argies' weapons had been confiscated much earlier. Laughable to us but not to the Argies was that their officers had told them that if they were captured by the Ghurkhas, they would be killed and eaten. Officer POWs coming aboard with small arms wanted to keep them (possibly for protection from their own troops) but they were given up under protest. All prisoners went through a process of being frisked, followed by having their belts and bootlaces taken off them. Once they had been 'vetted', they were taken away and given accommodation.

Whilst all this was going on, new friendly faces kept appearing and disappearing on and off the ship. One particular character, a mysterious type who didn't conform to what seemed the normal military way, was to make his presence known. Among the prisoners there were lots of hard-nosed, defiant types. You could see the hate in them, not so much at us but at their situation as prisoners. If a prisoner wouldn't co-operate, the mysterious character was called in. He went by several names, mostly Rodrigues or Gonzales. He was a Spanish speaker and apparently knew the Argentinian accent. I witnessed him addressing an awkward Argy in a demonstrative manner to try and get his message through. I just about followed the exchange, being able to speak a little Spanish myself, as did other crew members who'd picked it up on their travels. Our mysterious Rodrigues would wade into any defiant Argy prisoners and tell them that their mothers were 'cocksuckers' or words similar. For any race, this is an insult, but particularly for Latinos. It seemed to work. I realised this was a psychological tactic to bring the Argies down to the level that he wanted in order to control them. On one occasion, an absolutely defiant Argy just wouldn't accept his situation. As already mentioned, there were many containers on the car deck. Close to where the prisoners were held were refrigerated food containers that had motors running to keep the contents refrigerated. One of these had been kept running but without any food inside. It was opened up and they threw the defiant Argy in and closed the door. Five minutes later they let him out. This was done in full view of the other Argy prisoners to let them know that the Brits wouldn't stand any nonsense. It worked because the Argy was now a totally different person – he co-operated. This incident aside, the Argies were well cared for and the Geneva Convention fully complied with. We later found out that the mysterious Spanish speaker on our side was either SAS or SBS … or maybe he was both!

I wondered what we were going to do with these people. It then emerged we were to take them to Montevideo in Uruguay, a neutral friendly country. This meant we would leave cold rough seas to head north to warmer climes. Good, let's do it! One hope was that we would have free passage, uninterrupted by Argy aircraft, but I wondered if submarines could still be a problem. Whatever, a northerly direction it was to be.

When we sailed, although still technically a darkened ship, after the second night at sea the ship's navigation lights were allowed. This would play a major factor in what was shortly to happen. As well as the prisoners we had a real mixed bag of troops from different regiments. On the second night when lights were allowed, I was going about my business and as I passed a soldier, he told me, 'I have just seen somebody jump over the side. Did you see it?'

'Oh, bloody hell, no, I didn't,' I said. I went to the aft of the ship when somebody else said, 'Yeah. I saw this guy climb up and he's gone over the side.'

With that, one of the ABs, Mike Failey, confirmed that he'd also heard that someone had gone over. He then went to pick up a lifebelt and in vain hope he threw it over the side. I went to the nearest phone that I could find and I rang the bridge. It was Chris Cammish, the 2nd Mate, who took my call. 'Someone has gone overboard!' I said with urgency. I'd figured that someone else had surely made the same call. There was a pause and Chris replied, 'Okay, leave it with us.'

So, I left it at that. Shortly after this, I felt the ship turning around going through what's known as the Williamson or Anderson turn, a manoeuvre used to bring a ship or boat back to a point it had previously passed through. For such an emergency, a number of men are quickly assembled on the lifeboat deck. One of the Assistant Pursers, John Graham, suggested that I go on the bridge in case I was needed, which I did. In this situation the ABs would be manning the number one boat, known as the 'crash boat', which was the smallest of the lifeboats on the ship. Luckily, this was the first night that lights could be shown, which was paramount in this situation. Bright lights from the wing of the bridge were shining directly onto the lifeboat as it was lowered by Billy Hookem, the bosun. A heavy swell was present at the time, making it dangerous work. Bob Lough, the Chief Officer, was in charge as coxswain of the boat. With him were ABs Paddy Dolan, Mike Failey and John Laycock. For all of these men it was a brave but mandatory task to take on. But would it all prove fruitless? Would the person still be alive?

Once the lifeboat was in the water, the ABs dismantled it from the ship and it cruised off to conduct the search. The procedure was for it to travel so far in the direction we had come, switch off the engine and listen, proceed further and listen for noise again. It was a tense situation. On the bridge we could only hope that whoever had jumped overboard had survived the fall into the sea. If they had, we hoped they would be shouting for help, but then again, why would they shout for help having jumped in the first place?

Amazingly, the start/stop/listen procedure worked, for a voice was heard in the dark and someone was picked up from the water. It turned out to be a Royal Navy rating, who had been shouting out for his mother. His life had been saved. The lifeboat returned to the ship and was hauled back into its place from the heavy swell, which had caused Paddy Dolan to receive an injury that later on he discovered was a fractured shoulder, which he'd ignored to carry on working through the pain. With the job done, the *Norland* continued on its journey. The appropriate personnel from the survivor's unit took over his care. One way or another, he was a very lucky man to have survived. What an experience to go through! In the middle of night, in the middle of an ocean, in the middle of a war, the *Norland* and its crew had succeeded in an emergency situation that had saved the life of someone falling overboard or, as was the case here, jumping. Full marks to the lads involved in what can only be described as great seamanship. This was recognised by Captain Don Ellerby, who invited them to his cabin to say thank you and I am sure that included a tot of rum.

10

SUCH JOY BUT SUCH SADNESS

A couple of days after the man overboard incident, we arrived in the mouth of the River Plate on 12 June. The weather there was more welcoming. We dropped anchor several miles out from Montevideo during daylight hours before heading into port when it was dark. As we tied up alongside, the prisoners started to disembark immediately. This process took a few hours. Some of our lads were on the open deck watching it happen. We weren't allowed to go ashore. We had hoped to because it is a vibrant city, typical of Latin America. Many of the crew had been there before, but going ashore was not to be. After we'd taken on fresh water, rations and fuel, on 13 June we were back at sea on a course, once again, heading south to the Falklands.

That evening, engineer John Dent came up to the restaurant for a natter with Dave and me, as he often did. It was just after midnight and he told us something terrible. 'Oh, wasn't it a shame to hear about Chris?' he said.

'Chris who?' I asked.

'Chris Dent,' he said. 'You know, Captain Dent.'

'What about him, what's happened?'

'He got killed,'

'Oh no! Not him as well!' I felt shocked. This news was so sad for me to hear. In fact, everyone felt sad and not just about Captain Dent, but also about news of the dozen or so other casualties that was filtering through, all of whom somebody from the crew would have known. The same for John, who had also befriended Chris Dent, and although he had the same surname, he wasn't related. All the times Chris and I had jogged and chatted together flashed through my mind. I really liked him as a person and I wouldn't be seeing him again. This was a strange thought to process. In a way, I didn't expect the officers to be killed.

The next morning, a profound incident took place and electrician Brian Burton picks up the story:

> After carrying out some of my daily checks, I happened to be up on the bridge when I decided to have a brew with the makings that were in the chart room, which was a small area enclosed by a heavy curtain. With urgency, the navigating officer on watch, Alan Woof, shouted out loud to me, 'Brian, did you just see those two planes?' I rushed out to look, but they were gone. The ship's position around this time was about 100 miles or so off the coast of Argentina and this was a moment for great concern. Panicking, we both wondered whether to sound a general alarm. The two aircraft suddenly appeared, this time very close up to the ship and flying at the same speed as us, but to our relief they were British Sea Harriers. Now positioned only a few metres away, the noise of their engines was incredible as one flew on the port side, the other on the starboard side. Did this mean that we were in trouble and needed some kind of military escort? To our amazement, the Harriers did a flamboyant manoeuvre with their wings, which was in fact a 'victory in flight roll'. They then flew off, not to be seen again. The Harriers' action hinted that something positive was afoot. Half an hour later, news of the surrender came through by signal. It was reckoned that Admiral Sandy Woodward, on the flagship HMS *Hermes*, had given the order for the Harriers to find our ship and give us this acknowledgement.

As night stewards, if we didn't turn to by 9.30 p.m., someone would check on our whereabouts. On the evening of 14 June, I had been in my cabin resting before my evening duties when my cabin door swung open around 8.30 p.m. Dick Johnson, a fellow steward, stood there and yelled, 'Reg, I have got some news for you.'

'Sod off, will ya? It's not time for me to turn to yet!' I yelled back.

With excitement, he said, 'Listen, it's real good news. The Argies have surrendered and we've accepted it. Get yourself dressed and get in the bar. We're all having a beer.'

Since the start of hostilities, I'd decided not to drink and I'd stuck to this promise. However, I could indulge now that hostilities had ceased, or at least the Argy ground forces had surrendered because it wasn't initially clear if their Navy and Air Force had also surrendered. Whatever the exact situation, this news was too good not to celebrate. It wasn't a case of a booze up, as Dave and I had to be on duty at 10 p.m. But, anyway, we went in the crew's mess where it was a happy atmosphere, with everyone looking relaxed for the first time in a long time. The change in mood of everyone on board was overwhelmingly positive. Dave and I briefly joined in, but with our night shift to do we couldn't over celebrate.

So, the fighting in the Stanley area had stopped, though this news didn't stop us resorting back to a state of darkened ship as we journeyed south. The impartial weather wasn't interested in the outcome of events on the Falklands and we continued to slug it out against heavy seas. The ship's destination was San Carlos Water, yet again, where we would be preparing for more prisoners. The surrender supposedly meant no more air raids and, without this fear, we took on several hundred Argy prisoners, but everyone still had their guard up. Our next order was to head for the metropolis known as Stanley, the Falkland Islands capital. On arrival there, to put it mildly, it was a bit of a let-down. From where we were anchored, a mile or so off shore, all we could see from the confines of the ship was merely a collection of wooden houses. The town's dominant feature was a church with a small tower and classed as a cathedral. I can only say it was one of the smallest cathedrals in the world I'd ever seen. Our first priority was to take on fuel and water, as well as limited amounts of foodstuff, whatever was available. But what we mostly took on board were more prisoners. I wondered where they were all going to go because there were so many of them coming aboard. The procedure of confiscating belts, bootlaces and helmets – not forgetting the command of 'rapido' – was repeated. Separate to the prisoners, I also saw a group of our soldiers come aboard who were limping or walking uncomfortably, which had my curiosity. These British soldiers were in a condition that one would describe as the walking wounded. Some didn't have proper footwear on – socks and slippers but no shoes. One evening, several came into our mess room for a drink. I recognised a couple of them from 2 Para. Soldiers from other regiments were present as well. 'Are you alright, lads?' I asked.

'Not really, we're on sick,' came the reply.

'What's the matter?'

Two of them looked awkwardly at each other and one said, 'We've got trench foot.'

'Eh, surely trench foot is from the First World War,' I said.

'No, it's not. Living in rain-soaked trenches and dugouts, and the weather being as bad as it was, somehow it just happened.'

One of them was a familiar face to me and I was trying to figure out why. Then the penny dropped: the conversation I'd had weeks before about my walking boots, which somebody had wanted to buy. He was one of these men. He spotted me and came over to ask, 'Do you remember me?'

'Yes, I do.'

'Well, I wanted to buy your boots which you wouldn't sell me and now look at the fucking state I'm in. I've got trench foot. Why didn't you sell them?'

'I kept hold of them because I didn't want to get trench foot as well.' What else could I say to him?

'What, on board a ship?'

'Had we got hit, we might have had to go ashore,' I said.

A short pause followed. 'Fair enough,' he said.

For the lads with trench foot, it was all over for them. What an odd way to end one's participation in a modern war, at least it seemed odd to me. Some of the senior Paras criticised those with trench foot; it was seen as self-inflicted and incompetent.

To accommodate the number of prisoners we had, six were put into four-man cabins, one each on the four available bunks and two on the deck. In a two-berth cabin, this would have four prisoners placed in it, again two sleeping on the deck. The doors were kept locked from the outside. The armed Marines were taking no chances. In a conversation with one of the Marines, he was very pissed off at having to do this guard duty. He wanted to have been in the thick of the action, fighting.

Every available space was used to accommodate the prisoners, even in the Forward Lounge and Bar area. I wondered how the hell the ship would be able to feed all of these people. Red Cross representatives were now present to ensure the Argies were properly looked after. It amused me that the Red Cross had no interest in our crew's welfare or even the welfare of our own soldiers, injured or not. The Argies were given two main meals a day. The galley was flat out as usual. The Purser asked if I would come off nights, leaving Dave on his own, so I could help during the day. I, of course, said yes and I was detailed to work with the Marines carrying out guard duties by serving food to the prisoners. The Geneva Convention dictated that they were to have a balanced diet. Can you believe it, these prisoners in the cabins were not just getting a balanced diet but room service by stewards! A great number of other prisoners were sleeping on the decks in the lounges. They obtained their meals by queuing up, soup-kitchen style, with the stewards and the barmen doling it out. For those in the cabins, we used a trolley to carry the right number of portions for the right number of prisoners. We were escorted by an armed Marine, who would check his prisoner list before opening a cabin door just enough for me to hand the food over for someone to take. It was decent food, rice, vegetables and meat. An allocation of two cigarettes for each man was allowed. When pushing the trolley along an alleyway on B-deck with food ready to serve, I stopped at a door when my Marine escort looked at his list and said, 'In this next cabin I only have one man named.' The Marine opened the door, leaving just enough room for me to hand over the food. To my great surprise the person inside was wearing a dog collar. He was a man of the cloth, probably a Catholic padre. Knowing there was only one man in this cabin, I handed over a single portion. He looked at it and spoke in Spanish to us. '*Senor, necesito más.*' The Marine asked what he said. I told him it meant, 'I need more.' We looked at each other and both shook our heads. I guessed that the padre might speak English and I told him, 'Look, you're all the same to me. You are one person so you get one person's allocation.' He didn't look happy at hearing this. The Marine said, 'That's good enough for me,' and he slammed the door shut. I never saw the padre again. The Marine and I both thought it unusual to lock up a man of God.

The war was over for these Argentinian prisoners arriving to board the *Norland* for safe passage back home to Argentina.

We had been at sea for a couple of days and I'd stayed on day shift helping out with this meal routine as the ship headed towards their homeland. We were to repatriate the Argies in southern Argentina at a port called Puerto Madryn in the province of Chubut in Argentine Patagonia.

The Purser's opinion of the Argies was that they were not as well trained as our soldiers. 'That's all well and good but they could still fire guns and kill people,' I said. Yet, in some way they evoked a kind of sympathy in me to see them in their passive state. Sure, they were mostly young men, conscripts, not professionals. However, the Purser, like me, recognised that there were some hard-case types among them. It needed to be remembered that the Argies had a very professional faction to their army and these professionals were also fighting against us. The Purser spoke of his own connection with not one padre but two, when he told me:

An Argentine officer who spoke English approached me to run a church service. I had no problem with it. Two little old timers were wheeled out and I wondered who on earth they were. They were nothing like Major

David Cooper, the padre of 2 Para, who happened to be one of the best shots in the battalion and who used to teach the troops how to be a sniper. To me, these two old codgers were more 'last rites' administrators, not fighters or military trained. One spoke a little English and I asked what he was doing in the military. It turned out that he and the other padre each lived in a remote village, then one day the military came around and just took them. They were forced into serving and ended up in the Falklands. As a Catholic nation, I was more than happy to see them having a religious service; it would take their minds off any possible rebellion.

Not long after this conversation with the Purser, I was on the lower decks and it was there that prisoners in different stages throughout the day were allowed some exercise on the car decks. Two hundred at a time would be allowed a half hour stretch to walk about. One time, whilst this was taking place, the sound of prisoners collectively shouting and bawling broke out. I went down on the car deck to have a look. The Marines were present to witness some kind of spokesman who, on behalf of the Argies, was egging on others to act up. Word had wrongly got out to the Argies that the containers with the motors running on the car deck were gas chambers. The Argies feared they would be put in them and their bodies dumped over the side. The guards were trying to keep control. I got the sense this could easily get out of hand. In the middle of the crowd, the Argy spokesman causing the agitation was standing on a box or something, waving his arms about, getting everyone wound up. There was a kind of excitement that, to me, was typical of the Latin temperament. The Marine I was standing next to was anxious to say the least. He was a big blond-haired kid and as concern began to mount, he pulled out a sidearm. He then barged his way through the Argies, heading towards the spokesman. The other Marines closed up and had their weapons in a ready-to-shoot state. 'Bloody hell, what's going to happen?' I thought. The big blond-haired Marine had waded his way through hundreds of prisoners and on reaching the spokesman he grabbed him with one hand by the throat and with his other hand he held the revolver to his head. This action frightened me as I thought he was going to shoot him. It equally frightened the Argies looking on, which was the point of the exercise. The Marines cocked and aimed their weapons in support. 'I'll blow your fucking head off if you don't shut up,' shouted the Marine into the spokeman's face. He went limp as the Marine released his grip on him. The Marine then barged his way back to where he was originally standing by me and, amazingly, a calm descended. The white-faced Argy spokesman shut up alright. This intense situation was resolved and I had to admire the Marine's actions. For all that the Marines might have been pissed off at only having guard duties over Argy prisoners, they were doing a hell of a good job of keeping them in check.

Not long after this incident I was in our mess having a chat about it with fellow steward, Frankie Green. His attitude towards the Argies was not hostile at all. Indeed, his comment was, 'All these good-looking young men trying to kill each other, I don't get it. 'What a stupid waste of life.' I thought about Frankie's words and they were so typical of him and his empathy towards others, whoever they might be, enemy or not.

On the day we approached Puerto Madryn, without any Royal Navy escort, we didn't sail straight into the port. The same procedure was used as when we disembarked the Argies in Montevideo – we had to wait until dark before doing so. I was now back on nights and when the ship finally tied up and lowered the gangway, I couldn't resist looking to see what was going to happen out on the open deck. The deck was lit but not with bright lights, merely courtesy lights for the crew's use. With that, several Royal Navy officers appeared. The figure I mostly recognised amongst them was Commander Esplin-Jones, wearing his greatcoat and imposing naval hat. He approached the gangway and stopped several yards short. Those around him stayed a couple of yards back. I was standing well to one side, waiting to see what would unravel. A car pulled up at the bottom of the gangway. Several military people got out of the car and a single figure, also wearing a greatcoat, walked up the gangway first, followed by a couple of henchmen behind him. Judging by the amount of gold braid on his hat, the leading person was clearly of high rank. When he stepped aboard, something was spoken in Spanish. Esplin-Jones stepped forward to shake hands. The Argentinian officer refused to put his own hand out to take up the gesture. In fact, he placed his hands behind his back in a sign of arrogant defiance. 'Hell, that's awkward,' I thought. Something else was said in Spanish and Esplin-Jones stepped back. More words were spoken and then a process of disembarking the prisoners took place. The injured and sick were taken off first. A military person was standing at the top of the gangway with a counter, clicking away for each prisoner who left the ship. The ship's accommodation decks were emptied one by one, and this went on for two to three hours. Transport down on the quay took the Argies away, which I learnt was approximately 2,300 prisoners. The whole ship was relieved to see them go. Information emerged that after the last prisoner left the ship the Argentinian authorities informed our ship's captain, without any courtesies, that 'he could leave – immediately!' The ship had requested a fresh water resupply but this was apparently refused.

Just before dawn, the ship pulled out of Puerto Madryn. This time we had an escort, not a Royal Navy ship but an Argentinian Navy frigate. Even though the surrender had been given and it was seemingly being agreed to, an uncomfortable feeling circulated the ship. We didn't trust the Argies. We were in their waters, they could still sink us, especially now that we didn't have any of their troops aboard. I wasn't witness to it but apparently the Argentinian frigate was waving its guns about in a threatening manner. By now I had gone to bed and was disappointed to be later told that in answer to this threatening behaviour, an announcement was made over the ship's tannoy by Lt Cmdr Hughes. In deliberate, measured tones, he informed all on board: 'This British ship, the MV *Norland*, is now heading back to the British Falkland Islands.' The music of *Rule Britannia* then followed. Both the announcement and the music could be heard by anyone listening on the nearby Argentinian frigate before it finally broke away to leave us sailing south-east, this time with big grins on everyone's faces. Just prior to all this happening, hopefully a smile would have befallen the faces of our families at the 'Newsgram' updates sent on 19 and 20 June to Hull. Key extracts from both Newsgrams are as follows:

Dear Wives and Families,
… At long last the news appears to be good and our thoughts can perhaps begin to turn towards a journey home, although there is presently still much work to be done down here with vast numbers of Prisoners of War to move.

… Since our rapid departure from our homes and normal drafts, we have all been kept very busy on our mini Aircraft Carrier and have certainly done our share of the work, although we have not made the news as much as the *Canberra* and *QE2*. We are proud to say that we were the first Merchant Ship into the Falklands on the night of the landing and have been in the thick of things throughout.

… We have landed over 300 helicopters on our two decks and shifted literally tons of stores and hundreds of men, ship to ship and ship to shore. We have also found that we can turn our hands to a variety of jobs which would not normally be ours to do. Job wise the Deck Department are all fine, Cooks and Stewards all okay. The Galley and Cafeteria looks like a combination of Kings Cross Station on Cup Final Day and Aldershot on a Saturday night.

… We are sorry to say that the mail system from you has been constipated but we are hoping our letters get home to you. Do please keep writing. We are all fit and well, send fondest love and look forward to seeing you soon, please keep paying the bills.

The ship's Radio Officer, Brian Lavender was witness to a wonderfully amusing communication exchange between the monarchy and the ship. Prince Charles and Lady Diane's first child (later to be christened William) was born on 21 June 1982. Not long afterwards, 2 and 3 Para apparently sent a message of congratulations which must have included a cheeky suggestion. The *Norland* received a teleprinter message back on 25 June addressed from Buckingham Palace that read:

All three of us send warmest and appreciative thanks to all ranks of the gallant 2nd and 3rd battalions for their splendid message.
 We can assure you that our son will not be called Stanley.
 Charles and Diana.

11

WE'RE GOING HOME ...
AREN'T WE?

Having left Puerto Madryn on 21 June, and with our Argentinian naval escort having departed, we realised what a state our ship was in. The prisoners had left lots of their personal equipment behind, as well as rubbish of one sort or another that included human waste. Our ship needed a thorough cleaning and it was left to the stewards to sort out all of the accommodation and public rooms. The ABs had their work cut out too, having to clear the outer decks and the two car decks, where tons of webbing and thousands of helmets had to be disposed of. A decision was made to drop the stern ramp at sea. Paddy Dolan, John Laycock, Mike Failey and Ray Scruton were tasked with throwing all the Argy equipment overboard to let the bottom of the sea deal with it. Interestingly, the British Army has a word for describing their equipment, which is 'kit'. Everything that they had or used, if they liked it, they would say, 'That's good kit.' One bit of kit that could be useful to me was an Argentinian fold-up spade used for digging trenches. Not that I would ever be digging trenches, but I thought I might find a use for it in the boot of my car for who knows what. Anyone could have gone down to the car decks and helped themselves to the Argy equipment, if it had been of any interest to them. One soldier actually helped himself to six Argy helmets. What on earth he was going to do with them, I don't know.

The ABs given the job of disposing of the Argy equipment did so either by throwing it overboard from the stern ramp or by having a bit of a laugh and kicking most of the Argy helmets like footballs into the sea.

When they got down to the last half a dozen or so, a soldier happened by and said, 'I hope you've checked inside all those helmets before getting rid of them.'

'What for? They're mostly full of lice,' answered one of the lads.

'Ah but that's where the Argies would have hidden any money.'

The ABs looked at each other and said, 'Shit, it's a bit late to check them all now.'

Once the big clean had finished and the *Norland* resembled something like it used to be, an air of relaxation descended and nobody deserved a break more than the galley staff. All that had happened up to this point had put an understandable strain on the crew, with several feeling it more than others. The ship's hierarchy commented that everything we had done had been to the best of our ability and they were more than satisfied with our efforts.

No matter how satisfied the crew may have felt at their efforts being recognised, everyone on board was totally fed up with the water situation. I decided to do something about it for myself. Anyone who has been denied something as simple as good clean water will understand what I did. I went to see the navy lad who was running the desalination plant. It was the middle of the night and I was sitting nattering with him for a while. He knew that I was after something more than a chat, and I knew that he knew this. My eyes kept drifting to look at the small freshwater system he had going, which I had seen the first time that I'd visited him. This was a small separate water system to the one that came out of the ship's pipes, which always tasted lousy.

'So, that lovely fresh water that you have there, how about some of it for me?' I dared to ask.

Like at my previous visit, he repeated, 'No!' With a certainty to his resolve, he added, 'I told you before and I'm sorry to tell you again, I just can't do it.'

I wasn't going to give up. 'Look,' I said quietly, 'there is only me and you here having this conversation, which no one else needs to know about. You might like to know that I have the keys to the food store and there must be something in there you'd fancy.'

'I can't do it, whatever you've got to offer.'

'It just so happens that there's a couple tins of Crawford's Biscuits waiting to be eaten. Some are chocolate biscuits.'

There was a pause. He was thinking hard, bearing in mind the food situation at the time wasn't at its best and the treat of sweet sugary biscuits was a hell of a temptation. The long pause was broken.

'Okay, it's a deal, providing it's just between me and you.'

My cabin was on the next deck below, where I had a bucket already waiting. 'I'll be back in a minute with the goods and a container,' I said. Each crew member usually has a bucket under their cabin sink for washing their clothes. We call it a doby bucket. Hardly anybody was up at this time, so to be walking with biscuits secreted away and a bucket in open view wasn't a problem. I handed over the biscuits and he took my bucket.

'Thanks for these,' he said, 'but I also think you're a bastard because you got me.' He filled my bucket three-quarters full with that lovely, fresh, clean water I had been longing for. The deal done, we shook hands and wished each other well. I took the bucket back to my cabin and locked the door. Getting onto all fours, I dunked my face into the bucket and began to drink … slowly. Such nectar. I drank maybe a pint of this precious stuff. I then put the remaining water into a smaller container and went to present it to Dave. He wondered how on earth I had got hold of it. A little later, in the galley, we put on a small pan of this lovely, fresh, clean water to make a decent-tasting cup of tea. What bliss!

When we arrived back in the Falklands area, we learned that we were to accommodate 2 Para. This pleased us greatly for they felt special to us. Then shortly afterwards we heard that they might even be going home to Britain on the *Norland*. If 2 Para were going back to Britain, we assumed that we would be taking them. So, our time in the Falklands looked to be over. We dared to allow ourselves to think this and what a feeling it was!

Once we were back in Stanley, 2 Para began coming aboard but not en masse. Sometimes it was two or three, sometimes a dozen or more. They didn't seem to be the same 'gung-ho' people we'd said farewell to a month earlier on disembarking the ship. I say this because many seemed to have lost weight – some had clothing on their backs rotting or almost falling off – and they all looked extremely tired. They had a cheer about them but you could tell they'd had a tough time. As more and more came aboard, the main question asked by our crew was 'Did so and so make it?' The individual friendships built up between us and the Paras meant that it was quite emotional for the crew to know that their friends were okay. One of the Toms Dave and I had spoken to many times was Stuart Cardy. We were familiar with him from the coffee-drinking breaks on the way down to the Falklands. He always kept himself in top condition and was good company to be with. As more Paras appeared on the scene, together with soldiers from other units, we kept asking if anyone had seen Stuart. No, was the answer. We feared the worst because we knew there were lots of casualties. Many of the Paras who weren't coming back onto our ship were hopefully on the hospital ship, SS *Uganda*. I hadn't spotted the return of the young Tom who had taught me weapon training and live-firing. The best I hoped for was that he was injured and on the hospital ship. I asked one of the sergeants if he'd made it through in one piece. It seemed like an eternity before the sergeant quietly said, 'No, he didn't.'

I felt a bit numb at this. The sergeant could read my face.

'He got taken out by a sniper; it was a head wound. But, hey, we managed to get the bastard who did it. Yeah, we got the bastard good and proper.'

If this comment was to help me feel better, it didn't. I may not have known the lad that well but at the times we met up, I warmed to him. I enjoyed his company and when we were invited to fire weapons, it was always him that I waited for to be my instructor. He was one face of so many that our crew members had become familiar with. Now it would be a face I wouldn't see again.

For those returning, we were pleased that we could offer a clean ship, especially considering all that they had been through. A lot of personal reunions took place between the Paras and the crew, not just at our level but with the officers up on A-deck as well. It was towards the end of the final numbers coming aboard when Dave and I were in the restaurant and a bedraggled figure approached us. We didn't recognise him. The figure said in a quiet voice, 'Alright lads, any chance of a coffee?' Bloody hell, it was Stuart! We greeted him like a long-lost brother. How good it was to see him.

During this period the Paras told us that the military hierarchy wanted to fly them home. Thoughts were given to splitting up 2 Para, with some heading back to Britain by different means, getting them home as best they could and as quickly as they could. However, it was unanimously requested by the 2 Para Toms and the officers that they travel home on the *Norland*. The military agreed to this, which gave our crew a very proud feeling.

Whilst in Stanley we took on supplies of food, fuel and water. Chris Sutcliffe, the storekeeper, told me that at times we were so low on food, how we'd got away with it was nothing short of a miracle. He'd had a hell of a balancing act making ends meet. With hostilities ceased, from now on we wouldn't struggle as much to get what the ship needed and, indeed, what the ship probably deserved. For sure, the one thing that was needed to help the troops unwind was a resupply of booze – and plenty of it. Booze can bring its own troubles but without it there could have been a lot more. Not only did we have 2 Para back on board, but the whole of 3 Para joining us too. Some sort of rivalry might be in the offing. With the ship's compass set for north, our first stop would be Ascension.

On 25 June, we were back at sea. 2 Para were familiar with the workings of the ship and its layout, so it didn't take long for everyone to fall into the routine that they had previously known. 3 Para took time to adjust. In the restaurant some of the lads would turn up as before, looking for a cup of coffee during the nights. Conversations ensued, mainly about the troops' experiences fighting the Argies. When not in direct conversation with the lads, we overheard many of the stories they were telling each other. Frequently these were shockingly graphic. Many had gallows humour about them. We didn't yet know the full loss of personnel for the whole war or how many were injured. One death alone was far too many for me. What I can comment on is that the main concern was the loss of life in 2 Para. The Argentinian loss of life was touched upon but our troops were there to do what was needed: overrun military opposition, which required the need to kill or be killed. To me, that is the whole basis of a soldier and, in particular, highly trained elite forces such as 2 Para. This was their area of expertise. It was mentioned that several hundred, if not near to 1,000 Argentinians, were believed to have been killed at Goose Green alone. One Para commented that there is no way the Argentine authorities will admit to the true number of their casualties.

On the night when the Paras first disembarked from the ship, I'd had a conversation with one of their sergeants. He had been ready for action but he had reservations about one of his younger platoon members, a 19-year-old recruit from Yorkshire. I caught up with him and asked how the lad did. 'Fucking hell, he would have killed Argies all day long,' the Para sergeant said. What he meant by that I wasn't sure but the sergeant added, 'Let's just say, the lad did good.' A lot of the time when talking to the Paras, I felt that their frank honesty was a release valve to get things off their chest. Conversations that I overheard, or was directly involved in, talked of wondering how the hell some of them had got away with it. They couldn't believe their luck but at the same time they felt distraught at losing their mates. One young lad couldn't shake off the thought that he had got through it but his best pal hadn't. I think he had what they call 'survivor's guilt'. The wounded were out of the game early. Some who had gone the full way were not in the best of health either, due to bad shoulders and backs through the heavy weights that they had carried and long distances they had covered on foot. Sitting around in a coffee shop atmosphere listening to their war stories felt unreal. Many admitted to saying they had shit themselves. All the training they'd done was one thing but proper war was something else. The elements of extreme weather had not helped the situation, because it was winter in the Falkland Islands.

'Not long after we hit land, I wished I was back on the ship,' remarked one seasoned Para. 'Mind you,' he said, 'when we saw the ships getting bombed, I thought thank God I'm on land because at least I can dig a trench to shelter in.'

His mate chipped in to say:

In truth, we thought we would never see the *Norland* again. This wasn't because we might get killed or anything but because we thought it would have been you lot who wouldn't have survived the ship being sunk, especially with the amount of ammo and explosives you still had on board.

I heard one young lad ask, 'Did you kill using a bayonet?'

'I killed 'em any way I could,' came the answer.

In another conversation, on a regroup after an attack, a Para sergeant told me that he asked one of his young lads, 'Are you enjoying this or something?'

'What do you mean?' the young lad replied, confused at the question.

'You seemed to be doing more than your bit ... and without much bother,' the sergeant said to him.

'Well, what the fuck are we supposed to be doing, if it's not to kill the enemy?' was his unapologetic answer.

'He was right,' admitted the Para sergeant.

Stuart Cardy reckoned, however hard you train, the real thing was tougher and scarier. With the chance to sail home it would give them a cooling off period and time to reflect.

The killing that had gone on was still in the forefront of their minds. I knew that I would never want to repeat in conversation all of the experiences they inflicted or endured, not mentioned here. It would be up to individuals to divulge their own accounts of war, should they ever wish to bare their souls. It would never be my place to talk about it on their behalf. Besides, anyone serving in the military has to be guarded about what they say because of exploitative lawyers ready to take out often bogus cases against them, when all they'd been doing was their duty, fighting for their country and for their lives.

What we learned regarding the land fighting is that 2 Para was the only unit to go twice into battle, which was at Goose Green and Wireless Ridge. All the other land troops had fought in one battle each. These were: 3 Para at Mount Longden; Scots Guards at Tumbledown; 7th Duke of Edinburgh's Own Gurkha Rifles at Mount William; and the Royal Marines at Mount Harriet and Two Sisters. They'd faced enemy rifles, machine guns, mortars, snipers, artillery, aircraft bombing, aircraft cannon-fire and land mines.

The function of 2 Para on leaving the ship was that of protecting the British forces' beachhead by digging in on Sussex Mountain, which overlooks Bomb Alley from the south. A week later they marched 20 miles or so, further south to Darwin/Goose Green. On engaging the Argies in a 14-hour struggle, the first and the longest battle of the war ensued. On the way, most of the ground that they covered in biting winds and rain was featureless, sodden and energy-sapping. Heavily outnumbered, it was reckoned that they shouldn't have succeeded. In the end they captured the entire Argentine garrison at Goose Green – a superior sized force to theirs. This was partly due to the tactical genius of Major Chris Keeble, who took over military command of 2 Para after the tragic death of Lt Col 'H' Jones. He outflanked the enemy defences through the outstanding bravery of the 2 Para Toms, and subsequently offered the defeated Argentine soldiers the opportunity of an honourable surrender, to avoid further bloodshed and save imprisoned islanders in Goose Green, who had been locked up in a social club. Considering that the odds were one Paratrooper to every three Argentine soldiers, it was one hell of a gamble. But it paid off and saved further loss of life – on both sides. 2 Para's losses were fifteen airborne killed and sixty-four wounded, plus two personnel attached from other units. It was thought that this victory and the capture of around 1,200 Argy prisoners were an inspiration for all the other units waiting to go into battle. It also gave those back home some positive hope that we could win the war.

Their next job was to help with the wounded and dying soldiers who were brought off the two ships, RFA *Sir Galahad* and RFA *Sir Tristram*, which had been bombed by three Skyhawks in Bluff Cove while attempting to reinforce British positions at Fitzroy. A total of forty-eight soldiers and crewmen were killed in the explosions and subsequent fire on *Sir Galahad* and two crewmen in the partial bombing of *Sir Tristram*. All of the Para's first-aid training was put to use on the gruesome fallout of horrific injuries suffered by Welsh Guards from the air attacks. On leaving Fitzroy and Bluff Cove, they marched north to Wireless Ridge, located about 5 miles outside of Stanley. After the battle of Wireless Ridge was won, the Argies finally ran for it, all the way back to Stanley, where shortly afterwards their whole land forces surrendered. 2 Para losses in this battle were three airborne killed and eight wounded.

3 Para, who travelled south on the *Canberra*, had dug in around Port San Carlos, which overlooks Bomb Alley from the north. They then marched a northern route east towards Stanley, capturing Teal Inlet and

taking some prisoners on the way. Like 2 Para, braving the tough terrain and terrible weather, they continued on to what would be their key battle: the taking of Mount Longden, a strategic military location overlooking Stanley. Commanded by Lt Col Hew Pike, 3 Para's losses were twenty-three airborne killed and forty-seven wounded. This twelve-hour battle was as brutal as anything 2 Para had been involved in. In all of this, bayonets had been fixed and hand-to-hand combat engaged in.

Dave 'Charlie' Brown, a private in C Company (Patrols and Recce) in 2 Para, who also carried out the duties of Company Clerk and HQ Medic, said of his experiences:

With our D-Day-style beach landing, I thought that the Marines would have been ashore first, but it was 2 Para that went in to secure it for them! Our *Norland* issued lifejackets were day-glow orange coloured; they needed to be a colour that could be seen if civvy passengers ever ended up in the water, but they also made a good target for Argies to spot you. Fortunately, we got off the ship during the semi-dark and ignoring orders to keep the life jackets on, everyone took them off and threw them onto the car deck.

On not so dry land, it was a gruelling introduction to the island's terrain when making our way 10 miles to dig in on Sussex Mountain, where for several days we had plenty to look at as the Argies bombed everything in sight in Bomb Alley. On first seeing them, I stood up out of my trench and fired my SMG at the nearest passing aircraft. It was more of a 'fuck you' gesture, because such a weapon has nowhere near the killing power of a GPMG or Rapier missile system, but I felt good that I'd made my point. We got orders to go and secure Goose Green roughly 20 miles away. In the dark, all the kit we were carrying made it a challenge over every one of those 20 miles. We arrived at a forming-up place called Camilla Creek House. Lt Col Jones was mad as hell because the BBC had apparently leaked news of our mission while we were there. Fortunately, the Argy commander at Goose Green thought our proposed attack wasn't for real but some kind of tactical ploy. Leaving our Bergens at Camilla Creek, we went forward in fighting-order of smock, webbing and steel helmet, but the Signals platoon and Medics still had to carry their Bergens.

C Coy went ahead to set up the battle 'start-line' for the rest of the Battalion. On 28 May, in the early morning dark, we did what we were trained for, we all went in with violence. 2 Para got it as tough as it was ever going to get and when we received the order to fix bayonets, I thought, 'Battle of Waterloo job here!' At one time, C Coy was trapped on the forward slope of Darwin Hill at Goose Green during the day. Regarding casualties, we managed to get some evacuated, which was by our blokes dragging them off the battlefield back to a safe area. Later on, at night, I went back down the slope to retrieve some secret signal instructions from the body of Pte Mark Holman-Smith, a dead signaller, who was a best friend of mine. In the pitch black, I was trying to burn the instructions, which included important 3 Commando Brigade codes and battle plans. The papers wouldn't light because they were soaking wet, but I couldn't work out what the liquid was. When I woke up the next day, someone said, 'you've got blood all over you'. I checked to see if I was wounded but then realised it was blood from Mark, my best mate. I was utterly heartbroken at his loss.

Of this battle, I have to mention Major Chris Keeble, who saved a lot of lives; us and the enemy. He bluffed the Argies on the strength of our rapidly depleting troops and got a surrender out of them. What a brilliant tactic and the seasoned soldier that he is, it also reflected his humanity.

If the bloodbath at Goose Green wasn't bad enough, there was more to come when we witnessed the bombing of RFA ships *Sir Tristram* and *Sir Galahad* at Fitzroy and Bluff Cove. 2 Para helped the horrifically wounded survivors off the ships and administered first aid. Surprisingly, the carnage there didn't affect me as much as I thought it would; that's because we'd been blooded at Goose Green and, to be blunt, it was because I didn't personally know any of the survivors, I could detach myself from their suffering. I thought of the *Norland* and its crew and hoped that they hadn't received a similar fate.

Our second major battle was at Wireless Ridge, the last Argy defensive position before Stanley. It was another tough fight but we only lost three Paras there, one of them from friendly artillery. The enemy finally surrendered and I made it into Stanley in one piece! In C Coy HQ, I was part of a six-man outfit and by the war's end, there were only two of us who hadn't been killed or injured. On 14 June, by helicopter, the first troops into Stanley to receive the surrender were: Major General Jeremy Moore, the British senior Royal Marine officer and Commander of the land forces; his Spanish-speaking Intelligence Officer, Royal Marine, Captain Rod Bell; the Commanding Officer of 22 SAS, Lieutenant Colonel Mike Rose; and two signallers.

At the same time as the surrender, 2 Para were on their way into Stanley from Wireless Ridge, along with Brigadier Julian Thompson, Commander of 3 Commando Brigade. Whilst the talks were ongoing, we were ordered to stop and wait. This was on a road close by the island's First World War Memorial, located near Government House. The signal sent by Brigadier Julian Thompson was 'Hold Fast'. (The Road later became officially known as Holdfast Road.) When ready and released, 2 and then 3 Para were the first of the infantry units to march into Stanley.

We also wanted to be the first troops back to the UK, but we had to wait two weeks until the *Norland* arrived back from Puerto Madryn. It was worth it, for we were really eager to be looked after by the crew, who had been there for us all the way and who had been in a few close scrapes themselves. Looking forward to the same excellent food that we'd received on the way down south, to our great dismay, all we had on board to eat was rice, which was leftover food stores from feeding the Gurkhas and the Argy prisoners. Potatoes were not available on the island and any potatoes that the ship had in their stores had a limited shelf life and had gone off. Not so with rice and its longer shelf life, which accompanied every bloody dish served up. There was a standing joke when we asked what's on the menu. 'Chinese potatoes', was the answer. When back in the UK and enjoying some home comforts, I'd be ordering an extra-large, extra thick, cheesy-pizza takeaway; no bloody way would I be ordering a Chinese.

I thought back to the last major trek that I had taken part in, which was the Lyke Wake Walk. Our small group covered 40 miles in decent weather, over well-trodden terrain that was landmine free. We were happy in the knowledge that no one was going to ambush us and on reaching the end we would have a hug and a kiss from our loved ones over a pint. Overall, the Paras had marched further than we ever had and in the knowledge that when they got to their destination, it would be a life-or-death situation when engaging with an enemy. One couldn't help but have total admiration for them. What really struck me was the guts of the Paras to rush head-on at the enemy when being shot at. Several Paras spoke of being scared, but as Stuart Cardy said, 'No matter how scared they were, it scared the Argies even more to see us running at them, enough that it made the Argies run away.' I think this courage was something that partly helped win the war – a war that had affected the Para lads in different ways, but one common ground that everyone had agreed on was being grateful it was over.

The corporal who had been valued for his welding skills and his assistant sergeant made a safe return to the ship. A less tragic and quite curious account of an adventure had by them during the land battle was told to electrician Brian Burton. Apparently, during one of their many movements forward across the island, they passed through a settlement and caught the eye of two girls looking out of a window. A quick conversation was had and the corporal and sergeant told the girls that they'd come back and see them if they wanted, to which the girls said yes. A short time later, the corporal and sergeant commandeered a motorbike on which they made their promised return. The girls were pleased and allegedly 'accommodating' to them, before the two lads took off on their bike to re-join their unit. Feeling high after their 'getaway' experience, they lost concentration while riding and crashed the bike, resulting in them receiving minor cuts and bruises, along with torn combat clothing. More importantly, one of their rifles got a bit mangled in the process. Managing to get back to their unit, they arrived during an air raid. When the check came through after the air raid asking if anyone had been injured, they tried to pass off their personal predicament as a result of the air raid. Nobody was buying it. Had it been a peacetime exercise they would have been in big trouble. Due to it being war, when every available body was needed, allowances were made and they got away with it. Their mates were probably envious at their initiative, having enjoyed some of the 'spoils of war' that many of them wouldn't be experiencing!

We'd been at sea for two days when, one morning, I went onto the car deck. It was crowded with troops, with some of them back doing light training. Of all things, I heard a dog barking. I spotted a make-shift kennel with a dog tied up to the outside of it. I was approaching it when a soldier said, 'Careful, it's a bit nasty.' He was right. As I got closer it growled menacingly. I left it alone and didn't think anything more about it. The next morning, I had cause to go back down on the car deck and was in the same area near the dog kennel. This time the dog was wagging its tail and was as friendly as anything. 'Is this the same dog as yesterday? Why is it so friendly now?' I asked one of the troops.

He said:

Oh, didn't you hear what happened? The SAS fella who has been on board went up to the dog and put his hand out to stroke it. The dog snapped at his hand and the SAS fella called it 'a little bastard'. He made a move and grabbed the dog by the back of the neck. He then bit it, hard enough that the dog yelped. All of a sudden, it became a friendly dog.

I did find this amusing. What I couldn't figure out was why it was there in the first place. Apparently, one of the Para sections had come across the dog during the heat of battle. Everyone likes dogs, I suppose, but one of the Para officers said to his troops, 'Don't muck about with this thing. Just shoot it and let's get moving.' Whoever was in the immediate area of the officer must have felt they couldn't find it in them to carry out the order. The officer was adamant that it was to be sorted. The two lads left to do the job argued with each other about who would pull the trigger. Neither could do it and one way or another it ended up on the ship. What struck me about this incident is that it makes you wonder about human nature because these fellas wouldn't shoot a dog ... yet they had no qualms about shooting men.

Commander Chris
Esplin-Jones RN,
MV *Norland*, Senior Naval
Officer.

Major Chris Keeble, Acting
Commanding Officer, 2nd
Battalion, The Parachute
Regiment.

Catering
Department,
Purser, John
Crowther.

Above: One of our ship's secret weapons to keep up morale: Roy 'Wendy' Gibson conducting a singalong. (Courtesy John Foster)

Dave 'Charlie' Brown,
C Company, 2 Para.

Sgt Larry Little, 3 Para Rear Link Signals Detachment.

Cook Pete McWatt celebrates his twenty-first birthday on board the ship and is excited about one of many unusual gifts given to him.

Frankie Green
and Roy
'Wendy' Gibson,
celebrating just for
the hell of it.

Stewardess Jean
Woodcock with
the ship's mascot
Pengi. (Courtesy
John Foster)

Reg enjoying valuable time with his family, Jean, Terry and Steven, whilst on leave after so long at sea. For many, their war duties were over early, but for the crew of the *Norland*, it wouldn't be until several long months later that our duties would finally end.

Ship's policeman, big Ron Marshall, wraps his large frame around Dave Aistrop and Reg Kemp.

The one that didn't get away! Reg smiling alongside fellow steward Gary Holt, whilst holding a small hammerhead shark caught in Ascension.

Steward Pete Sansom and Reg, taken during shore leave in Stanley, Christmas 1982, which was summertime in the Falklands.

From left to right: Chief Engineer Lloyd Newell, Falklands Governor Sir Rex Hunt, Captain Bob Lough, Lady Mavis Hunt and 2nd Engineer Jim Draper enjoy a drinks reception in Government House on cessation of hostilities.

Bob Lough, a captain in his own right, was personally selected by the skipper of the *Norland* to be his Chief Officer during the Falklands campaign. Afterwards, Bob was also selected by Tetley's Brewery to pull the first pint – and drink it – to celebrate the refurbishment of the Crow's Nest, an estate pub in the east of Hull. (Photo courtesy Bob Lough)

Left to right: Chief Officer Bob Lough, Chief Engineer Lloyd Newell, Captain Don Ellerby CBE and Managing Director of North Sea Ferries Graham Dunlop view a newly commissioned painting by maritime artist John Steven Dews of the *Norland* under attack in San Carlos Water. Thereafter it was displayed in the *Norland*'s Forward Lounge and Bar. (Photo courtesy Bob Lough)

12
BATTLE OF AIRBORNE FORCES DAY 1982

As the ship proceeded north, the climate improved. We began picking up good weather, cloudless skies and lots of sunshine, which we hadn't seen for several weeks. Wendy, our pianist extraordinaire, was doing the thing he loved: entertaining. The atmosphere was near to what it was on the way down to the Falklands. I say 'near' because one night, when Dave and I turned to, we were told there had been big trouble earlier that day. The Paras were happy to be going home and even happier that their bosses had allowed alcohol to be available, but alcohol inevitably brings trouble.

'Do you know what happened earlier today in the Continental Bar?' I asked the Purser.

He said, 'The Quartermaster warned me last night that today was Airborne Forces Day. With near to 1,200 soldiers bunking down on top of each other, getting on each other's nerves, something was bound to happen. And it did! There was an almighty punch-up between 2 and 3 Para. Inter-battalion rivalry, they call it. Haven't they had enough of fighting by now?'

'Well, it's in their nature isn't it?' I told the Purser. 'Maybe we should be glad of it. The way they are is what helped them win in the Falklands.' I later found out from the barman on duty that when trouble was brewing, he was advised by the RSM to put the shutters down, leave the bar sharpish and let it play out. Any damage would be sorted out by the battalion. What follows is as told by Private Dave 'Charlie' Brown of 2 Para:

It began when a well-known character with a lot to say from 3 Para stepped onto a table in the Continental Bar and began winding up a lot of the lads. He was also critical to some of the crew who were gay. 2 Para didn't like this at all and someone from C Company threw a full can of beer at him, which knocked him off his perch. Then everything kicked off. It was like one of those Wild West saloon brawls that you see in the movies, except this was for real. There was a flailing of 2 and 3 Para fists and feet, which resulted in bust lips, black eyes and several bones getting crunched, some seriously. It wasn't just 2 and 3 Para fighting each other, there were a lot of personal grudges settled 'in house' – some to do with events during the campaign, others had been long-standing feuds that could have been festering from before we sailed. During this mass brawl, Wendy, who was sitting at the piano, valiantly played on. Every now and again, whilst ducking his head, in a high-pitched voice he cried out, 'Please boys, please, stop … ooh, watch out for my piano … hey, watch my hair!' The whole thing was priceless! 3 Para will never admit it, but it was 2 Para who won the fight, resulting in an extra battle honour for us: which I reckon should go by the title: Airborne Forces Day 1982 – MV *Norland*.

Afterwards, the Paras were as good as their word about clearing up the mess. The Continental Bar didn't look too much out of order. Other than this incident, alcohol was enjoyed without too much further rowdiness. On the ship, the majority of those wearing red berets (or to be exact, a red-maroon coloured beret) were infantry-style soldiers. They could be identified by their coveted winged Pegasus cap badge. It was these soldiers from the Parachute Regiment who did most of the 'boots on the ground' fighting, and who'd suffered the most casualties. But not everyone's task in the Falklands War was to fix bayonets and charge the enemy. Within the Para Battalion, supporting the front-line troops were Para-trained soldiers from other regiments, such as Engineers, Artillery, Medics and Signals. They didn't wear the winged Pegasus but wore their own regimental cap badge. I'd learnt early on that, whatever one's cap badge, those wearing red berets have all passed something called P Company, which is an arduous selection course for the Parachute Regiment, as well as for those from other regiments. A joke in the Paras is that anyone not wearing a red beret is considered a 'crap hat'. Banter from so-called crap hats is that there are only two things that drop from the sky: bird shit and Paratroopers.

A Para-trained sergeant from the Royal Signals called Larry Little had come on board the ship with 3 Para. He'd soon got to know some of the crew and his view on the war was interesting. Larry's job was providing communications from his Battalion HQ to those fighting at the front and to those steering the war back in Brigade HQ. Some of the radios the Royal Signals used were vehicle and trailer-mounted; some were carried by the Royal Signals Para lads. Along with personnel equipment, ration packs and radio ancillary equipment, that also included batteries; the signal guys had Bergens weighing up to 130lb. The personal webbing around their waists was stuffed with ammunition that included rounds (bullets), grenades and at least two mortar bombs. Larry had 'deck-hopped' from *Canberra* to HMS *Fearless* and was scheduled to land in the small settlement of Port San Carlos in the dark. However, when getting on the landing craft from HMS *Fearless*, someone slipped and broke their back, causing a delay. When reorganised, it was in daylight that the landing craft Larry and others were sailing on stopped 50m short of actual land – the remaining distance was achieved by wading through the water. Larry is only 5ft 6in tall and with 130lb to carry, that was some challenge. One might think of Paratroopers being 6ft supermen types. Larry, a square-jawed Scotsman, looked as tough as they come and proved it's not size that matters but the aggressive 'can-do' attitude that Paras have about them. His experiences were as follows:

On reaching land, soaking wet and after walking not even a couple of hundred yards, a blue civilian Land Rover arrived. The driver, a farm hand, told me he had two dead bodies in it. They were from a shot-down Gazelle helicopter that had flown ahead of our landing party. I was given the dead soldiers' weapons to look after and at that point I knew I was at war for real. Thereafter, getting from Port San Carlos to Stanley was a mixture of helicopter rides and tabbing. [A loaded march is known as a 'tab' or 'tabbing' in the British Army and a 'yomp' or 'yomping' in the Royal Marines.]

I was witness to several important messages coming through on the radio during the fighting. I initially felt anger on hearing reports of casualties, but well into the battle I put feelings aside, apart from when a 'bogus' surrender was reported. I say bogus because an incident near Goose Green had seen a white flag raised, which had members of 2 Para going forward to investigate and getting killed. When good news came through about successfully taking objectives, this was met with pride and celebrated with a brew and a fag. On the final surrender coming through, the message was closely followed by a command to stay put in our current locations. A senior Marine officer in charge didn't want the Paras to be the first troops seen entering Stanley. I never had any real thoughts as to whether we'd win or lose the war but, from the information I was getting, every battle that was planned was a success – so from that I had to assume it would continue until we were in Stanley. It was well known that if we got there it would be over. As soon as we did, all I wanted was to get a message home to my wife Julie that I was okay. My communications link on the island was in use well after reaching Stanley. A huge amount of administration and logistics to get everyone in the correct aircraft and ships for the journey home was necessary. Once we came on board the *Norland*, my call-sign was one of the last to close down.

Larry was relieved a decision had been made to have the ship's bars open with what he thought was unlimited licensing hours. Having slept rough and lost a lot of weight, he reckoned a comfy bed and food came second to the idea of a good booze-up. He further revealed:

Duty personnel from each battalion have dealt with drunken incidents, many of which you haven't seen. There's no real malice for picking on each other, it's mainly rivalry as to who had the toughest battle and who'd performed better than someone else. A lot of attention was given to the Goose Green victory by 2 Para, which rubbed up 3 Para the wrong way because they'd had an equally brutal time taking Mount Longdon. But any scrapping on board the *Norland* has been no worse than travelling with two battalions of Royal Marines and 3 Para on the *Canberra*, where rivalry boiled over on a number of occasions. There was even tension in Stanley as well. Whilst most of the Falkland Islanders were grateful that we'd liberated them, I met some who were against the behaviour of our Task Force once the job was done. Many of our troops needed to let off steam. The lack of alcohol in Stanley saw logistics get into gear and an abundance of it gratefully arrived, donated by various British organisations. I have to say that our intelligence brief on the way south reckoned the Argies were not that well trained or motivated. Well, they were motivated enough to fight for their lives and shoot the fuck out of our blokes. We were also told that they were short of rations, yet when we got into Stanley there were containers lined up full of meat, vegetables and a variety of electrical appliances, mainly televisions. These were apparently to be used by the Argies to win the hearts of the islanders, especially the televisions. How weird is that, considering there is no television station on the island? Here on the *Norland*, for some it's ten days' rest and recuperation, and a chance to reflect on what has happened. I've been on countless exercises where it's all staged; proper war isn't too far off an exercise except that exercise deaths are imaginary, in war they're real. For sure it was heart-breaking to hear reports come through 'live' on the radio of losses – and especially on hearing that Lt Col Jones had been killed. But here's a thing, war can be extremely boring too. There were days when nothing happened and you almost hoped for an air raid just to pass the time, to have the chance to fire your weapon at something. Listening to a radio that had little traffic on it due to either a lull in the battle or an imposed radio silence was mind-numbing. Of course, it was anything but that for those at the shitty end of the fighting. Knowing what war is like, I hope I don't have to make the comparison between this or any other war that I might be involved in. For now, being looked after on the *Norland*, with Wendy on the piano, and all of us singing any old song that Wendy can string enough notes together to identify as a song, that's enough to keep us happy until we get home.

The question asked by our crew was whether we would be going home too. Nearing Ascension, we got our answer: no! 2 Para would disembark and then fly to Brize Norton and RAF Lyneham in Hercules transport aircraft, or if lucky in DC10s. Their job was done and they would be leaving the ship for the last time. The *Norland* still had work to do. This was a bit of a downer for us. An event on the ship that at least gave us some joy is best explained by Pete McWatt, one of our ship's hard-working cooks, who was the youngest serving member of our crew and who celebrated his twenty-first birthday on board the ship:

I thought volunteering to go to the Falklands would be a good little break from the normal run to Rotterdam and that once we got halfway there, it would be over. When the *Sheffield* got hit, I knew there'd be no turning back. When we went in to San Carlos Water, during the red alerts I headed to the bottom of the ship on G-deck. Sitting there, hearing the bombs and guns, but not seeing anything was agonising. After a couple of raids less people went down there, so I didn't bother either. I hardly ever went outside. I'm not embarrassed to say that on seeing the planes coming in for the first time, dropping their bombs and all the guns going off, I ran back inside. After that, for a lot of the raids, I nervously laid on my bunk trying to think of happier times. My worst moment was after the *Antelope* got hit. Watching her sink, I had tears in my eyes. I felt it would be a sight that would never leave me.

On my 21st birthday, happy that the war had ended and that we were heading to Ascension with 2 and 3 Para, I didn't think it would be much of a day for me to look back on, but I was wrong. I got up at 5.30 a.m. and was working with Dick Johnson, a funny and great crew member, whose first words were 'happy birthday', followed by him putting a beer in my hand. What an interesting start to the day! Later on, the crew had decked out the mess room with any red, white and blue material they could find. They'd put together a very large box and told me that I had to open all the presents inside. It was one of the strangest gift boxes anyone could ever receive. There were around thirty things in it: a cabbage, a bag of flour, a box of cornflakes, a small cassette player and even a sex toy. Where this latter item came from, I don't know, and I didn't recall that the ship's gift shop sold anything like that either. One present was a black and white striped rugby shirt of Hull FC. Considering I am a fanatic red and white striped supporter of Hull KR, this was obviously a wind-up; a bit like giving a Liverpool supporter a Man Utd shirt. But it showed the great sense of humour of the lads. You would have thought it was a lot of the crew's birthday as well, judging by the way they celebrated with me. But for a lot of us, it was the first big release of pressure after the war; it was the first time that we had all really relaxed to party ourselves and it reinforced what great camaraderie there was within the crew.

The last day before reaching Ascension was quite emotional. Soldiers who had buddied up with each other would be going their own way during a further rest and recuperation period back in Britain. We wouldn't be seeing them again either, not unless arrangements had been made to meet up at home. Of the lads I had befriended, one of them came up to me and said, 'Reg, you and your mate Dave, I'd like to shake your hands and thank you for what you have done.' One of the Para sergeants who came up to shake my hand told me, 'Without exaggeration, this ship and its crew has been one of the secret weapons of the Task Force. Loads of the other guys would agree with me on this. And I hope the Royal Navy realise it too.'

This kind of exchange was happening everywhere. Our catering department had a close relationship with the troops as we were serving them food three times a day, which had thankfully been good food. The stewards' interaction with the troops was always more prolific. At one farewell that I'd had, one of the Toms took off the military jacket he was wearing and disappeared somewhere. A couple of minutes later he returned and said, 'I've got something for you. I can't repay you in another way.' He handed me the actual airborne wings that he'd cut from his jacket. I was very touched by this.

Another Para did something similar. He took off his red beret, unclipped his cap badge (the winged Pegasus) and said, 'I can't give you much else but please accept this.' I was equally touched; I knew I would never part with these gifts.

What might be considered something more serious than the giving of small gifts of gratitude was the surprising number of small arms that had been taken by the Paras as spoils of war. They seemed to be everywhere. Whenever 2 Para came into contact with the Argies, on their capture they disarmed them. They took a particular interest in the officers, from whom they took their sidearms as mementoes. There were an awful lot of troops in possession of a pistol or revolver, or whatever sidearm it might be. One night as Dave and I sat in the restaurant, a couple of boozed-up Paras came in. One of them said, 'Can I have a word with you?'

'Yeah, what's the matter?'

'Look, we're on the piss but we've run out of beer.'

The bars were closed as it was the early hours of the morning. He then put his hand down the back of his trousers and produced what looked to me to be a German Luger – not that I was familiar with such a weapon, but that's what it looked like.

'Whoa, that looks interesting!' I told him.

'A case of beer and it's yours,' he casually offered.

By then I had begun having a couple of beers myself during this celebratory period heading up to Ascension. I did in fact have a case of beer in my cabin, as other members of the crew did.

'I haven't got a case of beer,' I said with my best poker face.

'Get us a dozen beers and this Luger is yours,' he insisted.

'I haven't got a dozen beers. But I can give you what I have got, which is half a dozen,' I said.

He looked at his mate, then back at me: 'Alright, fuck it, we want another drink. Six beers it'll have to be.'

Before I knew it, I was in possession of a German Luger. That exchange gives some indication of the quantity of unofficially issued small arms on the ship. Some of the Paras we knew had three or four different types of small arms. One had a beautiful looking Colt-45, the type that John Wayne would have carried in the movies. The Argies had been supplied with a lot of American-made gear and some of this had also been appropriated by our troops. That was the nature of war, I guess. What I was going to do with my Luger, I had no idea. It was something to hold on to for the time being. Apparently, other crew members also acquired some small arms weapons, one way or another.

On the morning of 5 July, we dropped anchor in Ascension. The troops disembarked rather quickly by helicopter or launch. By lunchtime the ship was cleared of all troops heading home. The rest of the day was spent making the *Norland* 'ship shape'. When the Paras first left us at San Carlos, we didn't know if we would be seeing them again on the ship. When they did return, that reunion was very moving. Now that they had gone for good, the feeling was equally emotional at saying goodbye for the final time. The following day, we received a welcome surprise – anyone who wanted to, subject to their duties, could go ashore for the day. We couldn't believe it. There was a lot of excitement. Bloody hell, they're actually going to let us go ashore! Everyone who could, took up the offer. We stood waiting on the open deck by the chopper platforms, from where a Chinook or a Sea King would fly us ashore. Like excited school kids we clambered on board. We touched down a short while later at Wide Awake Airport. I believe that was the first time we'd walked on land in seventy-two days. Most of the lads just wanted to find a bar and a bit of action. Once we had got away from the area of the airport it looked like a lunar landscape. Very dry, very barren, very rocky; the remnants of volcanic strata (layers of hardened lava). Five of us found ourselves on a road, Dick Johnson, Gary Holt, Karl Tungate, Les Marrow and me. We didn't know exactly where we were going as we ambled along. A truck with an open top at its back pulled over. Two of us joined the driver up front with the rest tumbling in the rear. We asked the driver, 'Where's the nearest bar?'

'On this road, up ahead there's a bar called the Red Lion, though it's a good way uphill,' he said. He then explained, 'Here in Ascension, if you are driving and you see somebody walking on a road, there's an unwritten rule that you pull over and offer a lift, like I've done.'

The driver dropped us off at the bar which was located about 1,000ft up the side of the island's dominating feature, called Green Mountain. We thanked him and he went on his way, as we went on ours. In the bar, the owner only had two cases of beer in stock for the whole place. We chipped in to buy both of them. My attention, however, had been drawn to the mountain we were on. I'd guessed that it was an old volcano. Having a drink with the crew was fine, but I was more interested in getting to the top of this island. 'Does anybody want to join me in going the rest of the way up?' I asked. My question was received with silence and a puzzled expression on the faces of the lads. One of them spoke for the rest when he said, 'You are kidding … aren't you?'

Knowing how they felt, I left them to it. In a way, I was pleased that no one wanted to join me, so I could have this little adventure to myself. I'd been canny enough to put on my walking boots in anticipation of this opportunity. Ready for the challenge, I took a track up to where I could start walking and, looking up, at around 1,800ft high, the volcanic rock had a green layer to it. This is where the moisture of the clouds had fed it to grow vegetation in nature's way. It wasn't too long before I had reached the start of this green belt. This is where the first signs of plant life began and they increased as I got higher. The tropical vegetation was fascinating to me. I had seen that much blue sea, to look at green plant life was not just pleasing, it was exhilarating. The track that I followed was getting smaller and smaller. I was absolutely in my element. I kept walking and stopping to turn around and look back at the view. I could see numerous ships in the bay and aircraft spread along the runways. On reaching the top, I saw there was a small pond. I figured the pond would have been where the lava spewed out of the volcano when it was active. I was thrilled to bits that I'd reached this point. I took in the view from all angles. In the pond was life in the form of frogs. There were sea birds flying at a lower level than the peak. I then noticed a small container box with a lid that was positioned on the top of a 4ft pole. I opened the lid of the box to see a rubber stamp inside by an ink pad. 'Hmm, what's this?' I wondered. I trialled the stamp on my arm and could just about read the words, 'Ascension Island, the peak, 2,900 feet.' I took out two five-pound notes and one ten-pound note from my wallet and stamped them all (I didn't have any other paper on me). If I was thrilled at getting to the top of this Green Mountain, I was equally thrilled at finding this stamp system, which was obviously there for climbers to record their ascent of it.

I thought to myself, standing there on the highest point of Ascension Island, in the middle of the Atlantic Ocean, just south of the equator, this was surely one of the remotest places on earth, and one that I had now happily experienced. Had I not been part of the Falklands War, it was something in my seaman's career I would have probably never got to do.

When I returned to the Red Lion pub, all the beer had gone and morale was high. For my high, I didn't need alcohol; it had come from my mountain walk. As a happy group, we made our way back to the airport to find that

On the left-hand side of this old £5 pound note, you can see the ink stamp that I used when arriving at the peak of Green Mountain on Ascension Island.

some of the lads from other groups were missing. We got back to the ship, but the missing ones didn't. Storeman, Kevin Hornsby picks up the story:

My group had tried out the pub on the hill before moving on to an American forces bar further below. Getting into the flow, we cut it too fine to catch the chopper back to the ship. Mick Wingham, Pete O'Mahoney, Bobby Gair and me were stuck and would have to sleep somewhere on the air base until the next day. Alan (Chuddy) Eastwood then rolled up. We spotted an aircraft and decided to sleep under it. There was a ladder leading to an open door of the aircraft, so we accessed it. Inside, one of us slept in the pilot's seat, three of us used hammocks that were available, and one slept outside on the tarmac under a tarpaulin. Next day, with unease, we caught the chopper back to the ship. There was a welcoming committee of crew members lining the decks and applauding, though the navy personnel on board wanted us to be court martialled and sent home! Our skipper, Don Ellerby, refused and said he'd deal with it in his own way. It was unreasonable of the navy to be so strict, considering it was our first time ashore after seventy-two days. Nothing further came of it from the skipper and so nothing else was ever mentioned of it again.

13

THE AFTERMATH OF WAR

In Ascension, we exploited whatever leisure time we could. I put together some basic fishing gear. This consisted of a strong line and a large hook borrowed off a crewmate, Paddy Dolan. I had a small towel to protect my hands when letting out and pulling in the line to stop rope burns. For a float, I used a white plastic gallon container. Of the varied fish swimming about the place, I had a special target. It was night-time when I put a big chunk of meat onto my hook in the hope of catching a hammerhead shark. The meat sank about 5ft down in the water, held at this depth by the plastic float. Anchored in the shallows, sitting there, on the open stern ramp, with the ship's cluster lights shining brightly down onto the sea, all was nice and peaceful in the warm tropical weather. I wasn't alone, as some of the other lads had the same idea. One of them was a really keen fisherman, Mick Wingham, who had decent equipment and was looking to catch a tuna. Having sat there for a while, it was nearing midnight when I decided to go and get a couple of cold beers. I asked Gary Holt, a steward who was sitting with me, to keep an eye on the float.

'Okay, but what do I have to do?' he asked.

Pointing to the float, I told him, 'If that moves about, especially if it disappears under the water, pull the line as hard as you can.' I left and returned about five minutes later. Just as I walked up to take the line from Gary he shouted, 'Hey, Reg, you know that float thing, it's just gone under.'

I quickly put the beers down, grabbed the line off him and pulled it. It was a genuine bite. Clutching the hand towel, I worked the line, allowing it to surge through my hands before pulling it tight. It felt like something substantial was on the hook. Gary helped me and together we tried to pull it in. Just under the water level we could see it was a small hammerhead shark. We managed to get it up onto the stern ramp. It was near to 6ft long and how exciting it felt to have caught it. Once we had the shark on the deck, our intention was to get the hook out and return it back to the sea, hoping to get a photograph of it in the process. Then something inexplicable happened. As it thrashed around on the stern, one of the lads appeared on the scene and took a close look. Maybe he thought we wanted to skin and eat it because, seeing a heavy piece of timber lying close by, he picked it up and struck the shark with great force twice on the head. It died instantly. Slightly shocked, I asked, 'What are you doing?' He didn't reply. In fact, he shrugged his shoulders and wandered off. This seemed really out of character for someone normally quiet and unassuming. I thought it must have been some kind of release for the personal journey he had been through.

Our keen fisherman, Mick Wingham, looked on with envy, not at the shark's fate but that we had caught it. His time came later when he bagged a substantially large tuna. Don't let anyone knock fishing as a pastime; this way of relaxing felt wonderful after the intense time we'd all been through. The tuna that Mick had caught was presented to the galley, who did a magnificent job of cooking and displaying it. It laid in state with all the trimmings and the crew had the chance to help themselves to an exotic food experience, which was a lot different to what we had when the rations were running low.

The next day we heard that two stewards, Ernie Fuller and Steve Chapman, were going home. They hadn't been in good health and it was thought best to have them replaced. I didn't know if I should feel envious or not that they would soon be back in Britain with their families.

For the rest of us, we were to be heading back to the Falklands. We took on board groups of different troops and it was the Queen's Own Highlanders (QOH) who were the dominant contingent. Most of them were, of course, Scotsmen. The privates and NCOs seemed to be the usual type of keen, tough, young men, and being Scottish they spoke with tough-sounding accents. The officers, however, seemed to be a bit 'lah di dah', speaking with posh English accents and acting rather aloof. Once the ship had everyone assigned to their accommodation, on 9 July we headed south.

When the QOH first came aboard they had no idea what to make of our crew. We were dressed in jeans and T-shirts and many of us had long hair with beards. I wondered if the QOH thought that they had arrived to be part of some sort of hippy commune at sea.

The QOH officers were very different from the officers we'd experienced in 2 Para. They were forever giving orders. One day when walking down an alleyway towards two officers, I had just walked past them when a voice called out to say, 'Hey, you there!'

It was in a tone of voice that I didn't much like, so I carried on walking without reacting. With more urgency, the voice barked out to me, 'DID YOU HEAR ME? I SAY, YOU THERE!'

As I continued to ignore him, all full of himself, he demanded, 'YOU THERE, COME HERE!'

Getting further away, I managed to hear the same voice who had called out to me say to his colleague, 'Did you see that? Who is that man?'

What I thought was, 'I am that man … and being that man, you know what, fuck you!' This incident confirmed, at least to me, how different QOH officers were to Para officers. The QOH lads were, however, down-to-earth types.

In conversations with the soldiers of the QOH, knowing we had experience of being in the Falklands, they were naturally curious to learn from us what they could. They were, in fact, put out at the thought of having to go there now that the Argies had surrendered. What would be their job? They had been geared up to see a bit of action. I guessed they would be used as garrison troops in place of the troops already sent home.

We couldn't tell them much about the islands themselves, as we had only seen Stanley from the ship. The QOH wrongly believed it to be quite a big place and fun to visit.

Sometime after midnight, when Dave and I were doing our rounds, I was on G-deck where it was usually quiet. I got to a certain area when I heard the sound of voices. One of the cabin doors was ajar. There was

The QOH pipes and drums practising on the ship's heli-pad. (Courtesy Chris Esplin-Jones)

rowdiness coming from inside. I popped my head in for a look. A group of soldiers were sat around and when I asked if they were alright, one of them said, 'Aye, come on in, pal. Have a beer.'

I was handed a beer, which I took out of politeness, but I didn't leave immediately because something odd had been going on before I had got there. A couple of young soldiers had an older sergeant in charge of them. Another soldier said, 'We're just watching something, pal.'

At that, the sergeant said to his young soldiers, 'Go on, drink it!'

The two soldiers had a glass each. At first glance they looked to be half filled with beer. The sergeant said, 'Dinna fuck about, laddie, just get it down ya.'

They were hesitating and I couldn't figure out why. This must have been some kind of army tradition or QOH tradition. It transpired that the sergeant was testing them to drink his piss. As a young recruit, apparently, this was the kind of thing to be initiated in. I was glad that I hadn't joined the army. I only had one mouthful of the beer handed to me. Putting it down, I made my excuses and left, leaving them to their own entertainment.

Making good headway towards the Falklands, the crew got an invitation to the ship's radio room. We were told we could have a very brief phone call via a special satellite link back to the UK. Security was still paramount. Though a surrender had been agreed, it was emphasised that even at this stage we should be staying alert. We were still going through the darkened ship procedure.

Standing in a queue in front of me, one of the ABs made his call and I heard him say to his daughter, 'Hello, love. It's your dad, is your mother there?' There was a pause, then he said, 'No, I don't want to talk to the dog.' I thought this to be a strange conversation. He later told me, 'Our lass wasn't in and when I asked my daughter if anyone else was there, my daughter told me, no but the dog was!'

For our phone call home, we had to write on a message-form no more than thirty words. This would be checked and words were crossed out that were compromising. On my form, among the words I had written to my wife I had mentioned 'South Atlantic'. This was then vetted by a naval security person. Upon a quick glance at my message, he crossed out South Atlantic.

'You can't use them words,' he said.

'But that is where we are,' I challenged him.

'You are not to identify your presence wherever it is in the world and you cannot use these words. And that is that,' he said with finality.

I had to accept what he'd told me. It was no big deal that he had corrected it. We were also told that we would be cut off immediately if we didn't stick to what we had written on the form. I made my call and was lucky that my wife, Jean, was home. The phone call was brief but at least it was something. Up until then, this was the first communication we'd had with our families back home. It was a welcome morale boost.

Several days after leaving Ascension, we dropped anchor in Port Stanley; it was mid-July. The QOH went ashore, some by chopper, most by landing craft. It was reckoned that their job would be to mop up after 2 Para at Goose Green.

The next day, all kinds of different groups of military personnel departed and our crew received a big surprise. Depending on our jobs, we could go ashore. Wow! This was a big deal. We went in a launch to Stanley, which was a service provided by the local authorities. There was no recognised dock, so all ships had to anchor off Stanley in the inlet. The launch I was on had eight of us aboard.

In Stanley, the debris of wartime was very visible. Thousands of rifles were piled up, smashed pieces of military hardware littered the place, vehicles were left abandoned. I saw a shot-up Argy helicopter. The nearest I had been to this kind of scene was on television news reports showing conflicts from around the world. It had a feel of the newsreel footage that I had seen of Korea in the 1950s. We were told, if you drift away from the town, be careful of trenches or dugouts and be careful what you touch or tamper with, there might be booby traps. I ended up in the company of Graham Edwards, a steward, who went by the strange nickname of 'Hoss'. I'd no idea where that name came from. He was known for taking pictures and he had a good camera with him. 'I want to go up into the hills and take some snaps from there,' he said.

So, there we were strolling up a road towards the high ground. Even on the far reaches out of the town, there were trenches with machine guns or artillery pieces still in place. We drifted off the road and I'd noticed some coloured flags periodically sticking up in the ground around us. We were too busy enjoying this freedom and strolling about to take any real notice of them. We then heard the sound of a horn and looked to see an open-top Land Rover coming towards us at a good speed on the road. It slowed down when about 300yds away. There were four soldiers in it. One of them was standing in the open back of the vehicle, shouting. As there was nobody else around except Hoss and me, it must be us he was shouting at. I thought, 'What the hell does this fella want?' The vehicle was still coming up the road but really slow by now. Then it stopped a short distance away. He was close enough that we could hear him.

'What's the matter?' Hoss shouted to him.

'You're in a fucking minefield!' he warned. 'Those red flags are telling you that you're in a red zone.'

We froze. What the hell were we going to do now? We were scared.

'What can we do?' Hoss asked the fella in the vehicle.

'Gently walk out towards the road,' he advised.

I looked at Hoss and said, 'One of us has to go first and the other one has to follow behind.' Anxious words were exchanged that ended up with me being the one to go first. Hoss was behind me, walking in my exact footsteps. We got away with it. Once we were out of the danger area near to the vehicle, the soldiers looked at us with contempt and drove off. They didn't need to say anything else.

On our way back to town, we speculated that maybe the soldiers in the vehicle had been winding us up and they'd had a good laugh at our expense; maybe there hadn't been a minefield at all. We consoled ourselves with this thought. What an introduction to Port Stanley that was.

The next day, again we were allowed ashore. Those who had finished their work took full advantage. After my night's work, I slept through the early morning and then took myself off to Stanley in the early afternoon. There was talk of a pub that had some life in it by the name of the Globe. With excitement, a gang of us arrived to find a makeshift drinking place built of a deep, dark-red structure with a corrugated aluminium roof. Inside, it was as basic as you could get. None of this mattered: the important question was 'does it have good beer?' The place was packed with military types and the odd islander. The locals were naturally welcoming and easy to speak to. What struck me is that they had no noticeable accent to their speech. Without doubt, they appreciated the sacrifice that had been made to free the islands of the Argies. The energy in the bar was boisterous and busy. I had a couple of good hours in this watering hole, my first time going for a drink in the metropolis of Stanley.

We still had a lot of QOH soldiers aboard and they were later disembarked near to the Goose Green area. As we had suspected, their task was mopping up after 2 Para, to account for and bury dead Argies. What a grim job that would be. They were not very happy about it. Another job for us was to sail near to an Argentinian cargo ship that had been blown aground in bad weather in Fox Bay West, on West Falkland. It was believed to contain large stocks of ammo. Tugs were in the same area to tow it off the rocks and make it safe. Troops were coming and going, on and off the *Norland*. It was a floating hotel providing accommodation, and once again presenting reasonable food in the restaurants as resupplies of stocks were now less of a problem. I had no real idea who was passing through or what our many varied tasks were, not that it was my place to know all of this anyway.

It was around this time that the reality hit home of what the ship and its crew had been through. I had a strange sort of sympathy for the QOH who were disappointed that they had missed out on the action. Many thoughts went through my mind about young lads wanting such a thing, but then they had been trained for warfare. All our training was geared to safely carrying civilian passengers and vehicles, yet here we were in an area of conflict. For all the bravado in our mess room when we excitedly exchanged stories about what we had witnessed, there was no denying that, at times, it felt terrifying. This feeling related to the fact that, when standing on the deck of the *Norland* watching Argy aircraft come in on their bombing raids, though it was mesmerising, it was all beyond the control of any of us. That for me was the scariest part.

Worthy of a mention is that the Falklanders were having their own period of reflection. An island newspaper called *The Penguin News* had been on the go since 1979. Until the war, it was published monthly. Post war, to cover the 'news rich' environment, it was published fortnightly. In one copy, I was interested to see that some column inches were given over to the subject of war trophies as follows:

RELICS OF WAR

It is of great importance that one of everything brought into the Islands by the Argentine invaders should stay here for our museum.

The British Forces are taking helicopters, planes and armoured cars back to their bases in Britain, and of course they should be able to, but let's make sure that in twenty years' time, when the scars of war have all healed, we have a museum packed with everything from Pucara aircraft to mess tins.

It is not important that we do not have room to display these items at present. At least have them stored away safely for the day when we do have the room.

Being able to see and touch the actual hardware of the Falklands War will give future generations of Islanders a fuller understanding of the most important period of our history.

Editor – *The Penguin News*

(Issue 22, dated July 1982)

A rumour had it that on behalf of the military the *Norland*'s Chief Officer, Bob Lough, had 'okayed' the storing of a large war souvenir in the form of a Mercedes vehicle, which had been issued as an Argentine Forces staff car. (Apparently, Bob had been personally invited to a slap-up, compo-sausage-luncheon on the island by the RAF and then hijacked with the request, proving there is no such thing as a 'free lunch'.) The MOD actually frowned at the removal of war trophies from the island. On board the ship heading to Ascension, the over-officious Scots Guards complained about it. Mid-voyage, the vehicle disappeared! It was said to have been got rid of overboard and the matter was forgotten. The vehicle was, in fact, secreted away in an empty food container, until quietly getting offloaded at Ascension and then sent to a military unit back in the UK. Information came to light from Mercedes HQ in Germany that they hadn't received payment from the Argentinians for the vehicle in the first place, so its confiscation was somehow justified. In the end, because it hadn't been paid for by the Argentinians, the RAF were glad to hand it over to the MOD for them to sort out.

14

YOU'RE GOING HOME ...
MAYBE!

Towards the end of July, I was in my cabin when a commotion ensued. I was woken up by someone yelling and bawling in the alleyway outside. It was accompanied with a knocking on cabin doors. I tried to hear what was happening. The voice then became clear. 'We've got mail aboard. Listen up, everybody, mail has arrived.' With that I could hear cabin doors opening and closing as the crew made their way to the mess room. Things were more relaxed and so I'd now started to fully close my door. Someone knocked and opened it. Sporting a big grin, Dick Johnson said, 'Kempy, get your pants on, there's mail.' Arriving in the mess room, there was a score or more of the lads. One of the main mess room tables had a large pile of letters being sorted on it. Someone saw me and said, 'Here, Reg, three letters for you.' What a surprise. I knew straight away they would be from my wife, Jean. This was the first time we had received mail from home. I went back to my cabin to open my letters. In general, my two lads and the family were bearing up. There were lots of loving words from Jean, which I read again and again. Jean was a very good writer, but I could tell from her tone she was troubled by all that had happened. At sea, we didn't know what had gone on back home from their point of view. Reading between the lines, they'd had it tough themselves. Their uncertainty was probably greater than ours. We were always too busy to think of the ultimate consequences, but back home they had all the time in the world to imagine the worst. The British television news had reported events in full and they probably knew more about the war than we did. For sure, I detected the pressure that my wife and many others had gone through. The main thing was that Jean and my two kids, Terry and Steven, were okay.

One of the lads couldn't have been happier to get mail until he opened it. Seeing his expression, we asked if he was alright. 'No, I'm not alright. I've got a Dear John.' The mail wasn't always so good for everyone!

My mate Dave didn't get any mail at all. A couple of the other crew didn't either. The next day another load of mail arrived by chopper. Two bags were deposited. One bag was for the crew, the other for the officers. I wondered who had sorted out the mail between the crew and the officers before this drop. On this second round of mail I received another letter, yet there was still no mail for Dave. This went on for quite a while and I really felt for Dave. It was tough that when everyone else was so excited to have received letters from back home, he hadn't. The mail drops then became more regular and one day someone shouted, 'There's a letter here for Dave Aistrop.' A loud cheer went up. Dave wasn't present to hear this announcement. As his pal, I was asked to look after it. I thought of how best to give it to him. I could wait until the evening when we turned to or I could go and wake him up. I felt it was too important not to wake him, so I headed off to his cabin. However, waking Dave up in the middle of the day could be quite a delicate procedure. I opened his door, underneath which he always placed a black carrier bag to stop the light from the outside alleyway shining through. Taking this obstacle into account, with the door wide open, I asked with anticipation, 'Are you awake, Dave?'

Stirring, he drowsily answered, 'Yeah. What's the matter?'

'You've got a letter.'

'Oh, right … okay … thanks,' he softly muttered as he took the letter, still half asleep.

I left it at that. A couple of hours later another bag of mail arrived with another letter for Dave. As the previous time, I took it on behalf of Dave. Ah, but do I leave it until he turns out later or, like before, hand it to him in his cabin? I decided to take it to his cabin. I opened his door and asked, 'Dave, are you there, are you awake?'

'What's the matter now?' he asked, slightly annoyed.

In the light of the alleyway outside, I held up another letter and said teasingly, 'Look what I've got!'

'Oh, bloody hell, not another one!' he moaned.

At this, I just tossed the letter inside his cabin, closed the door and laughed to myself at his reaction.

An interesting letter was received by our ship's captain. It was sent by the most senior general of the British Army, Sir General Edwin Bramall, who as a young soldier landed on the beaches of Normandy. Apparently, back home in Whitehall, London, he had the responsibility of masterminding the campaign to take back the Falklands. I wasn't around at the time when he came on board the *Norland* to address our troops. He said a thank you to the Parachute Regiment and then to the ship's crew. I later managed to get a copy of his letter, which bore a sender's address from the Ministry of Defence and was stamped with the seal 'Chief of the General Staff'. In his letter was another thank you along with best wishes for a safe journey home.

So far, our journey hadn't come to fruition. It was now early August and, though we had no firm indication of what the exact future of the crew and our ship would be, some important news came through. One evening, when routinely carrying out our tasks, the Purser came to see Dave and me. He told us that most of the major ships in the Falklands area – of which he reeled off several names – had gone home. Their crews would all be enjoying an extended run of leave. These ships included the *Canberra* and QE2 and I was pleased for them. Yet we were still here. We had accrued a good number of days' paid leave. But how were we to take them, with what seemed no chance of the ship going back to Britain in the immediate future?

Then our role was made clear to us by the Purser and it wasn't something we wanted to hear. Until further notice, the ship's new task was to act as a ferry, looking after military and civilian personnel, cargo and freight, between Ascension and the Falkland Islands. We had done a couple of trips in this role already. Finally some good news came. The Purser, to his relief, was happy to tell us about a scheme of going home on leave that the officers up on the bridge had devised.

The plan was that half of the crew could go on leave for twenty days, while the other half would stay and work alongside a relief crew. After the twenty days of the original crew going on leave and returning, the crew that had stayed behind could go and return. (Twenty days was the length of time it would take for the ship to sail from Ascension to the Falklands and back.)

'Why can't we go home and have the whole crew relieved on a permanent basis?' we asked.

'Because it's vital to have the original crew in place for continuity,' said the Purser. It was further explained: 'You are all experienced hands, mostly from Hull, and we want to keep it this way. It works so well as it is.'

This was the company's overall point of view. To me it was outrageous. Blackmail even. What could we do? Alright, some might see it as a compliment that we were doing a good job; I saw it as taking a liberty. But I realised that if we didn't come back then the other half of the crew couldn't go on leave. That was the deal, no discussion. In the end, the ratings settled for it, as well as the officers and engineers.

It took a bit of working out who would be in the first group to go home. Names were supposed to be drawn out of a hat but a compromise was agreed. Dave and I both opted to go in the first group. The Purser, after sorting out the catering department, decided he would also go home in the first batch. He took with him his Assistant Purser, John Graham, whom he'd been mentoring and who had learned an enormous amount on this memorable trip. It just so happened that the Purser's daughter was getting married around the time that he would be home, which worked out nicely for him. He told me he'd had a conversation with one of the Para officers who'd mentioned that back home there was a rail strike on. Major Farrar-Hockley of 2 Para had said to him, 'We haven't been through all this to be denied a train. If there isn't one available, then we'll just damn well take one over.' John laughed at this and he really believed that they would have done it if necessary.

Established seafarers to replace our first group had been recruited from different ports of the UK. They would fly from Brize Norton to Ascension. Once they'd arrived there and were ready to come aboard, we could fly from Ascension to Brize Norton. Before we left the ship for Wide Awake Airport, we had plenty of ribbing from our crewmates telling us to make sure that we came back, otherwise they wouldn't be allowed home. Finding ourselves on the tarmac of the runway, we only had small amounts of luggage with us, the rest having been left behind. Before finally boarding the aircraft, we were checked through an RAF security tent. Officials addressed us and, in no uncertain terms, they warned, 'Before you get on this flight back to the UK, I will ask you something. Is there anyone here carrying firearms?'

I had totally forgotten about the Luger that I had acquired. I had stashed it away in the bottom of a drawer in my cabin back on the ship.

The warning continued. 'If anyone has got a firearm, just go through that side door there and leave it. Nothing will be said. If you don't and you're found in possession of a weapon, once you get past this point, you will be in serious trouble.'

A couple of men went through the side door, no doubt to dispose of what they were carrying. I made a mental note to do something with the Luger on my return. A Royal Navy lad directly in front of me was stopped and asked, 'Anything to declare?' He said, 'No', but upon being searched he was taken aside. By the time I had been seen to and was leaving the customs area, I saw the Royal Navy lad with a scared look on his face and his hands behind his back, as though they were ready for handcuffs.

After that interesting pre-flight procedure, we made our way onto a DC10. Run by RAF crews, it was a basic flight with no alcohol. Nine hours later we touched down at night-time and we were all getting tired. In between flights, I was pleased to get to talk with electrician Brian Burton to pass the time. As Brian was one of the ship's officers and someone more in the know than we ever were in the catering department, I griped to him about how we'd never got told anything during the war. Brian's reply was revealing:

As the ship's officers, most of the time we wouldn't have had anything to tell you, Reg. Cmdr Esplin-Jones and his naval team kept everything to themselves. Esplin-Jones was often on the special communications telephone back to Northwood in the UK. He had the unenviable job of passing on orders, presumably given by the military staff back home in the UK, which never seemed to be anything definite. Regarding

Esplin-Jones giving information to Northwood, I believe that at one time, he hinted the ship's crew were in a mutinous mood. Also, I think you were asleep at the time when he got the crew together for some kind of pep talk shortly before we went into San Carlos Water. His opening gambit was, 'If this goes awfully wrong, we shall expect to take up arms, go ashore and sort these Argies out.' To me this was Boy Scout stuff. One of the ABs replied, 'Hang on a minute, we got you here, I think it's your turn now.' Esplin-Jones then looked carefully around the gathered group. Suddenly, pointing at Frankie Green, our quick-witted, long serving gay steward, he asked him, 'Could you kill a man?' Without hesitation and giving a pouting smile, Frankie answered, 'Yes, love, I suppose I could … eventually!' The room erupted with laughter and the meeting fizzled out prematurely. We all headed back to our workplaces feeling better than we did at the start of the pep talk. I think it was a bit strong to suggest we were mutinous; mischievous yes. It was only that our attitude as civilians had us questioning decisions being made on our behalf by the Royal Navy. Regarding the military-running of the ship, I know he was the senior rank with immense responsibility and doing his job, but Esplin-Jones didn't like to be questioned or contradicted. As we were civvies and he was the senior Naval officer, it had to be that way, I suppose. None of that matters now, and one can only say that Cmdr Esplin-Jones had done a great job because we came through it.

And do you know the one thing that in my opinion helped us get through it … we had a lucky skipper in Don Ellerby! Even with the doubts over the ship's capability, the pressure put on the crew and the alarm at seeing ships around us getting bombed all the time, I always thought that Don Ellerby, who was known as a lucky bloke, would see some of his luck rub off on our tricky situation – and it did. It's not as though this trip hasn't been without its laughs; characters like Frankie on good form proved that. Another laughable moment was on discovering that in the early days when we first began zig-zagging, our navigation team went 'zigging' instead of 'zagging', which had us temporarily lost from the main Task Force. But the one memory that will always stick with me is when I went up on the open deck to watch the scene of jets coming in and being shot at by small arms and getting blown up by missiles. It was hypnotic. However, it was the noise of war that surprised me the most. You could actually feel it. I thought I was used to the sound of heavy noise from years spent in engine rooms but the noise that comes out of fighting a war is like nothing else; it's a power in itself. Overall, though, I tell you, Reg, even with the welcome bonus of earning two and a half times our normal pay, the time that we have spent away and all the stress that our families will have been through, to me, I'm sorry, but it hasn't been worth it. And knowing what I know now, if asked to volunteer to do it again, I wouldn't.

I know that Brian wasn't saying such words out of any fear he ever felt during our time in the Falklands, because he's a tough bloke and someone with an easy-going, positive attitude to life. Neither would he have ever thought that the sacrifice of anyone getting killed was worth it. He probably felt that he'd rather have spent his time doing something more positive that wasn't connected with the waste of life in a war, whether that war was justified or not. I reckon that several other members of the crew felt the same as him.

When called to our aircraft, we went through the same warning procedure at Brize Norton about illegal weapons. Customs didn't care if you had 100,000 cigarettes over the limit; their only concern was weapons. There was also an interest in finding a new piece of kit that had gone missing – a night sight known as an image intensifier. This was the latest bit of technology at the time, and the military security were hoping it would turn up in someone's luggage. It wasn't a weapon, but its potential was equally lethal in the wrong hands. It wasn't found amongst us. Thankfully, there was no drama to delay us. We then made our way onto a propeller aircraft that would fly us direct to our local airport, Humberside.

The 50 per cent of the crew in this first group were taken from all departments on the ship, including the skipper, Don Ellerby. We were all wearing civilian clothing. It was noticeable that the skipper went on the aircraft first, followed by the ship's officers who all sat at the front end. We sat in the middle and to the rear. I thought this would be a short flight, probably without alcohol, but I was wrong. Glasses were handed out and champagne corks popped. The Superintendent of North Sea Ferries, Mr McCarthy, had made the effort to be on the plane to welcome us in person. We were all drinking bubbly and when our glasses were empty, they were refilled by stewardesses. This really was all very nice. The flight only took an hour. When the pilot announced 'fifteen minutes to landing', some of the ship's officers checked themselves, ensuring they were properly dressed in their Merchant Navy uniform ready to face whatever reception there might be. It got me thinking of what they might say if any media were there. I also got to thinking of the many different stories that our lads would be telling their families and friends.

Pete McWatt on the aircraft heading home, sitting with fellow cook, Karl Tungate. Pete is proudly and protectively holding his twenty-first birthday 'key to the door' present, which was hand-crafted by the ship's carpenter. (Courtesy *Hull Daily Mail*)

15
BACK HOME THEN BACK TO SEA

On landing at Humberside airport, we emerged from the aircraft to a crowd of cheering people. Leading our crew was the skipper, Don Ellerby, followed by the heads of each of the ship's departments, the officers and crew, and not forgetting our mascot Pengi. The latter was carried affectionately by Dave, who sported a big grin at being given this responsibility. It resulted in them both making for a fun image in all the local papers. One by one we made our way down the stairway and into the crowd below. We didn't need the champagne that we'd drunk to feel good or to give us all a big grin; the hundreds of people greeting us were enough. Cameras flashed as everyone made their way to somewhere or other. I headed into the crowd not knowing where to go exactly. Wading through people, I had gone about 20yds when I felt a hard tug on my shoulder. I turned around to see Jean and I instantly wrapped my arms around her. I kissed her and she kissed me, as only she could. What immediately struck me was that she had lost weight. She held my hand and directed me to a vehicle I was familiar with. It belonged to my father-in-law, Arthur. Suddenly he appeared in front of me. We shook hands as he said, 'Welcome home.' I saw my two lads, Terry and Steven, whom I embraced, kissing them on their foreheads. They both said, 'Hiya, dad.' What a lovely sound to hear. I then said, 'Come on then, Arthur, do your stuff and let's go home.' The magnificent Humber Bridge had just been built and thankfully we didn't have to go the long way around through Goole.

I lived on Bransholme, supposedly Europe's largest housing estate at the time. It's located in the east of Hull. As we arrived home, a balloon was on our gate as well as a banner with the words 'Welcome Home Reg'. 'The neighbours have put something out for you as well, Reg,' said Jean. I thought it was a bit over the top. I honestly didn't want any fuss.

It felt strange to be in my house, which I hadn't seen for five months. The first few days of leave were like a blur. I didn't really want to go anywhere. I was happy being with Jean and my two lads, Terry and Steven, who were quite blasé about my Falklands trip. They didn't have any searching questions to ask me; they just wanted to be out playing, like kids do. As the days wore on, Jean revealed that while waiting back in Hull, news had come through of the sinking of a large merchant ship with loss of life. This had been announced on the loudspeaker in the Telstar Club on the Bransholme estate. The rumour had spread like wildfire across the estate and the rest of Hull that the *Norland* had been sunk. This was terrible news for families and friends of the crew. The ship that had been sunk was, in fact, the *Atlantic Conveyor*.

Fortunately, something else happened which gave our families some comfort that the rumour had been false. A day or so later, BBC news correspondent Brian Hanrahan did a report from the Task Force. He was bringing the public up to date with events. During his bulletin, in the background a distinctive sound was heard. To those familiar with the *Norland*, it was the 'ding dong ding' of the ship's tannoy system. Therefore, on hearing this, people would know the ship must be safe for him to be doing his bulletin from either on it or within its vicinity. Shortly afterwards, Mike Booth, the North Sea Ferries personnel manager, made phone calls to confirm that the *Norland* was safe.

After a few days at home, I got restless and felt I needed to get my family away. I hired a caravan and took us off to the Yorkshire Dales. It is a part of the world l have loved all my life. Near to the North Pennines, the similarity of the terrain to the Falklands is uncanny. One day we were out walking in pleasant weather and a low-flying jet passed overhead. It approached from behind and, when I first turned to look, I got a feeling of wanting to take cover. It was a horrible feeling. My wife had noticed that my expression had changed to one of apprehension. 'What's the matter?' she asked. I think I'd involuntarily flinched, ducked almost. It was an awful sensation that took me back to Bomb Alley. I passed it off as nothing to Jean, not wanting her to worry more than she already had. It did occur to me that some of the other lads might have been affected through similar incidents whilst on leave.

In Hull, the wives had been placed in groups of six. Each group had a leader who liaised with the company office in King George Dock. Jean was a nominated leader who'd informed the rest of the wives and families of any news. This system saved the office in King George Dock having to contact hundreds of individuals. I didn't realise how much some of our families had worried for us, until my wife let something slip. She was with a friend whose husband had also sailed on the *Norland* when they bumped into someone who blurted out, 'They're all gonna die, you know!'

'Who said that to you?' I asked in disbelief.

'It's okay, it doesn't matter.'

'It's not okay,' I persisted. 'Who the hell would say such a thing?'

'One of the crew who didn't go,' Jean confessed.

So, Jean and the friend she was with had to live with this thought all the time we were away. This brought home even more what our families had been through.

What Jean didn't tell me is how much she had truly worried whilst I was away. It was enough that she often had a little crying session. She tried to hide this from our kids, but they had noticed her tears more than once. Now I was home, they quietly told me about it. I could only hope that with the fighting over and me back safe, she would be more at ease. She wasn't at all happy that I would be going back, though. As the days ticked by, towards the end of my leave I got a haunting feeling that soon I would be receiving a phone call from North Sea Ferries telling me it was time to report. Before this phone call came, I went to visit my mother and father. We chatted as we always did, over a cup of tea, when inevitably we got onto the subject of my going back. I didn't want to but when I looked at my father, this man in front of me was one of the merchant seamen who had been through six years of sailing in North Atlantic convoys in the Second World War. I felt that the Falklands Conflict and what I had gone through were a mere sideshow in comparison to what my father and many others of his generation had experienced in the supreme seafaring 'Battle of the Atlantic'.

Sure enough, the phone call came from Mike Booth. When we were away in the South Atlantic, Mike had done a great job keeping families up-to-date with whatever news he could pass on, giving support where and when needed.

We had to meet on King George Dock in Hull at the North Sea Ferry terminal to be picked up by a coach. In conversations I'd had with Jean about this, she asked me, 'Reg, you're not really going back, are you?' Each time I told her as apologetically as I could, 'Sorry love, but we've got to.' Of course, she knew about the deal we had struck so that the remainder of the crew could have their leave, but she wasn't satisfied with it. I wasn't alone in not wanting to go back; two crew members completely ignored the deal and didn't turn up. Jean accompanied me to the terminal, thinking we must all be crazy to want to return – but we had to. The original skipper, Don Ellerby, would not be with us as his stint was over. He was relieved by Derek Wharton, one of the other regular skippers of North Sea Ferries. John Crowther, the Purser, was another who wouldn't be returning. It turned out that he was wanted to work on the relief ship covering for the *Norland*. On the coach waiting to depart, seated behind me was Malley Gelder. His wife Jose was looking up at the window, and so was my wife. As the bus pulled away, it was awful to see them with tears in their eyes. I felt that Jean would never forgive me for going back.

It was only a couple of miles outside of Hull when the driver told us he was pulling over and this would be the last chance for the toilet before heading non-stop to Brize Norton. On the seat in front of me was Brian Willow, who had brought a parcel on to the bus, which turned out to be a case of beer. Brian opened a bottle when we got going again. He offered me one. I declined. Anyone was welcome to have one of his beers. He'd drunk a couple of bottles when he leaned over to tell me, 'I'm dying for a pee.' I said, 'Sorry, Brian, I can't help you.' He then pissed into one of the empty bottles, which he stood under the seat in front of him. Half a dozen bottles had been emptied of beer and filled by his piss. Near to

Brize Norton, the driver had cause to slam on his brakes. With that, there was a loud clinking of bottles. Everyone at the front of the bus wondered where all this fluid had suddenly come from. I figured he might just as well have pissed on the floor of the bus in the first place. The driver was not a happy man when he discovered what had happened. Getting off the bus as fast as we could, we had a hotel room waiting for us until the flight the next morning. Feeling low at having left my wife and knowing she was upset, I turned in early.

The next morning at breakfast, Derek Wharton, the new skipper, was hopping mad. He approached me and asked, 'Was you one of them last night?'

'One of what?' I said.

Now addressing all who were in earshot at the breakfast table in the restaurant, he pointed his finger at them and angrily said, 'If I find out who has been rowdy, I'll make sure you don't go. The noise from your drinking session kept me awake half the bloody night.'

This was laughable, because none of us wanted to go anyway. We did chuckle at his rash statement. As he walked away, I'm sure he realised what he'd said and a smile came to his face as well.

After breakfast, we boarded a DC10. It was a pleasant flight even though, once we left the English coast, there was nothing to view out of the window except for sea. Wide Awake Airport was there to welcome us, which we quickly passed through to find ourselves on a chopper heading back to the ship. On the ship, something wasn't right. There had been a change. The atmosphere was different, but naturally so. This change was due to new faces from other parts of Britain, who were complete strangers to us. Some were from Hull, but even with those from our hometown it meant we would have to go through a process of getting to know and used to working with them. I was confident, though, that it wouldn't be long before we all got into the routine that was needed.

The crew waiting to go home for their twenty days' leave shook hands with everyone and quickly departed. Dave and I went straight on to nights. The next day we took on passengers, who were now mostly civilians, as well as the usual military. The civilians were building contractors, along with fellow Merchant Navy lads joining ships in the Falklands.

A lot of these civilian passengers soon found the crew bar. All the main bars were still open and doing a roaring trade. Wendy wasn't there entertaining on the piano because he'd gone on leave with the second group. As night stewards, Dave and I realised that the civilian passengers fuelled with drink were wandering around the ship, helping themselves to whatever they could. We had to lock up things more carefully. Some passengers wouldn't conform to what was asked of them, such as when we told them the restaurant was closed and the area out of bounds. Brazenly, they would try to help themselves to food. The military on board still had their self-discipline. They tried to exert this same discipline on the civilians, but it was to no avail. As the civilian passengers disembarked at Stanley, we were glad to see the back of them.

I got some sleep and woke up early in the afternoon to find we were allowed shore leave. Four of us decided to go ashore on the launch and I was surprised to see the place was still being cleaned up. The build-up of the army was very noticeable. We headed for a drink in the Globe. I didn't know what its opening hours were, but I figured that the landlord was making a fortune as it never seemed to close. Like the last time I was there, it was full. Locals having a drink were as happy as ever with the military presence. It struck me that with the days and months quickly passing by, the Argies wouldn't be taking measures to try and regain the Falklands by force. The bar was full of energy with army and navy fellas having a good time without baiting each other, the way members of the military so often do. A face in the bar then caught my eye. I thought I'd recognised someone I knew in uniform. I racked my brains for who it might be, but I couldn't recall. He nodded to me. 'I must know him,' I thought. He then came across the bar and said, 'Hiya, how are ya?'

'I'm fine,' I answered, still puzzled as to who he was.

'You're in civvies,' he stated.

'Yeah, we're crew members off a ship,' I explained.

'Ah, right. From where do I know you?' he queried.

'I don't know. I'm looking at you thinking the same,' I said.

It didn't go any further than that. He went back to his mates and I sat there with mine. I glanced over now and again to notice he was doing the same to me. He then came over to me again and said with a grin,

'Well, bloody hell, I've just realised how I know ya. Where I've seen ya.' There was a pause.

'Well, go on, tell me,' I urged.

'It was on the North Yorkshire Moors. On that walk, the Lyke Wake Walk.'

What a coincidence! He was one of the four soldier lads whom I had met earlier in the year when I and the other lads of our crew had done that walk. We both put down our drinks and spontaneously embraced like we'd known each other all of our lives. We talked about one thing and another, and then he said, 'Do you know, the countryside here and the terrain on the North Yorkshire Moors, how similar it all is?'

'Exactly,' I agreed.

It was a very unlikely encounter that had us chatting for a while, before he headed back to his mates. After a few more beers he left the pub. What were the chances of that, meeting someone I didn't know, yet, somehow, I did? Should we meet again, hopefully I won't be scratching my head wondering who the hell he is. And seeing as I had got the beers in, next time we might meet, it would be his turn.

Back on the ship and ready to sail, we headed to different parts of the main island, picking up and dropping off different personnel. Lots of vessels from the UK had arrived and could be seen in the local waters. Massive amounts of supplies were constantly being shipped in. Our job was to continue as a floating hotel and we got back into the routine of heading from the Falklands to Ascension. Once we were back at sea, Dave and I found that, again, an unruly element of passengers was making life difficult for us after the bars had shut.

Heading back to Ascension, early morning around 2 a.m., I was making my way to the Continental Bar on D-deck to tidy up. The bar had closed and a few stragglers were hanging about the place. I noticed two soldiers in uniform finishing off their drink. As I approached them, I nodded and asked, 'Are you alright, lads?'

'Oh yeah, we're fine, thanks,' came the reply.

As I was walking past, one of them called after me, 'Have you got a minute, mate?'

I turned back. 'What's the matter?'

'Have you heard about one of your stewards getting beat up?' one of them said.

'Who's that?'

'You know, the gay guy. I think they call him Francis. He's been worked over. He's had a right hiding.'

'When did this happen?' I asked, upset at the thought.

'Just a couple of minutes ago.'

'Where is he now?'

'We don't know. He picked himself up off the floor and made off somewhere.'

I knew who it would be: Frankie Green. I thanked the two soldiers for the tip-off and went to look for him. I checked around the bar area. Not seeing him and worrying he might have collapsed and be laid out somewhere, I checked the men's toilets. He might have gone there to clean himself up. I noticed traces of blood in one of the sinks. He wasn't there or anywhere else obvious. I guessed that he must have gone to his cabin. It was all quiet as I made my way down to G-deck. I tried the door of his cabin but it was locked. I looked through the keyhole and I could see there was a key on the inside, so I knew he was there. I used my pass key, hoping to push his key out so that I could use mine to open the door. After carefully managing to do so, I opened the door to see him laid on his bunk. The light was on. I called his name but there was no response. The first thing I noticed was his face. It had severe swelling, but most noticeable was that his nose was pushed way over to one side. I tried again to get some response out of him. He was either unconscious or flaked out from too much drink. The drink had likely done him a favour, possibly dulling any pain he would have felt. He was, hopefully, not going to feel the pain from what I was about to administer. I checked his breathing, which was okay. I thought, 'When he wakes up and looks in the mirror, he will die of fright.' I then did something that I wasn't sure was the right thing to do. I held his head with one hand, and with my other hand I pinched his nose and pushed it back into a straight position with a crunching sound. The action I had taken worried me, but his nose looked to be in a normal position. With that, Frankie groaned and stirred. He then fell back into a deep sleep. I put him into the recovery position, placed a blanket over him and left without locking the door. I made my way to the information desk and asked if one of the military units on board had a medic who could check on him. People soon got to know of Frankie's situation. It was awful that something like this could have happened. The word was out and it was reckoned that Frankie had been beaten up by someone in uniform. This was the first time there had been a fallout between the military and the crew, and we were greatly disappointed. Frankie wasn't seen for several weeks, nursing his wounds in his cabin.

A troop sergeant told some members of the crew that they were so sorry for what had happened. He added, 'Francis is a good bloke and didn't deserve this. We have found out who it was and though he reckons he doesn't like homosexuals, that is absolutely no excuse. We'd appreciate it if you can leave it with us to sort out ... and believe me, we will. The wrongdoer will get his comeuppance.'

With this reassurance we left it at that. It wasn't until two weeks after administering my version of first aid to Frankie that I saw him again. All the bruising was coming out but Frankie himself was not. He'd holed himself up in his cabin. Some of the crew were taking him his meals and attending to any other needs. During my visit, I couldn't have been more relieved to see his nose looked okay. I was pleased with myself and that my handiwork appeared to be successful, for his nose was thankfully straight.

Not long after what happened to Frankie, another incident that had fists flying took place, this time between a bolshie soldier and one of our no-nonsense crew members. A disagreement developed which had them 'offering each other out'. The result was that our crew member knocked down the soldier, who had apparently been mouthy. Laid on the deck, the soldier was told 'Don't get up.' He was wise enough not to and our crew member was honourable enough not to take it any further. The outcome of the fracas was that it earned a new respect for our ship's crew and, in a way, it redressed the balance with what had happened to Frankie. It soon got around the rest of the soldiers on board that they shouldn't take us for granted. The soldier who'd got laid out had a reputation as a 'tough guy' but he kept a low profile afterwards.

16

TAKING CONTROL OF THE SHIP

With the business of the bolshie soldier and Frankie's trouble in our minds, Dave and I agreed that something radical had to be done. Generally, the military had some self-discipline, but our main problem now was that our passengers were mostly civvies who enjoyed no limit on drinks allowed per night. Their attitude was 'you can't tell us what to do because we're not in the army'. We figured we knew exactly what we had to do to prevent this 'attitude'. We went to see the old man, Derek Wharton. One morning after breakfast, when we knocked on the door of his day room, he invited us, in wondering what the matter was. He asked us to sit down and make ourselves comfortable. 'Well, this is a rare thing, you coming to see me about something. What is it?' he asked with a look of concern.

We explained the late-night problems with drunkenness and how lack of discipline with civilian passengers was starting to get out of hand at night.

'But things are not totally out of control, are they?'

'They soon could be,' I said. 'Dave and I are too busy with our normal jobs without having to sort out drunken behaviour as well.'

'Behaviour like what?'

'When the passengers leave the bars, they're drifting into the restaurant because they know that's where the food is. They're ransacking whatever they can and we can't stand guard because we need to be elsewhere.'

'What do you suggest?' asked the skipper.

'We need a ship's policeman back on board. We know from our normal run across the North Sea that passengers take notice of someone in police uniform. You could send for Big Bob or Ron Marshall.'

'Which one are you thinking of?'

I replied, 'No disrespect to Bob, but we would like Ron Marshall. There's nothing wrong with Bob, but Dave and I have worked with Ron more closely. Ron is a former Marine with nine years' service and he'll easily relate to what's going on here. He has that presence of being a policeman, because that's what he was after his military service, a bobby on the beat.'

The old man hesitated before answering. 'Right, let me think on this and I'll let you know my decision shortly.'

The next night, a group of drunks were roaming around the restaurant, heading towards the breakfast buffet that we'd prepared. It was covered over with white cloths, but that didn't matter to hungry boozed-up revellers. They took off the cloths and began helping themselves. At that very moment, we couldn't believe it when the skipper walked in to witness it.

'Hey, what do you think you're doing?' he asked them with authority.

They looked at him with no care at all. One of them said, 'What the fuck has it got to do with you?'

The skipper was taken aback at this remark, especially as he was wearing four stripes on his epaulettes, which obviously made no difference to them. There was an uneasy stand-off. The three of us then closed in together and the drunks must have thought better about the situation … they backed off and drifted away.

The skipper looked at us and, nodding, he said, 'Okay, I agree with what you're suggesting. I'll sort out this matter straight away. You've got yourself a policeman.'

At the time of this incident, we were only two days away from Ascension. Once there, when passengers had disembarked, as usual the ship was made ready for our next run south. The following night, Dave and I turned to and while sitting in the restaurant, we were surprised to see Ron Marshall walk in. The skipper had been as good as his word. Within three days, Ron had received notice, sorted out his affairs, caught a flight to Ascension and here he was, ready for work. He knew what he had to do, having often done the same on Hull to Rotterdam crossings, when some of the passengers on those sailings could be tricky to handle. Considering that he was a policeman, Ron was popular with the crew at all levels on the ship.

We left Ascension with the regular mixed bag of military and civilian passengers. A rumour emerged that this trip to the Falklands and then back to Ascension would be the last one before we headed home for good. Our reaction due to previous rumours was 'yeah, yeah, yeah'. When Ron heard this rumour, he was justifiably annoyed, as he had just arrived. He needn't have worried because, as per normal, it was just a rumour.

Around this time, I went to my cabin and locked the door. Kneeling, I opened the bottom drawer of a desk. Pulling the drawer out completely, I found the weapon I'd acquired, secreted away in a space below. I undid the hand-towel that I'd wrapped it in. A hand gun is a strange thing. It's a tactile thing to hold, as well as frightening to be in possession of. This First World War – possibly Second World War – Luger in my possession no doubt had an interesting history. It would likely be worth money if sold legally at an auction. It could also be worth money if sold on the black market. Neither of these options was my intention. I had made up my mind what its fate would be. Hiding it on my person, I made my way to the stern of the ship and without ceremony I threw it over the side into the Atlantic. What I was doing with it in the first place, I could only put down to being an 'in the moment' decision when offered it – and for the cheap price of six beers. What some of the Paras did with their small arms war trophies, I don't know. I just felt a great relief at having got rid of mine.

Many weeks earlier, when first heading from Ascension to San Carlos Water, our ship's funnel had received a half-finished paint job. Between then and now, the funnel managed to receive several completed paint jobs, which were mainly in the form of a tribute to the different regiments we had carried. It had also had PW written in large letters upon it, which was to let the Argentinians know that, at the time, we were carrying their prisoners of war. Like a military person wears headwear with a cap badge, our ship's funnel was our version of headwear, and the cap badges that we displayed over the last few months were of military insignias. Every couple of weeks when I caught a glance of the funnel, some neat artwork had been carried out by AB Tommy Clark, who was handy with a paintbrush. On reaching double figures of various regiments having been painted in, and painted out, Bob Lough, the Chief Officer, called a halt to this procedure as it was taking up the ABs' valuable time. It was also causing arguments between different regiments wanting their insignia to be bigger and better than the last one. Opposite is the 2 Para insignia. The three crowns shown underneath it is the coat of arms for the City of Hull.

On our arrival in the Falklands, Ron was keen to be shown about the place. Ron, John Foster and I went ashore and we figured that the best way for Ron to get a feel of the place would be to visit the Globe. There were other drinking places in Stanley, but the Globe was thought the best choice as it was the shortest walk from the jetty where we landed in our launch. Enjoying a drink, we discovered a new word had emerged to describe the local people. This word was 'Benny'. The locals didn't have live television on the island and therefore didn't know about the programmes in the UK. Back home there was a soap opera on TV called *Crossroads*. A character in this soap was a big, slow-thinking individual who always wore a woolly hat and went by the name of Benny. Initially the islanders didn't pay any mind to this term until the real reason for it was pointed out that they supposedly resembled the Benny character off *Crossroads*. I felt the label of Benny was a bit unfair because the islanders were good people. Some islanders were annoyed by it, some weren't.

Next day, back on the ship, a barman called Pete Smith with the nickname of Smoko was called up to the radio room. His 21-year-old son Kevin was serving on the aircraft carrier HMS *Hermes*. Smoko was informed that as a goodwill gesture the military wanted them to meet up. He couldn't believe this offer. He was given the day off so that he could get to Stanley where Kevin would be helicoptered in. A couple of the crew, myself included, went ashore with him by launch. He met up with his son to have some personal time, whilst we went off to the Globe. A short while later, Smoko and Kevin rolled up at the pub with big beaming smiles. It was a good feeling to see this reunion. We all had a good day together, but come 5 p.m. in the afternoon we needed to get back. Weather in the Falklands could be unpredictable and transport to the ship could be a problem if strong winds had whipped up. Luckily, the weather held and as we sat in the launch to return, Smoko got emotional at having to say goodbye to his son, who was left on the jetty. As the launch pulled away, his son walked along the jetty as far as he could, watching his dad leave.

A scene from Stanley, ravaged by war, in which Argentine vehicles became British war trophies.

Smoko said, 'If you get home before me, son, give your mam my love.' The walking space on the jetty had run out for Kevin as the launch pulled away. Kevin shouted, 'And you do the same if you get home before I do. Give mam a big hug from me … I love you, dad.' As these last words were said, everyone in the launch had a lump in their throat. I think Hollywood couldn't have done better for the emotion that we all felt at this parting scene.

When in the Stanley area and sailing around the coast, picking up and dropping off civilians and military personnel at various locations, we went back to San Carlos Water (Bomb Alley). It seemed a long time ago now since all the drama that had taken place there. It was in that area that I was in a conversation with a steward called Nigel Dickenson, who had flown out as a relief from the UK. Nigel went by the nickname of Blossom. (I have always been amused at where some people's nicknames come from.) Whilst chatting away with him in the restaurant, a figure came into view. Straightaway I recognised him. He looked at me and as he approached, he had his hand out, which I warmly shook. Standing in front of me was Trevor, the helicopter pilot whom I had looked after when he and his team were in need of some food. We had a little natter and I learnt he'd recently been home on leave before returning back to helicopter duties. The island was now equipped with different armaments to counter any threat from the Argies, in particular the Rapier anti-aircraft system. Unexpectedly, Trevor said, 'By the way, I owe you one.'

'What's that?'

'Because of the favour you did for me. Can I repay you by offering a quick tour of the island in my Sea King?' he said.

'Wow! That'd be great,' I said.

Trevor said:

I tell you what. In the morning at 10 a.m., be on the after deck heli-pad, and stand so that when I land, I can see you. I'll be transferring different crews with their baggage for the Rapier system deployed around the island. When I've landed, just keep your eyes on me. My helmet and mask will make it difficult to see my face but it'll be me as I am the only one flying a chopper tomorrow. As soon as I give you the okay by putting my thumb up, just climb in. Don't hesitate and don't let anybody obstruct you. You're my guest, so you can get on board, no problem. Once inside, stand behind me and stay there. I'll fly over the route that the Argy pilots took when they came in on their raids.

'Alright, I've got all of that. I'll be there.'

Blossom, whom I was standing with, cheekily asked, 'Can I come along as well?'

'Is he a mate of yours?' asked Trevor.

'Yeah, I know him.' What could I say with him standing there next to me? I then added, 'Yeah, he's a good mate.'

'Okay, make it the two of you, but stick to that.'

Blossom was thrilled, as was I at his offer. Ready for 10 a.m. the next morning, we made our way to the pick-up point near the heli-pad, when at the same time the skipper appeared, strolling about the ship. He came towards Blossom and me and with a curious look he asked, 'Reg, what are you doing here?'

'Oh, just a bit of sightseeing,' I weakly offered.

At that point, the helicopter came into view.

We talked with the skipper about nothing in particular, then as the helicopter came in to land, the skipper put his arm in front of us and said, 'I don't mind you being here for a while but stand well away.' He moved us back to what he thought was a safe distance from the heli-pad. Though he carried on telling us about something or other, I wasn't listening for I had my eyes fixed on Trevor the pilot. A Rapier crew quickly got off with their equipment. The noise and the downdraft were very powerful.

'Now, don't forget. Keep well away, keep well back,' shouted the skipper with authority.

The pilot put his thumb up, which Blossom and me both saw. One minute we were in conversation with the skipper, the next minute we had mounted the heli-pad and climbed aboard the helicopter.

'Hey, Reg, what do you think you're doing?' the skipper called after us, his voice straining above the noise.

Once inside the helicopter, I stood behind Trevor, as he had told me. Blossom stood at the other side of me. I looked back through the doors of the helicopter and I could see our skipper with a confused look on his face. I grinned broadly as the helicopter pulled away from the ship, and though tempted to salute our skipper, I didn't. Thereafter, any conversation with Trevor was limited due to the noise made by the Sea King. Trevor swung the thing about in the air, which was exhilarating. The view was amazing through the open doors and especially over Trevor's shoulder through the windscreen. We hovered near to the ground of a Rapier site and some personnel jumped in. We then pulled away. With that, coming in from the west, we flew over the brow of a hill and laid before us was the full stretch of San Carlos Water. We made a sweep past Fanning Head, that dominant feature which could have been our downfall all that time ago on first entering San Carlos Water. Various ships at anchor were dotted about. We were flying at roughly the same height as the Argy aircraft had flown and we swept the full length of where we had been anchored during the bombing raids. The *Norland* was currently anchored slightly to our right. The thought that really struck me was 'how the hell we didn't get hit, I'll never know!' I shouted this to Trevor, who nodded. The *Norland* stood out like anything as I viewed it on our flight. I mentally blessed our luck that during the times when it was no fun, we'd managed to come out of it unscathed. Twenty minutes or so later we landed back on the ship. I patted Trevor on the shoulder and thanked him. What an experience and what a thrill!

The next night shift, I had reason to go up onto A-deck where the officers had a noticeboard in one of the alleyways. Further emphasising our luck in not getting hit by Argentinian aircraft was a hand-written letter on the noticeboard, sent to our ship's skipper by a survivor from the less lucky HMS *Antelope*.

13th June 1982
Dear Sir,
I am writing to convey my sincere thanks and gratitude to the Officers and Crew of the MV *Norland*, which transported the Ship's Company of HMS *Antelope* from San Carlos Bay to the relative safety of South Georgia on the 24th May 1982.

The hospitality, sympathy and cheerfulness afforded by your ship's company to ours will remain etched in my memory forever.

Your crew are operating in extremely hazardous conditions and are held in the highest esteem by all the Royal Navy personnel who have had the honour to have fought alongside them in the Falklands.
Yours Most Sincerely
D G Hawkins
Chief Petty Officer, HMS *Antelope*

I was impressed with this letter's content. It was a heartfelt thank you and its powerful words made one reflect. It invoked feelings in me that I'd had during the war when, on an almost daily basis, we heard of ships getting hit. Whilst we were not getting a lot of news coming through of the wider picture, what couldn't be kept quiet was the loss of our navy's ships during the war. It was very disturbing to hear about these losses at the time. In all, seven vessels were sunk and seventeen suffered varying degrees of damage. A total of 174 British people had died at sea. Perhaps the luckiest ship was MV *British Wye*, which was being used as an auxiliary support tanker. Eight bombs were dropped on it from an Argentinian Hercules. Only one hit, which bounced off into the sea, causing minor damage. The seven vessels that didn't make it through the war were:

HMS *Sheffield* – Destroyer
HMS *Coventry* – Destroyer
HMS *Ardent* – Frigate
HMS *Antelope* – Frigate
SS *Atlantic Conveyor* – Container Ship
RFA *Sir Galahad* – Landing Ship Logistics (LSL)
Landing Craft Utility (LCU) from HMS *Fearless*

One time, when sailing into Stanley, I spotted RFA *Sir Tristram*. It was in a hell of state, yet it had survived. Its decks had been strafed and two of its crew had been killed. A 500lb bomb had penetrated its deck but, like so many other instances in this war, an Argentinian bomb had failed to explode on impact, which allowed the remaining crew to be evacuated. Following the later explosion of the bomb, the ship was abandoned. After the surrender, it was towed to Port Stanley to be used as an accommodation ship. (It was then later rebuilt and put back into service.)

How fortunate were we to have come through it unharmed? This is best answered by the Chief Officer, Bob Lough, who, in an interview, gave an account of an incident when we were in Bomb Alley:

> We were in our designated anchorage, very close to land under a hill and the weather during the night saw the ship drag her anchor. So, we all had to turn to. We got the engines started and put the bow thrust on and we re-anchored the ship, but it was about 300–400 yards from where it had been at sunset. At first light the next morning, two Skyhawks came over the hill and released bombs and the bombs went in where the *Norland* had been [originally] parked. And I'm convinced they'd had the ship spotted. This was a change of plan as far as they were concerned; they thought they would come in and have a go at one of the transports, but of course we weren't there!

The Falklands War lasted seventy-four days. It claimed the lives of 255 British, three civilian Falkland Islanders and an estimated 650 Argentine servicemen. Most casualties, on both sides, occurred at sea. The figure of British ships sunk could have been higher had it not been for several Argentinian bombs failing to explode on hitting their targets.

RFA *Sir Tristram.*

The number of Argentinian ships either sunk, damaged or captured, which included support, supply and spy ships, was estimated at eighteen. Argentina admitted to 100 fixed and rotary wing aircraft lost through a combination of being shot down, damaged or captured. British figures were ten fixed-wing aircraft and twenty-five helicopters, resulting from air battles, flying accidents, being on board ships that were hit, and one that was through self-destruction for tactical reasons.

A Royal Navy ship that would become known as 'the forgotten ship' was HMS *Glamorgan*, a destroyer. On 12 June, she had been supporting 45 Cdo in its battle on Two Sisters and as she moved away from the coast to join the Task Force, she was hit by a land-launched Exocet. Fourteen of the crew died. The ship managed to sail back to Portsmouth for repairs. It was the last British ship to suffer damage and loss of life, but at the time it received little recognition because the surrender dominated the news two days later.

The eight other ships from Hull requisitioned by the MOD, in addition to the *Norland*, included United Towing tugs *Irishman*, *Salvageman* and *Yorkshireman*. In the early stages of the war, during the recapture of

South Georgia, the Argentinian submarine *Sante Fe* was damaged and partly sunk alongside a jetty in Grytviken. At the war's end, it was floated and beached in the harbour due to efforts of the *Salvageman* crew and Royal Navy personnel. It was later towed into deep water and scuttled on 10 February 1985.

Trawler owners J. Marr & Son provided *Cordella, Farnella, Junella* and *Northella;* British United Trawlers provided *Pict.* Whilst the tugs were manned by local Hull seamen, the five trawlers (used for mine counter-measures work) were manned by Royal Navy personnel. All of the ships came back undamaged with no casualties.

17

A BELATED CHRISTMAS PRESENT

The second half of the crew had returned from their leave to re-join the ship and the rest of the year began to pass by quickly. The pattern was backwards and forwards between Ascension and the Falklands. Interestingly, the islanders took advantage of the fact there was now a ferry service between the Falklands and Ascension, for they made up most of the passengers, no doubt travelling on to the UK. Any aggro on board, Ron sorted it out – not in an adversarial but in a friendly way, which was his style. His powers of persuasion were a great skill that he had nurtured through the years. Mail was regular, there was no more darkened ship and we were back in our steward's attire. Our routine was familiar and life felt normal, or as normal as it could be, not knowing how long the ship would stay requisitioned by the MOD.

In September 1982, in San Carlos Water, Dave Aistrop got a message to go up and see the skipper. The upsetting news he received was that his mother had died. It was a credit to the system that he was so swiftly returned to Britain. He flew in a Hercules from Stanley Airport to Ascension and then on to Brize Norton. Dave returned to the ship and ended up on a different watch from me. I saw very little of him after that and he was greatly missed. He was a good workmate and an equally good friend to know.

The end of October came and we were offered leave again. It was the same deal, half go, half stay. I went home in the first half, this time for a lengthy period from the beginning of November to mid-December.

Having been home for such a long period, we thought that whilst we were back in Hull the ship would surely be released from duty. No way! We had to return. For those of us in it for the long haul it was the hardest time. Being away for the festive season, the feeling of missing home was at its worst. The leave system was such that being part of the first group I was back in mid-December, but the second group was lucky and they got both Christmas and New Year at home. During all the coming and going on leave, though some members of the crew had changed, the majority of the original crew that had served in the Falklands were still with us.

On Christmas Eve, when at anchor in Stanley, there was no atmosphere on board to talk about. Okay, there was plenty of drink on the ship but that didn't make up for being away from home. Regardless, we all pretended that we were enjoying ourselves. On Christmas Day the cooks pulled out all the stops to make it as pleasant as possible. Prior to our meal, a message from the skipper informed us that he was going to come down with a couple of his officers to serve us personally. Malley Gelder, the Chief Cook now in charge due to the absence of George Rimmer, had put on a good show with some turkey for us to tuck into. But being 8,000 miles from home and my family, I have to say this Christmas dinner memory would stay with me for a long time as probably the worst of my life, mainly because of where we were. But credit to the skipper and his officers for serving us. Service included the pouring of wine into our glasses, for which we complimented them at not spilling any.

Come New Year's Eve, we were still at anchor in Stanley. We'd all had a good drink and, one way or another, a group of us ended up on the bridge alongside the Officer of the Watch. It is a tradition on New Year's Eve that all ships blow their horns at the stroke of midnight. One of our group got the privilege of doing this, signalling the end of 1982 – and what a year it had been! The weather was calm and still, because in the Falklands it was their summer. That said, no matter how the weather was one minute, the next minute it could change dramatically. The expression 'four seasons in one day' was very apt for that part of the world. However, on New Year's Day, the weather was very pleasant. I spent some time with Pete Sansam, a good friend of mine. The conversation was mostly about what our families might be up to back home.

A fun incident that took place on New Year's Day that I wasn't part of, but which was told to me by electrician Brian Burton, concerned, of all things, a lifeboat race. This was dreamed up on New Year's Eve at a communal booze-up between members of the nine ships that were anchored in Port Stanley. During the celebrations, it had been agreed that each ship would launch one of its lifeboats the next day in a race across the harbour.

The basic rules were that, whatever size of lifeboat was used, it could be manned by any number of personnel using whatever oars were available. The second mate of the *Norland*, Jerry Walker, was a competitive sort. He decided that this was a challenge our ship was going to win. To make sure of it, he got a rush job done through the ship's carpenter, who nailed on some wooden blocks for the rowers to get a better purchase with their feet. With six (hungover) rowers, each one to an oar in our ship's sizeable lifeboat, on the start signal, the second mate navigated the ship on an immediate left tack. All the other lifeboats headed straight towards the finish line. Several minutes into the race, a slight breeze and strong tide pulled the other lifeboats off course. Our lifeboat then took on a right tack and it reached the finishing line first. The prize was free drinks in the Globe afterwards for the winning team.

But upon arriving at the pub, it was found to be shut. Banging on the front door brought no joy, so a bunch of thirsty sailors made their way around the back and Brian Burton was one of them. Banging even harder on the back door brought out an annoyed-looking landlord, who told everyone that it was a public holiday and the pub wouldn't be opening.

'But we'll pay double for our drinks if you do,' Brian generously offered.

'You could pay treble and it wouldn't make any difference,' said the landlord.

Brian noticed what looked like packed suitcases in the hallway behind the landlord. The landlord knew that his suitcases had been spotted and he confessed:

Gentlemen, I have made more money in the last eight months than I have done in the whole of the last eight years, I'm sorry but I don't need the business today, or any other day. I'm retiring to invest my money. I can see you've spotted the suitcases behind me. The truth is I am leaving the island and it might surprise you to know that it's in Argentina where I intend to make my investments. I did business with Argentina before the invasion and now it's all over, I am carrying on where I left off.'

Brian had fond affection for the Globe. The months spent on the ship were driving a lot of the crew stir crazy. Brian reckoned that for them the Globe was like a second home and he was kind of chuffed that on any visit, our crew were always the last to leave before closing time. The lads weren't too pleased at the landlord's actions, but they were understanding that the locals had to pick up the pieces and return life to something like it had been before the invasion. Brian best summed up this situation when he said, 'There is, of course, an irony in the landlord's personal circumstance in that he was probably one of several islanders who were now better off because of the war.'

Military-wise, establishing the Falkland Islands as a safe haven for the islanders appeared to have been accomplished. Less cargo and fewer passengers had been travelling with us and we figured that our South Atlantic ferry role was drawing to a close and we would soon be back in Britain. This was the thought we mostly hung on to.

A couple of days into January 1983, I went ashore with four of the lads. Inevitably, we ended up in the Globe, which had by now re-opened. Whilst enjoying a pint we overheard a word not familiar to us. The word was 'Stills'. What was it supposed to mean? Thinking it might have had something to do with illicit booze-making, we asked some military fellas to explain. It turned out that the islanders were upset at being nicknamed 'Bennies' and wanted it stopped. It came down as a directive from the top brass not to use the term Bennies anymore. The quick-thinking wit of the military never ceased to amaze me as the locals were now described by them as Stills – in the sense that they were 'still Bennies'. We were not military, we were civilians, so therefore no bloody army directive would tell us what we could and couldn't say. However, we liked and respected the islanders and were happy just calling them 'mate'.

Free time to go ashore was now more generous. One day on taking the launch to Stanley, the wind was noticeably strong. We hoped it wouldn't get too bad, but those thoughts were put to the back of our minds as we strolled around Stanley browsing the small array of shops. Then it was off to the Globe. After a few pints, we could hear the wind howling outside and this wasn't good news, for it meant the launch would be stopped from running. We finished our drink-time early and arrived at the jetty to find the launch wasn't there. Oh hell, what now? We were stuck. We had to get back to the ship to turn to for work. It was late afternoon and I was relatively okay because I didn't have to start work until 10 p.m. Maybe there'd be a change of weather and the launch would start running again. To kill a bit of time, we walked up the coast road, doing a bit more browsing. We came upon a smart-looking house, a big colonial-style building where Sir Rex Hunt, the Governor at the time, lived. It was set back from the road with a large grassy area to its front. If we couldn't get back to the ship, maybe he could help us. This was wishful thinking though. Suddenly we heard a helicopter, which was quite common for Stanley, but this one was about to land on the Governor's lawn. When it touched down, people got out and hurried into the Governor's House. One of the lads said, 'That's the only way we're going to get back tonight.' In response, I said, 'Well, I'll go and ask.' I ran to the helicopter. The winchman was stood on the grass taking bags out and throwing them down. There was a lot of noise from the downdraft when I gestured to the winchman. 'Can I speak with you?'

He took his headphones off and asked, 'What do you want?'

'Will you ask the pilot if he can give us a lift?' I said, getting straight to the point.

He shook his head and said, 'No chance.'

'Can you just please ask the pilot for us? We need to get back to our ship,' I insisted.

He paused and then, turning his head, he spoke into his mouthpiece while looking towards the cockpit.

'What ship is it?' asked the winchman.

'The *Norland*,' I told him.

The winchman then grabbed my arm and walked me to the front of the helicopter. The pilot, who I couldn't fully see because of his helmet and visor, then nodded.

'I don't know what the fucking hell it is that you've got but he's okayed it. Get the rest of your lot aboard,' said the winchman.

The lads must have thought there'd be no chance of getting a lift, but I'd somehow managed it. I don't know if it was the reputation of our ship or if the pilot was Trevor and he'd recognised me – whatever the reason, we had our lift. On arriving at the ship ten minutes later, the pilot didn't land but hovered a couple of feet up and we all safely jumped out. We signalled our thanks as we'd been saved from getting into trouble. We went straight to our mess room where the other lads had given up hope of seeing us that night. We were glad to tell them of our good fortune and they liked that the helicopter pilot and the winchman had looked after us.

Immediately after the illegal occupation of the Falklands, Sir Rex Hunt, his wife, Island Councillors and Royal Marines were flown out to Montevideo in Uruguay. For Sir Rex's return as Civil Commissioner, the MOD wouldn't let him travel together with his wife by Hercules. She returned sometime later on the *Norland* to be met by Rex. A well-liked couple, they often wined and dined on board when using it as a ferry. Thereafter, they always spoke in glowing terms of their relationship with the ship and its crew, and its long service to the island's needs.

Rumours were rife. 'We're going home soon', was the daily topic of conversation. Surely there had been some pressure from North Sea Ferries to allow the ship to get back to its normal role of sailing from Hull to Rotterdam. Maybe the sum of money paid by the MOD for requisitioning the ship was too good to worry about it taking up its civilian role. A replacement ferry was taking the place of the *Norland* back home, but what kind of job was it doing? Overall, we felt the company was on our side and that they wanted to get the ship to Britain. Mid-January, word came that this was it … the ship was to return home. We were anchored in Stanley and only a dozen or so passengers were living on board, so it was believable. Then a message came through that, yes, finally the ship was to be released.

Absolute confirmation that we would be heading home came when we had a visit from a very high-ranking British Army officer. Major

General David Thorne was appointed as the Commander of the British Forces in the Falkland Islands shortly after their recapture. He'd boarded our ship to give us what turned out to be a farewell thank you. He spoke of how teamwork had won the day and praised the care and attention we'd given when looking after 2 Para and 3 Para. What mostly struck a chord with me was when he said:

> We have four great pillars supporting our country, the Navy, the Army, the Air Force and you, the Merchant Marines. And should there be another crisis, I know I'd want the *Norland* to serve with us again, because the kind of service we'd receive would be unique, caring, good humoured and steadfast. I salute you all.

He then saluted us and to loud cheers he left, probably to have a tot of rum with the skipper.

The following morning the crew was buzzing with excitement. The weather was glorious without a cloud in the sky. I was on the outside deck talking with a couple of the lads and enjoying the day when one of the tugs called the *Yorkshireman*, which had been doing sterling work in nearby waters, came alongside. On the foredeck of the *Yorkshireman* was an army brass band, playing their instruments. They neared to about 25yds when one of our crew shouted, 'What's the band for? This is a funny place to be practising!'

Someone from the tug shouted back, 'The band is for you, the *Norland*. It's because you're sailing today!'

We realised it must be the army's way of saying farewell. I was quite touched by this. The band was merrily playing good-old, military-style, rousing music. It certainly roused me. We weighed anchor and slowly made our way out of the inlet towards open sea. In the distance, four aircraft then appeared in formation. As they got closer, you could see one was a Hercules flying quite slowly. It was escorted, either side, by two Harrier jump jets. Behind the Hercules was a Phantom. They flew directly over the ship and, about a mile away, the Harriers majestically veered off left and right as the Phantom went straight up, all dispersing into four different parts of their quartet.

BUCKINGHAM PALACE

I am delighted to hear that at long last Norland
is back from the South Atlantic. Welcome back to
your home port.

I, together with everyone in this country, was
deeply impressed by the performance of the Merchant
Navy in the South Atlantic campaign. I hear nothing
but the highest praise for the Officers and Crew of
Norland and of the superb contribution you made
month after month, often in dangerous, difficult and
disagreeable circumstances. I send my warmest
congratulations and best wishes to you all.

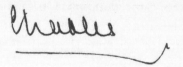

On reaching open water, we saw two frigates ahead of us. They began
sending water spouts up into the air. It looked quite spectacular, considering this effect was made by simple hoses. One of the ships, which I believe
was HMS *Plymouth*, made towards us, dead slow. The *Norland* was now
going dead slow too and it looked like we would pass each other very
closely, no more than 100yds apart. By now, everyone who was free had
come up on to the open decks. With the weather on its best behaviour, it
was a wonderful feeling to be standing there saying goodbye, knowing that
at last our job was done. A lot of activity was taking place on the frigate as
it neared to pass. Its deck was full of men, all lined up along its length on

their port side. A voice called out from the frigate, 'THREE CHEERS FOR THE NORLAND, HIP HIP HOORAY … HIP HIP HOORAY … HIP HIP HOORAY!' For each cheer, all the sailors lifted their hats in unison to one side and then finished by putting their hats back on. The voice then shouted, 'Have a good voyage home, *Norland!*'

This was one of the most moving things I had ever experienced. It was emotional enough that it had several of our crew with tears in their eyes. I know I did. What a farewell from the Royal Navy, which by my reckoning had suffered more than anyone in the Falklands.

There was now no doubt whatsoever that the ship was going home and we were going with it – hopefully to a peaceful life.

10 DOWNING STREET

THE PRIME MINISTER

Best wishes to the MV Norland, her Captain and crew.

The Norland was in the thick of things at the San Carlos bridge-head and, since the fighting, has played a vital part in supporting our garrison in the Falklands.

I join with the Hull Daily Mail, families and friends of the ship's company in welcoming the Norland's safe return to her home port.

Margaret Thatcher

Both royal recognition and government approval. (Courtesy of *Hull Daily Mail*)

18

LAYING GHOSTS TO REST

The journey of the *Norland* was epic in respect of the continuous time spent at sea and the distances covered. My account of that journey is just one of hundreds of stories that have since come out of the Falklands War. Everyone has a story in them about their experiences during and after that time, big or small. Of these numerous stories, I wanted to end mine on another memorable Falklands trip that was greatly uplifting for me; a trip that came about decades after hostilities ceased.

I had no desire to go back to the Falklands, but I was asked several times by my old shipmate Pete McWatt if I would. Initially I said no. Then he made it easy for me to say yes, when he offered to take care of all the arrangements. This was in 2014 and Pete had been back there several times already. On hearing about my intended journey, the Hull Independent Merchant Navy Association asked me to act as a courier on their behalf. Eddie Piercy, the Association's Chairman, said, 'Reg, you could deliver a letter to the Governor of the Falkland Islands on behalf of our organisation and its members, together with a plaque.' That was a good idea from Eddie and something that I would be pleased to do. It also gave me the idea to deliver another message to someone in the Falklands on behalf of a neighbour of mine.

Transport to the Falklands via Ascension was by an RAF DC10 for the bargain price of £250 – return. The aircraft was near enough full. The military has a system that allows eligible personnel to fly for a minimum price on their aircraft if seats are free, with priority given to veterans wanting to return. For my trip, along with Pete McWatt, the others we travelled with were three lads from 2 Para: Steve Harris, Jimmy Goodhall and Dave 'Charlie' Brown, together with professional photographer Paul R.G. Haley. Back in 1982, Paul was one of only three civilian photographers who were commissioned by the MOD to sail with the Task Force. As well as being a brilliant 'all round' photographer, he gives lectures on his varied career, which includes fascinating stories from his best-selling book of Falklands War images called *One Man's War*. Paul had been back once before to the islands, but this time he had a specific mission which none of us knew about. Pete McWatt's main reason for me to come along was not only to be company for him but to make up this group of six, which would be sticking together during an exploration of the island. Our group had a good balance of military and civilian personnel. It was three decades since the war and, on first meeting up, all of us showed our age. Surprisingly, the Para lads showed it more than most and seemed not to worry at being less in shape than they used to be. At the airport, initially we didn't recognise one another as everyone had changed so much. Once the stories got going, though, we realised who everyone was.

On arriving at the Falklands, our accommodation was at the Liberty Lodge, located a mile outside of Stanley. Purpose-built for returning veterans, it's a self-catering facility, sleeping up to thirty people and overlooking the bay. Our stay was to be ten days. Pete and I shared a room. Several other people were staying in the lodge as well. Not long after our arrival we were introduced to a local lady called Helen, who had been appointed as our tour guide and chauffer. Getting about the island would be courtesy of her 4x4 vehicle. Like Britain, driving is on the left in the Falklands. Beyond Stanley, which is the only town, other residents live in small settlements on remote farms, so nearly every vehicle on the island is a 4x4. It made me smile to see good old-fashioned red telephone boxes in Stanley and that the town is twinned with Whitby, North Yorkshire. The main language is English, with Spanish taught as a second language in schools. With a population of just over 3,000, the locals are all native-born and of British descent. The islands are a democratic and self-governing British overseas territory, not a British colony. They do, however, rely on the UK for the guarantee of their security with a military garrison providing defence, which has a strength of around 1,000 personnel. The local economy is financially self-sufficient and the only cost to Britain for the Falklands is security. I shouldn't think it is a dream posting for members of the military, considering there isn't a Kentucky Fried Chicken or McDonald's outlet anywhere. Neither is there a Costa or Nero's coffee shop. Other than an independent food store, there is no ASDA or Tesco supermarket. Thankfully, there are half a dozen pubs or so and we intended to visit them all. However, in time, we would find that we often didn't make it out of the first pub that we walked in.

The island is also visited by Argentinian veterans. From our group, on a previous visit in 2012, Charlie and his 2 Para friend, Geoff Johnston, were both wearing 2 Para T shirts in the Globe pub. A group of eight Argentinians were also present and as one of them came over, Geoff said, 'outnumbered again'. In broken English, the Argentinian asked Charlie and Geoff if they were veterans. An islander friend of Charlie's, called Pepe, volunteered to translate. The Argentinian's name was Dany Grau and he had fought on Wireless Ridge. Charlie asked how many friends he had lost. He said 'cuatro morte' (four killed). At that point, Charlie got emotional and needed to go outside. Dany and Geoff followed. Dany spontaneously hugged Charlie. The rest of the Argentine group, who were mainly conscripts at the time of the war, came out. The atmosphere was very friendly, with everyone sharing a beer and Pepe translating. Their group was initially wary of the two Paras, so they avoided them until Dany decided to break the ice. Charlie had some spare poppy pin badges with him and he offered them to the Argentinians, explaining they signified peace and remembrance. To this day, Charlie and Dany communicate via Facebook. When Dany sends pictures of his travels, mainly around Europe, he wears the poppy pin badge. Dany even took time out to visit the Para war memorials at Arnhem. What a lovely and respectful story of reconciliation.

A couple of days after our arrival, Helen arranged for our group of six to visit the Governor's House. The Governor wasn't there but Sandra Tyler-Haywood, the Deputy Governor, was. The letter of greeting and plaque of the Hull Independent Merchant Navy Association were presented.

As we sat around in the main lounge of Government House, the Deputy Governor, who is part of the UK's Diplomatic Service, talked of what she missed back home in Britain. Tea and biscuits were had, along with polite conversation, and one could tell she was used to entertaining visitors in these types of situations.

Charlie is second from the left. Geoff Johnson is fourth from the left with Dany Grau to his right. Argentinian wine is not sold on the Falklands and the bottle held by one of the Argentinian veterans was a rare vintage brought with them, which they gifted to Charlie and Geoff.

Hull Independent Merchant Navy Association

Chairman/Treasurer Eddie Piercy
22 Kings Bench Street
Hull
HU3 2TU

To the People of the Falkland Islands

Dear Friends

Greeting to all from all the crew of the Hull I.M.N.A; here in the UK, we hope that everything is going well for the people of the Falkland Islands and that those troublesome noisy neighbours of yours are behaving themselves?????

The bearer of this letter Reg Kemp is a former crew member of the MV Norland on which he and many other association members served during the liberation of your Homeland.
Reg would like to present the accompanying Association Plaque on behalf of all our members to the people of the Falkland Islands, to show our continued support and solidarity with our fellow members of the British Family of Nations.

The association wishes all the citizens of the Falkland Islands the very best wishes for a peaceful, prosperous and secure future.

Yours sincerely

Eddie Piercy
Chairman/ Treasurer

From left to right: Jimmy Goodhall, Steve Harris, Sandra Tyler-Haywood (Deputy Governor of the Falkland Islands), Charlie Brown, Reg Kemp, Paul Haley and Pete McWatt.

I refrained from telling how close I had been to knocking on the Governor's door shortly after the war for help to get back to the ship before a helicopter landed on the lawns and saved our bacon. The conversation became fascinating when she revealed a curious tradition relating to a snooker table in Government House. No one really knew how the tradition began, but she invited us to look underneath the table. We could see hundreds of signatures written onto its wooden-and-slate construction. She told of how Margaret Thatcher was invited to pull her skirt up, bend down and leave her signature. The thought of this was intriguing, but it wasn't confirmed whether she did or didn't take up the offer. It made us chuckle. Before leaving, our group signed it. It was good to know we had left our mark.

My other courier task was to deliver a personal message from a female neighbour in the apartment below me in Willerby, where I live on a small estate of fifty homes for retired people. One morning, HMS *Clyde*, a Navy A Class patrol ship, was on security duty around the island and it pulled into Stanley Harbour. Paul, Pete and I aimed to go aboard. The trouble was, an armed guard was standing at the top of its gangway. We walked up it and when challenged I said to the guards, 'I wish to speak to Officer Christopher Sharp.' A message was passed and an officer approached us. I introduced our group and repeated my request to meet Christopher Sharp. We shook hands and the greeting officer said, 'Welcome aboard. Somebody will attend to you.' It turned out that this officer was the commander of the ship. An exceptionally tall figure then approached and introduced himself as 'Christopher Sharp, Second-in-Command of HMS *Clyde*'. Once again, we went through the ritual of shaking hands. He was accompanied by two junior officers. 'Christopher,' I told him, 'I have an important message from your grandma. She hopes you are doing okay?' The officers accompanying him smiled. Christopher had a surprised look on his face, which broke into a broad grin. 'How is she?' he asked. I explained that his grandmother, Vera Clarkson, lived in the flat below me and that she was a good acquaintance of mine. Hopefully for Chris this was a pleasant interlude during his tour of duty and it also gave truth to the old adage 'what a small world it is!' We finished the morning with a tour of the ship but, disappointingly, without a tot of rum as the ship had imminent orders to sail.

The snooker table at Government House with signatures written on the underside.

Pete McWatt knew the score from previous visits to the Falklands and he'd advised us to bring fresh fruit, which on the island was always in demand. I'd brought half-a-dozen small oranges with me. The Falklands for the most part are hilly, rocky and covered with low shrubs and coarse grass, with hardly any trees for simple fruit such as apples and pears to grow. Worthy of note is that in Stanley, there is actually a wooded area called Memorial Wood located close to the Stanley Cemetery. It commemorates members of the British armed forces who had died. There is a tree for each life lost. Compost and fertilisers were specially brought in to help the trees grow and thrive. Trading with the nearest land source – Argentina – is limited. All fruit is expensive to import. I gave a family with some small children my stash of oranges and they couldn't have been more delighted to receive them. It felt like when bananas returned to post-war Britain in the late 1940s and young kids couldn't believe their luck at receiving a similar treat.

Of the various places to see, I couldn't wait to try out my old pub, the Globe, its full title now being the Globe Tavern. The outside looked pretty much the same, but the interior was less basic and resembled a cosy drinking joint. On our visit, some young locals in their twenties went out of their way to buy us a drink. This reinforced the feeling that the new generation of Falkland Islanders were also appreciative of all that had been done for them.

An Argentinian liner arrived whilst we were there and passengers came ashore. Relations between the Argentinian passengers and the locals were very cordial. In a souvenir shop, browsing around and looking at trinkets, the Argentinians were speaking in their native tongue. Listening in, I learnt that they couldn't figure out the local currency against the American dollars that they had. The local currency is the Falkland Islands Pound, which is worth exactly the same as a British Pound Sterling. In my best Spanish, I offered to help. They were very grateful and showed an interest in how I could speak Spanish and what my own reasons were for being there. I didn't explain why.

A real treat for everybody was the day Helen took us to see a penguin colony in her 4x4. In a remote location off the tourist track, it was a trip and a half to get there. Although there was no road to this out-of-

The Globe,
an old friend.

the-way location, Helen somehow navigated overland to it. She proved
to be a brave driver across challenging terrain and we had to be equally
brave passengers. We negotiated hillocks, narrow passages, steep inclines
and streams, all of which Helen merely scoffed at. I'll never complain
about women drivers again after witnessing her admirable driving skills.
Though we were buffeted around getting there, upon arrival it was
worth it. Helen emphasised that this beach was only ever frequented
by naturalists – determined naturalists, I would say. The penguins were
not used to people. Frolicking on the water's edge, on our arrival they
looked nervous and waddled away. Not so much later, realising we were
not a threat, inquisitively they came up close to inspect us. They were
pure entertainment. All that time ago when we had sailed into South
Georgia and I'd hoped to see them but hadn't – this made up for it. At
least the Falklands has something going for it in respect of an expand-
ing market in nature tourism. We also had the pleasure of seeing sea
lions and what enormous things they are. These ponderous creatures of
the sea might lie resting for most of the time, but we were warned not
to get too close with our cameras because they move a lot faster than
we might think. The tourist board is keen to point out that the islands
are also host to elephant seals, dolphins, killer whales and a healthy
black-browed albatross population. What really struck me, though, was
that the beaches were virtually devoid of litter.

Gluttons for punishment, the next day Helen took us on another challenging journey to a remote cottage near San Carlos Water where we

met an elderly couple who couldn't have been more delighted to have company. Whilst enjoying their hospitality, the war was discussed. Yet again they were typical of their fellow islanders in that they were very grateful for what had been done to liberate them. They had no television and the husband was really chuffed to be able to chat with us. I laughed when he referred to the islanders as 'us Bennys'. The implication was that this word did not offend him.

In the Falklands, traditionally peat was a main source of fuel. Kerosene had of late replaced much of this and I noticed wind generators also played their role. With the winds that are forever blowing in the Falklands, wind power is something to be exploited for natural energy. Though life was primitive at these remote locations, this existence suited those who lived it. I had no idea how most folks made their living in general, but they were happy. I never saw much that grew in the way of crops, but I did see plenty of sheep. It's reckoned there are near to 500,000 sheep on the island. No matter how great the excitement of our visit, this couple, like other homeowners whom we met, had something to do. No one on the islands loafed around and, after our conversations, they always wanted to get back to work. Ready to leave this lovely couple, I was taken aback as the old lady hugged us all and then kissed our hands as we departed. That heartfelt act of appreciation has always stayed with me.

A fun memory of the Falklands came about when we were travelling along the main road that comes in and out of Stanley. In the distance was a set of traffic lights. These were the only set of traffic lights on the island that I had seen. This main route was of a B-road standard with a width that just about allowed vehicles to pass either side of each other. The traffic lights had been erected due to roadworks for the construction of a small layby. Not reducing her speed, Helen approached the lights and shot straight through them on red. I was sitting up front and tried to keep quiet, but unable to hold my silence, I said, 'Helen, you do know those lights were at red.' With casual indifference she replied, 'Oh yes, but we don't take any notice of things like that around here.' She had been back to England so it's not as though they have never seen simple technology before. The islanders have a different attitude to the fast lives that we live back in our big cities. I liked her attitude.

One obvious part of our programme would be to take in a battlefield tour. For the Para lads this was going back to the scene of stark memories. We visited where Lt Col Jones was killed. Jimmy had told us prior to this visit that he wanted to bury the ghost. At the battlefield site, we could see he had a lot on his mind. Jimmy didn't talk much about his involvement. In fact, all three Para lads drifted around lost in their own thoughts. It was here that they had been in the thick of some of the fiercest fighting.

Our guide was a well-spoken civilian and former army officer who had studied the Falklands War. He didn't see action there himself, but he'd decided he wanted to spend his retirement as a tour guide. Explanations were given about the tactics of attack and defence. Many of the military terms mentioned were lost on me. 'That little pile of stones just there,' he said, pointing to a spot in the ground, 'is a marker for where Captain Chris Dent fell.' Having known Chris, albeit on a very casual basis, this stopped me in my tracks. The tour guide talked about how the actions of Lt Col Jones, though admirable in getting the job done, were considered by some to be near reckless. I don't know the rights and wrongs of all this and I'll gladly leave it to the military historians to decide.

Left to right, Steve Harris, Jimmy Goodhall and Dave 'Charlie' Brown strike a pose with some of the artifacts (SLRs) in the museum at San Carlos, which has now relocated to Goose Green.

Courtesy of the Royal Signals, the image below is from documents made available exclusively to this publication. It is taken from the actual logbook used on the radio link between the Parachute Regiment Battalion Headquarters in the rear, forward to 2 Para and 3 Para, located at the battle front. In the log, one of the most significant entries (recorded by Sergeant Larry Little of the 3 Para Rear Link Sigs Det) reports the death of Lt Col Jones. Received on 28 May 1982 at 2020 hours, the message reads: 'Sitrep on 2 Para: Sunray + Seagull dead, other casualties, mission totally successful, taken 100 prisoners and gone firm.' On British Army radio nets, for the sake of brevity and security, 'Appointment Titles' were used to refer to the senior officer in charge of a specific army unit or a specific arm of the military. Sunray was the title used for a Commander, which could have been any rank from Lieutenant to General. In the radio transmission reporting the death of Sunray, the appointment title of 'Seagull', meaning 'Adjutant', is also reported, which referred to Captain David Wood of 2 Para.

Continuing with our tour, the guide pointed out where Jones had fallen and there was a significant monument to mark this, unlike for Chris Dent and others killed near this site. (At Darwin, overlooking Stanley, is a memorial of bricks, a large wooden cross and a plaque with the names of all the fallen from 2 Para and supporting arms. In life, Chris Dent had followed 'H' Jones and in death it was the same, for his name was placed immediately after his commanding officer.) The Para lads with me were surprised at the wealth of knowledge and especially the candid revelations of the guide, who didn't shirk from telling how he saw it. He had praise for Major Keeble, who took command and saw the Battle of Goose Green through to the Argentinian surrender at that location. Of course, all of this had gone on whilst we were on the ship and it was fascinating to discover from an expert what the Paras had achieved, in particular the Toms, who were greatly praised by the Para officers.

We then moved on to visit the village of Goose Green itself. One of the main features is its village hall. This is where the Argentinians had rounded up about a hundred locals and imprisoned them inside. Jimmy was part of the operation to capture and secure the hall from the Argentinians. He hadn't referred much to this part of the war except to say, 'it was all a bit hairy'.

Nearby to the village hall is a large container, the type that you see transported by ships. Inside this container is a small museum with artefacts and information about the war. We went in for a look. I learnt that during the battle, when arriving at the village hall, the Paras heard noises coming from inside. They realised locals had been locked in. A padlock was knocked off the doors, which were carefully opened. The first person to step out through them was a woman holding a baby. Jimmy, who was stood in close proximity, somehow ended up holding the baby. A photograph was taken and it made for a strange scene to see Jimmy with his tired, rugged, bearded face against the sweet cherubic innocence of the baby's face looking at him. 'What's the baby's name?' Jimmy asked the mother. 'He's called Matthew,' the mother said. All those years ago, when this scene played out, it was photographed by Paul Haley, the very same photographer who was in our group.

So, there we were in this small museum looking at memorabilia and nattering away when, through a window, I could see some people heading towards us. Our photographer Paul saw them and said to me, 'Reg, just stay here and don't drift off. I want you to watch what happens.'

With that, the door opened and a big brawny local lad came in, looking unsure of the situation. Paul said to Jimmy, 'Hey Jimmy, I have got something to tell you. The guy who's just come in through the door, he's called Matthew.'

Jimmy shrugged it off and said, 'Huh, yeah, okay.'

Paul then said to Matthew, 'This fellow here with me, have you any idea who he is?'

Matthew said, 'No, should I?'

'Yes, you should,' said Paul. 'This here is Jimmy and he's the Para who held you after they took the padlock off the village hall doors back in '82. When your family was liberated, you were handed to him by your mother.'

There was a silence. Not an awkward silence, just a peculiar silence. Jimmy is a big bloke and tough looking. Matthew is a sizeable bloke and they stared at each other searchingly. Everyone else looked on in curious wonder at the unfolding event. Then realisation dawned about who each other was. Spontaneously they embraced. It was a beautiful moment to witness and there were smiles all round. Adding further poignancy to this meeting, it came to light that after the war, Jimmy got married and had a baby boy. He'd called his baby Matthew.

That evening we were offered a stayover in basic accommodation. Beforehand, the village hall, which serves as a social club, was converted into a bar – a free bar, I might add. We could drink as much as we wanted, which we did. Late in the evening, having had our fill, we emerged from the village hall into a jet-black night. There was no street lighting. Finding our way half-drunk to our accommodation was hilarious. It made me wonder how the hell the Paras fought their battles, which were mostly in the dark and far from hilarious. They weren't drunk on booze like we were. Back then they would no doubt have been drunk on adrenaline.

The next day we had another battlefield visit to where an Argentinian stronghold had held the high ground on Mount Longden. My admiration for other units, not just the Paras, increased on seeing how they also coped, winning battles against the odds that experts thought they shouldn't have won. Everyone in the Falklands War did their bit in what was a really close-run thing.

Though I have mentioned one of Jimmy Goodhall's war experiences, of the other two Paras in our group, Steve Harris was a private person and didn't reveal too much, whereas Charlie Brown, a very affable bloke (when not suffering inner turmoil), was more than glad to share his experience. By the way, Charlie is his nickname, not his birth name. Two members of 2 Para went by the name of Dave Brown and one of these two Daves had settled on the nickname Charlie. Regarding Charlie's introduction to the Falklands War, on the day that 2 Para disembarked our ship in San Carlos Water (21 May 1982), he had turned 21 years old. The celebrations he enjoyed were greater than normal for reaching such a birthday milestone. Indeed, to this day, Charlie has gone down in Airborne history as the Paratrooper who received a 21-gun salute courtesy of the Royal Navy, and a fly-past courtesy of the Argentinian Air Force. Charlie, a private in C Company (Patrols and Recce), tells here of his coming to terms with the war:

After the war, back in the UK, I only served for another three years. Going on exercise using blank rounds and smoke bombs and having exercise umpires tell you that 'you're dead, you've been shot', well, it seemed ridiculous. The lads who'd fought in the Falklands would say, 'no I'm not' and carry on. Once you've been under real gunfire, there's no comparison. On leaving the army, I hit the bottle and lashed out, which resulted in a prison sentence. Prior to my court case, I had been formerly diagnosed as suffering from Post Traumatic Stress Disorder (PTSD). On leaving prison, I set about rebuilding my life, with support from the Parachute Regiment Association and especially from Lt Col Simon Brewis, who had been my former CO in the Parachute Regiment Depot. For my recovery, I needed a variety of pills every day to calm my panic attacks, depression, and violent mood swings. I often shut myself away until the internal rage in me disappeared. This happened when I thought of all my mates who were chopped to bits by gunfire in the Falklands.

Alcohol masked the pain of the nightmares and flashbacks that haunted me. What the Paras teach you is to go in and cause as much damage as you possibly can. I was still fighting the war in my head for years afterwards. Many of the other lads' marriages have suffered through PTSD, as did mine. Tragically many of the lads have committed suicide. From the soldiers who served in the Falklands, more have since died by their own hands than those who did during the war. Those who came back from the Falklands but whose close pals didn't, many suffer from what is known as 'survivor guilt'. Salvation came for me when I set up the Northern branch of the South Atlantic Medal Association (SAMA 82). This was to take pressure off Denzil Connick, formerly of 3 Para, who despite losing his leg on Mount Longden and suffering PTSD, was the energetic founder of SAMA in 1997. This organisation exists for veterans of the Falklands conflict and one of its main aims is to give advice and support for anyone like me.

Trips for service personnel returning to the Falklands are called 'Pilgrimages of Veterans'. This came about through the famous military surgeon from the Falklands War, Rick Jolley OBE ODM, Denzil Connick and myself. We organised the first one for the 20th Anniversary in 2002. At the time, the MOD had no interest in helping veterans fly to the Falklands to 'lay their ghosts to rest'. When Rick Jolley saw the letter sent to me by the MOD stating this, he said with swearing that I dare not repeat, 'Well, we will just charter our own aircraft.' We fundraised and had financial support from Sir Rex Hunt and comedian Jim Davidson. The success of the 2002 Pilgrimage led to a Pilgrimage in 2007, commemorating the war's 25th Anniversary, which had 250 veterans attending. As an observer, the MOD sent Member of Parliament, Derek Twigg (Under-Secretary of State and Minister for Veterans) to report on its impact. His report resulted in veterans receiving support by allowing them greatly reduced prices on RAF aircraft.

This trip with Reg is my ninth visit and which brings me to say, it's not just the memories of my Para mates that I remember, it includes the crew off the *Norland*, whom I equally consider as brothers in arms. They are blokes who, in character, are as good as any Para.

Pete McWatt, a cook, first met Charlie on the 2007 Pilgrimage of Veterans 25th Anniversary Commemoration, when they became friends, and they have remained close ever since. Pete was the youngest member of our crew and, like Charlie, he had his twenty-first birthday down south. Here follows a brief account by Pete of his relationship to the Falkland Islands:

I first returned to the Falklands in 2007 with a fellow steward, Chris Sutcliffe. We were there as representatives of the *Norland*, and SAMA 82. The whole island was given the week off work to look after us. We were met at the airport by buses and accommodated through home-stays. Later, an unbelievably long convoy of 4x4's took us around the island to key battle sites, to attend memorial services and enjoy social receptions. I made so many friends on the island, all of whom were so grateful for their freedom, it made me see that the war was really worth fighting. I was lucky at meeting a new friend in Charlie as we hit it off immediately. The hectic visits and very emotional services that we attended were so overwhelming, during a quiet time, I took myself down to the beach at San Carlos Bay to be alone. Looking out across San Carlos Water, aka Bomb Alley, I suddenly started crying, I had never experienced anything like that before. Glancing down, by my feet I noticed a small pebble in the shape of a heart. I picked it up and I have since carried it with me in my wallet. Another incident that moved me was when I visited the Memorial Wood. Walking through it, I came across a Para who had been on the *Norland* with us. He was stood by a tree sobbing. I asked if he was okay and he said, 'See this lad here, Pete, I shared a cabin with him on the way down south. He had the biggest, smelliest feet you could imagine. Oh, how I wish he was here now.' I gave the Para the last bit of rum I happened to have with me and said, 'Have a drink with him,' which he did. There were many other emotional moments on that first trip and I wasn't in a good place when I came home. That's why I've returned so many times. I feel that the best I can do is pay my respects and try to keep the name of the *Norland* in people's memory.

Not long after my 2007 visit, with my partner Felicity (Fliss), we attended an invite to St James' Palace in London, in the presence of HRH the Prince of Wales. Prince Charles spoke to us and I mentioned about Fliss having relatives who had been held hostage in Goose Green. He asked if, during the conflict, Fliss was my wife, to which I answered 'no'. Because he'd asked this, it got me thinking. I looked at her and said: 'Do you know what Prince Charles just said about you being my wife … will you marry me?' I had no ring to offer, but thankfully she said 'yes'. We married over a year later. A while after that, we received an invite from SAMA 82, to go to Highgrove House, again to meet Prince Charles. He spoke to us and I said: 'You may not remember, Sir, but we met at St James' Palace and you asked if Fliss was my wife. Just after you walked away, I asked her to marry me.' Charles congratulated us and I said: 'There's one more thing, Sir, all my close mates now blame you for getting me hitched!' He laughed heartily and said, 'I have been accused of a lot of things before, but never that!'

Almost immediately after my proposal to Fliss, I rang my long-standing friend, Reg, who was the first person to know our news. Reg laughed out loud when I said that Prince Charles made me do it, but at least I can say 'I have royal approval!' Not bad for a lad from a housing estate in Hull, who also got to meet and shake the hands of former Prime Ministers, Margaret Thatcher and Tony Blair.

I also received an invite to a garden party at Buckingham Palace. Working as a postman at the time, I'd already had time off for my previous visit to St James' Palace. I now needed further time off and I wrote a letter to my boss which read:

Dear Paul,

As you know, last year I went to lunch with HRH Prince Charles. Charles has been speaking with his mother who has now invited me to her garden party, So by Royal Demand, can I please have two days off, because I do not think it would be fitting to refuse the Queen as she is so much looking forward to meeting me.

Thanks, I will pass on your regards.

Yours, Pete McWatt

In 1983, when at last our work in the South Atlantic ended, some of the crew flew home early. I wanted to be with the ship as it sailed into Hull. I felt it was a final act of sorts. I was with her when she left and I wanted to be with her when she got home. Some other crew members had the romantic notion of wanting to see the White Cliffs of Dover as we sailed by. When I first told my dad that I had volunteered to go, he was very

Their Royal Highnesses
The Prince of Wales and The Duchess of Cornwall
request the pleasure of the company of

Mr Peter McWhatt & Mrs Felicity Whittle

at a Reception
to mark the 25th Anniversary
of the Falkland Islands Campaign
to be held at St James's Palace State Apartments
on Tuesday, 26th June 2007

Time: 12.00 pm
R.S.V.P.   *Dress: Lounge Suit or*
on card provided   *Service Uniform*

The *Norland* crew were all made honorary members of 2 Para. For his work representing the ship, Pete was officially presented with a red beret and cap badge, with permission to wear it at official functions. Here he is accompanied by Fliss.

227

unhappy and said, 'Never volunteer for anything! You don't know what your mam and me will be going through now.' What I did know is that, even though we never really talked about the war afterwards, they were so proud when I finally got home safe to Hull.

Pete administers a Facebook page called *Norland* Crew, which provides communication for those with a connection to the ship. This reaches out to many people, not just the crew. He has always worked hard to keep the name of the *Norland* prominent by travelling the country as the ship's representative at SAMA 82 Annual General Meetings, and at various remembrance services.

Over our ten-day stay, our group of six had happy times hanging out together. A Scottish sergeant major from a unit in the military garrison based in Stanley also looked after us. We ate and drank sensibly and appropriately to our age. All too soon it was time for going home. But before we left, we held a humble service at the Blue Beach Military Cemetery in San Carlos, laying wreaths and small crosses at the headstones. The cemetery holds the remains of thirteen of the 255 British casualties killed during the war. Up until 1982, all British serviceman killed in action were buried and commemorated as close to the place of death as possible, and the Commonwealth War Graves Commission managed these graves. Families have since requested the repatriation of their fallen sons' bodies from the Falklands. On 16 November 1982, sixty-four of the dead (fifty-two soldiers, eleven Royal Marines, and one laundryman from Hong Kong) were returned to Britain aboard the landing ship RFA *Sir Bedivere*. The families of fifteen of the dead kept with tradition and preferred that their son's remains stayed on the islands. Thirteen are buried at Port San Carlos, with two more at isolated single gravesites at Goose Green and Port Howard.

We also visited the Argentine Military Cemetery which holds the remains of 237 fallen. It is located west of the Darwin Settlement, close to the location of the Battle of Goose Green. (There is a replica of the cemetery at Berazatequi in Buenos Aires Province, Argentina.) We didn't hold any kind of ceremony at this cemetery; we simply wanted to pay respects to the war dead of Argentina who, like our military, were just doing their duty.

I was surprised at how emotional my return to the Falklands had been. I was so glad that Pete McWatt had encouraged me to go, if only for having witnessed the meeting of Jimmy with the grown-up Matthew. Amongst all the carnage back in 1982, when Jimmy held baby Matthew it provided a moment of humanity. All these years later, Jimmy meeting Matthew again provided a similar moment.

Was the war worth it? That is a question many now ask, even some of them off the *Norland*. The families of those who died would probably say no. From those who fought, what I have discovered is that most say yes. Otherwise, the sacrifice made by servicemen killed and wounded in the Falklands would have been in vain. Having seen Jimmy's experience on his return to the Falklands, I believe that for him, and many others like him who have made the same trip, it has been a healing process. Whatever the rights and wrongs of the Falklands War, even though Argentina lost the conflict, it has benefited in another way, for it ditched its military dictatorship and gained a democracy.

On the islands, having visited the war graves, my thoughts drifted to other conflicts. For as much as the *Norland* and its crew had forged a bond with 2 Para, as well as 3 Para, and for as much as I felt great sorrow for the loss of life by other arms of the military, my feelings will always lean towards seafarers. I utterly respect what the Royal Navy do and I hold them in high regard, but it's the Merchant Navy that I lean towards. Through the decades, those who went before us saw more action at sea than we ever saw on the *Norland*. The Merchant Navy are non-military, but when called upon, they never fail to rise to the occasion. The ninety-three crew of our ship could have easily been any other ninety-three who happened to be serving at the time – I just happened to be one of them. To admit I am grateful to have had such an experience is a strange thing to say, but it's true. I feel for all the Merchant Navy seamen who answered the same call for their country, but didn't come back from the conflict they served in. The Royal Fleet Auxiliary is the largest employer of British merchant seamen in the world. It delivers worldwide logistical and operational support to the Royal Navy that can include war, counter-piracy, humanitarian and disaster relief and anti-drug running operations.

For the record, of the 174 who died at sea in the Falklands War, ten were members of the Royal Fleet Auxiliary and six were members of the Merchant Navy. With this sacrifice in mind, to conclude my story of the Falklands War and the small part that I played in it, I end with a citation dedicated to seafarers produced by the Hull Independent Merchant Navy Association. It appears on the war memorial shown below, which is located at the pier-head in the Port City of Kingston upon Hull.

They did what they were asked to do.
Dedicated to the men and women
of the Merchant Navy
who gave their lives for the freedom of others.
Many lay in foreign lands.
For most they have no grave but the sea.

The Hull Independent Merchant Navy Association memorial, where an annual service of remembrance is held on 3 September – National Merchant Navy Day.

EPILOGUE

The MV *Norland* returned to Hull from the Falkland Islands on 1 February 1983. Unlike the *Canberra* and *QE2*, she did not arrive home to the national hype of cheering crowds and flag waving, but this wasn't for the lack of trying. Though scheduled for an early morning arrival, she sailed into Hull's King George Dock late in the evening, during driving rain and a howling wind. She struggled not to flounder on the Humber sandbanks due to the terrible adverse weather conditions, which was ironic considering all she had been through. She had a welcoming committee of North Sea Ferry personnel, a small military contingent and the ever-dependable *Hull Daily Mail*. North Sea Ferries had wanted to make a big occasion of the ship's return. The idea was for those of the original crew who were already home, having flown back early, to go out onto tugs into the Humber and join the ship. A bus took them from Hull to Immingham where the *Norland* had hoped to tie up, but couldn't. So, the bus had to bring them all the way back again. Meanwhile, anyone with any connection to North Sea Ferries had come along to King George Dock to be part of the welcome committee. However, by the time the ship tied up late in the evening, most of the welcoming committee had gone home. Although it was all a bit of an anti-climax, the important thing was that, at last, the ship was home where she belonged. I reckon that when I saw her tied up, she gave a physical sigh of relief.

Captain Don Ellerby, Master of MV *Norland*, was honoured with the award: Commander of the Most Excellent Order of the British Empire (CBE).

The Purser, John Crowther, in a conversation with Commander Esplin-Jones, was asked about nominations for those he thought deserving of a mention in despatches. John suggested the Storekeeper, Chris Sutcliffe, and the Chief Cook, George Rimmer, who had both been excellent at their jobs. He also thought Chief Officer Bob Lough should have received an equal honour to Captain Don Ellerby. From the North Sea Ferry company's point of view, Bob Lough was rewarded, for in time he became the General Manager. Admiral of the Fleet, Sir John Fieldhouse GCB GBE, was appointed overall Commander of the Task Force and given responsibility for the mission to recover the Falkland Islands. He conducted the campaign from the UK-based Northwood Command Centre. Admiral Fieldhouse sent a letter of commendation to Bob Lough praising him on several counts: one was for the night of 10 June 1982 when: '… on passage he lowered and took away a lifeboat to effect the successful rescue of a man overboard'.

Commander Chris J. Esplin-Jones RN was honoured with the award: Officer of the Most Excellent Order of the British Empire (OBE). He was later promoted to the rank of Captain.

Two Victoria Crosses were posthumously awarded to Lt Col Herbert 'H' Jones, 2 Para, and Sgt Ian McKay, 3 Para. In total, some seventy-one gallantry awards for actions in the Falklands were made to attached personnel, members of the Parachute Regiment and former members on service with other units.

Major Chris Keeble's recognition for performing a crucial leadership role at a pivotal stage in the Battle of Goose Green saw him awarded the Distinguished Service Order (DSO). He said of his award:

> The victory, however, was H's. The inspiration of 2 Para came from him, and my role was merely to act on his behalf in his absence. For that I am the caretaker of an enamelled bit of metal, which I carry on behalf of every man in 2 Para, especially the junior non-commissioned officers and the soldiers.

Major Keeble was later promoted to the rank of Lieutenant Colonel. The Parachute Regiment received the following battle honours:

Falkland Islands 1982
Goose Green
Mount Longdon
Wireless Ridge

For her service as part of the South Atlantic Task Force, MV *Norland* received the battle honour: Falkland Islands 1982.

Two crew members of the *Irishman* tug received British Empire Medals (BEM) as part of the Falklands Honours Awards. They twice risked their lives when boarding the stricken *Atlantic Conveyor*, which was hit by Exocet missiles, to attach tow ropes. They were given their medals in a ceremony held at the Hull Guildhall.

A medal with rosette was issued to all who served in the Falklands War. The *Norland* crew members received theirs through the post.

A veteran's badge has been created for anyone who has served in the UK armed forces. The only variant of this badge is one that includes the Merchant Navy Red Ensign and is available to all Merchant Navy seafarers and fishermen who served in a vessel when it was operated to facilitate military operations by HM Armed Forces at any time.

The only entertainment available on the Norland was from Roy 'Wendy' Gibson who was very consistent with his piano playing and singing accompaniment. As Hull's Liberace, he did this in his spare time before or after his normal daily duties. Everyone warmed to him and he became a bit of legend for his good-natured antics. Sadly, he passed away in 2021, when The Parachute Regiment gave him an unprecedented honour by placing a brass plaque dedicated to him on the Goose Green memorial bench in Aldershot Military Cemetery, as well as a plaque in a Parachute Regiment pub in Aldershot - the Trafalgar Inn.

Stewardess Shirley Howlett was the girlfriend of the ship's union man, Bill Moody. They were always seen together and their relationship has endured through the years. Stewardess Jean Woodcock was very much an individual person who functioned in her own way. She liked a drink but was always there when needed. They were highly commended by many for their contribution.

When Chief Cook Malley Gelder was asked about the catering arrangements on board, he remarked, 'As long as the Paras had chips with their every meal, they were happy. Without exaggeration, over the ten months and the number of passengers we've carried, we have dished up about a million meals!'

The air travel distance from Britain to the Falkland Islands is equal to 8,050 miles. The *Norland* was at sea for 282 days on leaving Portsmouth; 287 days if counting the date of leaving Hull. It covered 66,325 miles – the equivalent of nearly three times round the world (or sailing four times to the Falklands and back). Shortly after the ship's return to Hull, it went into dry dock for extensive repairs and refurbishment over a six-week period. It was then employed back in its normal service from Hull to Rotterdam. In 2002, it was sold to Società Navigazione Alta Velocità (SNAV) as the SNAV *Sicilia* for service between Naples and Palermo. The ship was broken up in India in the summer of 2010.

After the ship's refurbishment and before it was scrapped, when back on its normal run and up until the day I retired, I had teamed again with Dave Aistrop on nights. As stories unfolded of our Falklands trip, we finally received an explanation for our mystery 'UFO incident'. The strange lights and noise we'd experienced in the middle of the South Atlantic, between South Georgia and the Falklands, were actually a helicopter. It had been specially fitted with extra fuel tanks for long distance flying. It made the exceptionally long journey to intercept and deliver hand-written instructions of the location in the war zone where the ship was to sail next, which was back to Bomb Alley.

The piano that had served the ship so well collapsed with exhaustion and found a fitting place for its retirement home, the bottom of the South Atlantic.

Several years after the Falklands War, I took a scuba diving trip to Hawaii and whilst there visited Pearl Harbor, where many ships were sunk or damaged by a surprise attack by the Japanese in the Second World War. I discovered that a ship which was heavily damaged but survived this surprise attack was the USS *Phoenix*. I also discovered that upon its repairs, it went into battle against the Japanese and helped to finish the war in the Pacific with proud distinction. After the war it was sold to Argentina, where it was renamed the ARA *General Belgrano*.

Pete McWatt was surprised to see the *Norland*'s bell on display on another P&O ship. It was in a public lounge of the P&O Dover to Calais ferry, MS *Spirit of Britain*, having ended up there after the breakup of the *Norland*. Historically, all timekeeping on board ships revolves around a bell. The close personal relationship of a bell to its parent ship can never be over-emphasised. Whilst delighted to discover it, Pete was annoyed that the bell was not on display somewhere in Hull. He determined that it should be returned to its rightful place. As a result of his hard work, with great assistance from former Assistant Purser, Keith Thomson, it now forms part of a Falklands War memorial in the Minster.

Like many others from Hull, Assistant Purser Keith Thompson is a member of SAMA 82. In April of each year since 2015, with help, Keith has organised an independent annual commemorative service for Falklands War veterans in Hull Minster. Furthermore, Hull Minster also includes a fascinating tribute to the part played by the city and its Merchant Navy men and women during the Falklands War, with a collection of civilian and military artefacts on permanent display.

Nearly twenty years after the Falklands War, a young Falkland Islander took a job on the *Norland* as an AB. When we were talking about the Falklands, I happened to have a few scrap photographs from the war lying around in my cabin. One of these photographs showed two children playing on an abandoned Argentinian gun. As the young AB would have been the same age as them back in 1982, on the half chance, I asked if he knew who the children were. He replied with astonishment, 'You are not going to believe this, but you see that lad there, he's my brother. And the other lad in the picture with him, that's me!' We laughed out loud at this coincidence and the AB was delighted to receive a copy of the photograph, the original of which is shown in this book.

When *Norland* took on survivors from HMS *Antelope* and headed to South Georgia, in appreciation of our crew's care, one of their ship's radio men gave our Radio Officer, Brian Lavender, his naval-issued survival suit to help see out the war. After 1982, Brian carried that same survival suit on every ship he worked on till his retirement in 2001. Brian always remained grateful to that *Antelope* crew member.

Before the troops left the *Norland* for the last time, 2 Para offered the crew arrangements to go to Aldershot, where they would be looked after before being trained for a 'one-off' parachute jump. It would be a static-line jump from a balloon at a height of 800–1,000ft. Full of bravado, about twenty crew members said, 'I'll do it!' A year or so after the Falklands War had ended, only one person remained from the original list of those willing to do the jump. 2 Para reasoned that it wasn't feasible to make good on their offer for only one person, so nothing came of it. The crew had dropped out through a mixture of reasons. Some had come to their senses once they'd returned to Britain and it didn't seem important any more. Some just wanted to leave any connection with the war behind them. Some had wives and girlfriends who told them they were not prepared to see them possibly get hurt, that it was a stupid thing to do and something only Paratroopers did!

Through the active service pay that he'd accumulated during his time in a theatre of war, on his return from the Falklands, Sergeant Larry Little of 3 Para, Rear Link Signals Detachment, treated himself to a brand-new Mazda RX7 sports car, which didn't please his wife too much. Shortly afterwards he was posted to Germany. Like many who had experienced the *Norland* in the Falklands and who later travelled to and from the Continent, Larry always booked the ship for his crossing. Once on board, he made himself known to the ABs running the car deck with a request to ensure that his prized motor didn't get scratched. He then made himself known to the stewards, which usually resulted in an invite down to the crew's bar for an evening of reminiscing. This actually pleased his wife because it meant she got to drive his beloved sports car the next morning as Larry was always too hungover. Countless individual reunions similar to Larry's took place through the years on the ship and, though the *Norland* has long since been scrapped, the relationship of those who were acquainted with it from the Falklands War is as strong as ever.

Royal Navy Commodore Michael Clapp was in charge of Amphibious Warfare with the South Atlantic Task Force and was directly responsible for landing Brigadier Julian Thompson with 3 Commando Brigade. In 2002, at a function on board the *Norland* held to celebrate its final trip as a North Sea passenger ferry, Commodore Clapp was invited as a guest. What follows is a truncated version of his speech:

Norland to me is arguably the most remarkable ship that went south. To many of us she became a great friend, and clearly from the numbers turned up (here) that's proved that one [sic], but she also earned an enormous respect and it's never easy to say goodbye to a friend ...

You might have thought there had been worries from our end that a merchant ship was put into this position, and we were then going to be in a position where we would be under fire. I have to say that not one of the naval officers that were attached to the ship came to me and made any real complaint. Yes, they said they were worried, that was quite understandable, but the Merchant Navy proved themselves as steady as they had been before. The fact that only six Merchant Navy men were killed out of some 174 that died at sea is quite irrelevant because they were as much in the front line as any of us. I'm enormously glad it worked out that way but it was luck, nothing else. They were more at risk than the rest of us partly because of the gaudy painting, which showed them up for miles away and partly, of course, because they were largely totally unarmed. But there was more to it than that, a merchant ship is not designed to be attacked and bombed and rocketed. It's not designed to fight the sort of fires that come from that, and this is what they had to live with ...

But who in *Norland*'s crew had signed on in the doubtful honour of being the first merchant ship to enter San Carlos Water?

Another claim to fame that the *Norland* can be proud of is having a crew member as the first person into the conflict. When the anchor is dropped, this is done by the ship's carpenter going forward into the bow. Normally, carpenter Derek Zeese would do it. As mentioned, he was busy elsewhere and the task was given to AB Brian (Shep) Sheppard, along with the 2nd Officer Alan Woof. Shep reckoned that because the *Norland* was in front of the escort ship, and because his position in the bow was ahead of Alan Woof, technically he could claim to be the first person into the Falklands leading the charge of the Task Force. This was Shep's belief of the situation and nobody was going to take it away from him. Good for him, everyone thought. The Royal Navy might dispute this, but as Merchant Navy civilians it's our story and we're sticking to it.

AFTERWORD

BY LIEUTENANT COLONEL (RETD)
CHRISTOPHER PB KEEBLE, DSO MSC FCMI

For my battalion, The Second Battalion, The Parachute Regiment, and all those sailors, soldiers, airmen, and prisoners of war who were sheltered within the hull of MV *Norland*, we were lucky.

It was the dedication of the Master of the Ship, Don Ellerby, and his crew of the P&O roll-on/roll-off ferry who, from operating in the tranquillity of peace between Kingston upon Hull and Rotterdam and Zeebrugge, responded to the call to arms and voyaged to war in the South Atlantic. Despite the shortage of preparation time, the complexity of logistics, the damaging seas, the Antarctic weather and the immense distances, *Norland* and its crew faced up resolutely to the uncertainties of combat.

Although we were a parachute battalion, the landing in San Carlos by 2 Para was its third amphibious assault since the Second World War; the previous being Suez in 1956 and Anguilla in 1969.

My abiding memory, as the military Commanding Officer from the UK to Ascension Island, and through the turbulent South Atlantic to our beachhead in San Carlos Water, was that we were not only lucky, but together were a happy ship's company. Somehow, the ruthless airborne soldiers blended with the adventurous attitude of the merchant seamen, to play their separate parts, in order to fulfil the task of ejecting the Argentine occupation, for the restoration of the islanders' liberty.

This mosaic of many memories is remarkable for its everyday insights into the difficult, challenging and at times exhausting task of caring for the people and the provisions, through arduous days and nights at sea, and over turbulent and dangerous seas; safely, expertly, and with immense good humour.

MV *Norland* may now be so many razor blades, but the memory of the fine British seamanship, working together against the odds, in a proud vessel so ill-equipped to be a naval amphibious craft and a troop ship during war and its aftermath, will live on.

These pages record the tenacity, fortitude and sheer dogged enthusiasm of a bunch of people who went well beyond the call of duty, to make a fighting ferry for the Falklands War.

I could not give greater praise than to say *Norland*, and especially its crew, lived up to the Parachute Regiment's demanding motto, Utrinque Paratus – 'Ready for Anything'.

NOTE BY REG KEMP

This book is a personal record of my small contribution to the events that took place in the South Atlantic in 1982. In agreeing to tell my story I wanted it to serve as a tribute to British Merchant Navy men and women with whom I had the privilege of sailing. I also wanted to recognise the strong bond that was formed between our crew and the Second Battalion, Parachute Regiment. The MV *Norland* was just one ship among hundreds of others, but Kingston upon Hull and its people can be proud that it was a major contributor to the Falklands Task Force, along with several other ships from the Port of Hull. Due to the passage of time, I may have to stand corrected on the chronology of certain parts of my memoir, but at no time have names been changed, characters invented or events fabricated.

As a mere ship's steward, I'll always remain impressed at how the deck department, engine room staff, catering department and officers performed. The *Norland*'s involvement in the war showed that the military could work alongside Merchant Navy men and women not in an 'us and them' situation but as a 'team'. Aside from all the grand words spoken about us after the campaign from senior military top brass, with whom I had no direct connection, it was important to our crew from the very start that the military, in particular the Royal Navy, recognised that we didn't need any help in the running of our ship. In fact, the experience of our crew proved to many in the Royal Navy that they could learn a thing or two from Merchant Navy men and women. Admittedly, there was the odd occasion when we may have learned something from them, such as the risky business of razzing, of which Commodore Michael Clapp said, 'It's a procedure at sea that any sensible seasoned navy person would wish to avoid for it puts you at the risk of collision.'

Overall, it was without fuss that our crew got stuck into every task in a cheery and professional way. My direct boss, the Purser, John Crowther, summed it up best for me when he once remarked that he couldn't have been happier on our Falklands voyage because, without complaint, his 'herberts' (the crew) did everything that was asked of them.

Though this has been my story, it would never have been told without Michael Wood, whose book this is as much as it is mine. Through Michael's crafting of my memories into a narrative and his securing of a publishing deal, it has been a fascinating process. His understanding and appreciation of the Merchant Navy's ways and the comradeship of those who serve in certain occupations gave me confidence to commit to this project. While designing the battle maps and the ship's blueprint, and organising the acquisition and order of images, together with his former military knowledge and contacts, his vision for this book's presentation never wavered. His ear for a story coaxed forgotten memories from deep inside me and other crew members, resulting in a book I had no intention of ever embarking on, but I am thrilled that I did. Michael's enthusiasm, patience, research and writing skills have also provided the opportunity to tell not just my story but, ultimately, the broader story of the *Norland*, its crew and the precious cargo (2 Para) we safely carried to and from war.

THE *NORLAND* CREW LIST

(MARINE VESSEL) MV *NORLAND*

Hull – Rotterdam Service 1974–2002

Overall Length	153.0m
Overall Breadth	25.2m
Service Speed	18.5 knots
Gross register tonnage (GRT)	About 12,500 tons
Passenger Capacity	1,244
Max Cars	520

Built 1974 A.G.Weser, Bremerhaven
Hull–Falklands, South Atlantic Service 1982–83

CAPTAIN

Ellerby, Donald A.

NAVIGATING DEPARTMENT

Lough, Robert B.	Chief Officer
Cammish, Christopher R.	2nd Officer
Woof, Richard A.	2nd Officer
Risby, David M.	2nd Officer
Lavender, Brian	Radio Officer
Hookem, William G.	Bosun

Zeeze, Derek	Carpenter
Shepherd, Robert B.	Able Seaman (AB)
Clark, Thomas	AB
Dennison, Raymond W.	AB
Dolan, Patrick	AB
Failey, Michael G.	AB
Kenyon, John	AB
Laycock, John C.	AB
Scruton, Raymond	AB
Temple, Michael S.	AB
Shirtliff, Raymond	AB

ENGINEERING DEPARTMENT

Newell, Lloyd	Chief Engineer
Draper, Ernest J.	2nd Engineer
Bales, David M.	3rd Engineer
Dent, John W.	3rd Engineer
Frizzell, Derek	3rd Engineer
Waller, Francis M.	3rd Engineer
Begg, Derrick	3rd Engineer
Burton, Brian L.	Electrician
Slater, Herbert	Electrician
Altoft, Frank	(PO) Motorman
Whitelam, John A.	(PO) Motorman
Slaughter, Kenneth N.	Motorman
Reeve, Robert	Motorman

CATERING DEPARTMENT

Crowther, John W.	Purser
Graham, John H.	Assistant Purser
Thompson, Keith	Assistant Purser

Foley, Christopher J.	Chief Cook
Gelder, Malcolm T.	Chief Cook
Rimmer, George	Chief Cook
Temperton, Alan J.	Chief Cook
Hardisty, Timothy	2nd Cook
Harry, Kenneth	2nd Cook
Lambert, John	2nd Cook
Tungate, Karl	2nd Cook
Wilson, Anthony	2nd Cook
Woolin, Neil	2nd Cook

STEWARDS

Sutherland, Harold N.	Shop Manager
Dixon, Harold	2nd Steward
Isham, Leslie	2nd Steward
Sutcliffe, Christopher	2nd Steward
Wilson, Brian F.	2nd Steward

Aistrop, David	Atkinson, Michael
Black, Donald	Butcher, Steven
Carter, Leslie	Chapman, Steven
Eastwood, Alan	Edwards, Graham B.
Evans, Martin D.	Foster, James G.
Foster, John F.	Fuller, Ernest
Gair, Robert	Gibson, Douglas S.
Gibson, Roy	Green, Frank
Holt, Gary	Hornsby, Kevin J.
Howlett, Shirley	Isham, Les
Isham, Steven M.	Johnson, Richard A.
Kemp, Reginald A.	Knowles, Peter B.
McMamee, Anthony F.	McWatt, Peter
Marrow, Leslie J.	Moody, William G.
Myers, Barry	O'Mahoney, Peter

Palfreman, Anthony
Robinson, Andrew N.
Rounding, Nigel
Smith, Peter
Suter, Cyril
Whincup, Ronald H.
Woodcock, Jean M.

Palfreman, Geoff
Robinson, Malcolm
Sansom, Peter
Stephenson Terence
Whelan, Joseph
Wingham, Michael R.

ACKNOWLEDGEMENT OF THE BRITISH PUBLIC

Worthy of mention here is a gesture not intended to promote alcohol. On the contrary, it merely highlights the important role that alcohol plays in life and, in particular, in support of the British Armed Forces. The bottle shown overleaf which is surprisingly unopened, forms part of Reg Kemp's South Atlantic Task Force memorabilia.

The production of a welcome Task Force Special Ale came about when a serviceman mentioned to his mother that British beer was greatly missed in the Falklands. She contacted the *Sunday Mirror* which, as a morale boost, campaigned for the creation of a brew to show the military how well they were thought of back home. This resulted in a 'mercy mission' delivery of 8,500 bottles to Port Stanley – one each for those serving in the South Atlantic. Produced by Newcastle Breweries, the bottle is now in demand as a collector's item.

Interestingly, when the *Norland* first began its South Atlantic ferry service, it was due to leave the Falklands for Ascension and alcohol supplies were alarmingly low on board. Former Chief Officer, now the ship's Captain, Bob Lough refused to sail until resupplied, which was twice denied by a nearby RFA supply ship in Stanley Harbour. The RFA ship then pulled away in the dark and a determined *Norland* closely followed her around the island to San Carlos Water, anchoring up nearby. At daylight, the RFA asked, 'What are you doing here?' 'Waiting for the *beer*,' came the reply. There was a stand-off ... *Norland* finally set sail but now with her bars fully restocked and smiles on the faces of thirsty troops.

GENERAL ACKNOWLEDGEMENTS

Photographs and images are courtesy of Dave 'Charlie' Brown, Brian Burton, John Crowther, Chris Esplin Jones, John Foster, Frankie Green, Chris Keeble, Reg Kemp, Brian Lavender, Larry Little, Bob Lough, Pete McWatt, Eddie Piercy, P&O North Sea Ferries, Brian Sheppard and Michael Wood. A special thanks is given to the *Hull Daily Mail* for photographs as noted.

Sources of reference include The Parachute Regiment data website; The National Museum, Royal Navy website; SAMA 82; *Norland* Crew Facebook Page; and Wikipedia.

We are grateful to all who have contributed either through review, inspiration or critique, and a special mention is given to Dave Beattie, Peter Fitzgerald, David Mitchell and Martin and Judy Ward for their invaluable feedback and encouragement.

We are especially grateful for the testimony and contributions from Derrick Begg, Dave 'Charlie' Brown, Brian Burton, John Crowther, Brian Lavender, Bob Lough, Chris Esplin-Jones, Chris Keeble, Larry Little and Pete McWatt.

The final acknowledgement of this book is given to recognising the Hull Independent Merchant Navy Association. It is a superbly-run organisation open to *all* seafarers. This is largely thanks to the original founders, Gordon Grady and Paddy Dolan, and others, together with the current hard work of Eddie Piercy the Chairman, Cyril Butler the

Secretary and the supporting committee. It provides the opportunity for its older members to talk about the good old days, as well as for its younger members to champion the merits of all kinds of seafaring in today's challenging times.

All pictures courtesy of the authors, unless otherwise credited.

ABOUT THE AUTHORS

Aged 16 in 1954, Reg Kemp attended the famous (though many would say infamous) National Sea Training School in Sharpness, Gloucester, where 70,000 passed through its gates. Part of the school was a ship called the *Vindcatrix*, moored in a canal close by. Known for very strict discipline, this was one of two main sea-training schools for ratings, the other being at Gravesend, Kent. After his training, Reg's first ship was the *Albano*, a Hull-based cargo vessel, and his first port of call was Stockholm, Sweden. In 1999, fittingly, his last port of call was Hull, Yorkshire, sailing on the *Norland*. Aged 61, he then retired early due to the tragic loss of his young wife, Jean. Unsettled by living on his own, Reg spent his time travelling the world, mostly by aircraft. Nowadays, his leisure pursuits of rock climbing and scrambling have given way to sequence and ballroom dancing.

Reg Kemp.

Raised in Kingston upon Hull and army-educated, Michael Wood served in the Royal Signals from 1972 to 1994, including four years as a Para on airborne exercises with 16 Para Brigade HQ. On leaving the army after twenty-two years' service, he embarked on a second career in the entertainment industry, taking on various acting and performance roles. Most notably, Michael became Town Crier for the East Riding of Yorkshire and also Hollywood, USA, winning national and international town crying championships. He now concentrates on writing.

Michael Wood.

ABOUT THE COVER PAINTING

Left to right are Larry Malkin (Chair of East Riding Artists Association), Reg Kemp, Eddie Piercy and Cyril Butler. Eddie and Cyril are the Chairman and Secretary, respectively, of the Hull Independent Merchant Navy Association. Larry, who specialises in sea vessel paintings, invited the group below to have the first view of the *Norland*, which was commissioned by Reg Kemp and Michael Wood to become this book's front cover. It was based on a photograph taken by steward Graham (Hoss) Edwards, a copy of which was given to Reg Kemp and has hung in his living room since 1983. The painting has more features than the original photograph and it reflects a post-war scene. It now forms part of the Falklands War collection in Hull Minster. In the painting we can see a Chinook helicopter and a Sea Harrier in flight. In the foreground is a decommissioned Argentinian artillery piece. In the background is Port Stanley overlooked by the low mountains, where many of the land battles took place in the final push to the capital and final victory.

IF YOU ENJOYED THIS TITLE FROM THE HISTORY PRESS

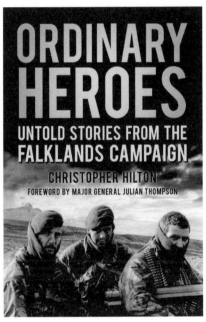

978 0 7509 9474 3

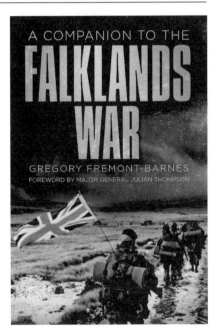

978 0 7509 8177 4